# Islam and the West African Novel

*A Three Continents Book*

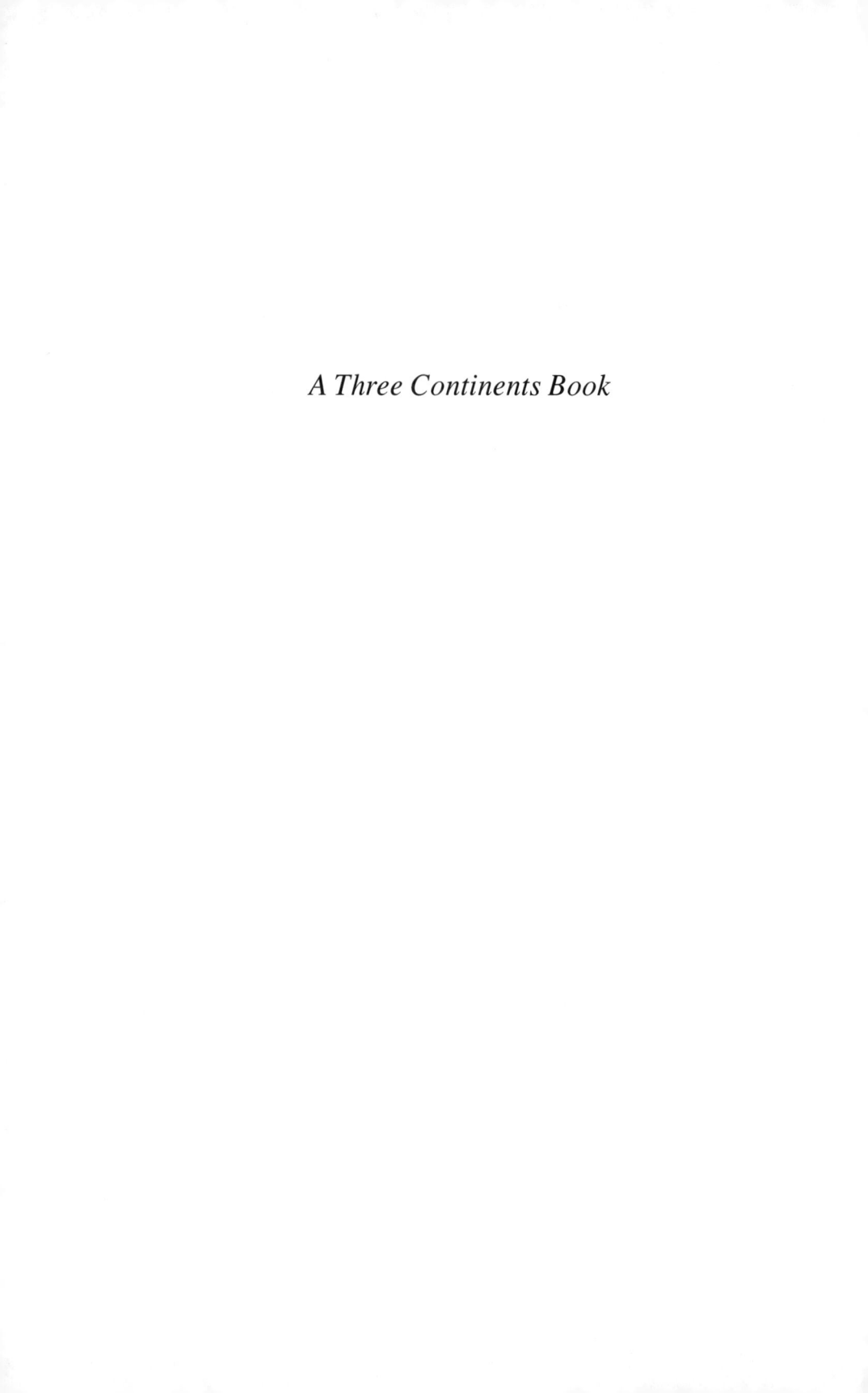

# Islam and the West African Novel

## The Politics of Representation

Ahmed S. Bangura

LYNNE RIENNER PUBLISHERS

BOULDER
LONDON

Published in the United States of America in 2000 by
Lynne Rienner Publishers, Inc.
1800 30th Street, Boulder, Colorado 80301
www.rienner.com

and in the United Kingdom by
Lynne Rienner Publishers, Inc.
3 Henrietta Street, Covent Garden, London WC2E 8LU

© 2000 by Lynne Rienner Publishers, Inc. All rights reserved

**Library of Congress Cataloging-in-Publication Data**
Bangura, Ahmed S., 1960–
　　Islam and the West African novel　:　the politics of representation　/
　　Ahmed S. Bangura.
　　Includes bibliographical references and index.
　　ISBN 0-89410-863-8 (hc　:　alk. paper)
　　1. West African fiction—History and criticism.　2. Islam in literature.
　3. Islam and politics—Africa, West.　4. Politics and literature—Africa, West.
　5. Islam—Africa, West—History.　I. Title.
　PL8014.W37B36　2000
　809.3'938297—dc21
　　　　　　　　　　　　　　　　　　　　　　　　　　　　　99-056007

**British Cataloguing in Publication Data**
A Cataloguing in Publication record for this book
is available from the British Library.

Printed and bound in the United States of America

The paper used in this publication meets the requirements
of the American National Standard for Permanence of
Paper for Printed Library Materials Z39.48-1984.

5 4 3 2 1

# Contents

| | | |
|---|---|---|
| | *Preface* | vii |
| 1 | Introduction | 1 |
| 2 | Africa, Islam, and the Legacies of Colonialism | 9 |
| 3 | Islam and Africanist Literary Criticism | 23 |
| 4 | Critical (Mis)Readings of Sembène Ousmane | 55 |
| 5 | Taming Islam: Aminata Sow Fall | 81 |
| 6 | The Quest for Orthodoxy in Ibrahim Tahir's *The Last Imam* | 107 |
| 7 | Conclusion | 131 |
| | *Glossary* | 149 |
| | *Bibliography* | 151 |
| | *Index* | 165 |
| | *About the Book* | 171 |

# Preface

My Arab friends owed me an apology. It was the late 1980s, and I was pursuing graduate studies at the University of Alberta in Canada. There, for the first time, I met Muslim Arabs, who happened to be students.

No Arab had ever been seen in Rogbap, my village in Sierra Leone. In fact, the words "Islam" or "Muslim" were hardly used at Rogbap, just *olaneh,* believer. To be a Muslim was like having a head on one's shoulders, just a simple fact of life. But after I left my village I met many Arabs and Muslims—in books of history, literature, and literary criticism. In Canada I met Arabs for the first time. And they owed me an explanation.

Their ancestors, horsemen with curved swords, had stormed Africa, my homeland, ravaged the land, enslaved some of the people, and forcefully converted many others. Their crimes against Africa cried out for reparation.

Some of my undergraduate professors of literature convinced me of the great violence and intolerance that accompanied the advent of Islam in sub-Saharan Africa. *Two Thousand Seasons* by Armah and *Bound to Violence* by Ouologuem featured prominently in our literature curriculum. Also, the works of Sembène Ousmane show what Islam is: a fatalistic religion, an opiate of the people, the explanation for the backwardness of African countries with a majority Muslim population.

As for those novels with no violent content, it was evidently because they did not have an Islamic theme. *The Radiance of the King* by Camara Laye was a Christian allegory. It did not matter that Camara Laye was, as I learned later, from a traditional Muslim background.

My Arab friends did not seek to defend the record of the Arabs in Africa. Before meeting me, most of them did not even know of a country called Sierra Leone. Their silence challenged the image of Arabs and Muslims that I had in my head. I was forced to revisit that image, its source, and its enduring influence on African letters and thought. That exercise yielded this book. Perhaps I should have, as a friend suggested, given it the title *The Imam's Grandson Writes Back*.

I am grateful to the people whose support and assistance guided me through this undertaking. Among them are my wife, Fatima Maju; Stephen Arnold, George Lang, Anthony Purdy, and Nasrene Rahmieh of the University of Alberta; and David Skinner of the University of Santa Clara.

My thanks also go to the director and staff of the Center for Black Studies of the University of California at Santa Barbara, where I did part of the research for this book. I am equally grateful for the support and encouragement of my colleagues at the University of San Francisco.

# 1

## Introduction

To those who still believe in the autotelic, self-sufficient, and self-referential character of the literary work, the imbroglio following the publication of Salman Rushdie's *The Satanic Verses* in 1989 must have come as a shock. The "word" decidedly intruded into the world. It unleashed an energy demanding the acknowledgment of the word's origin in the flesh (a real author). Then came the unambiguous if terrible choice between the destruction of the word and of the flesh from whose satanic sinews the word was believed to have originated. For many Muslims, including some of the very few who actually read the novel, this was an ultimatum to which Salman Rushdie has yet to respond satisfactorily.

At the center of this current problem is the question of representation, ideology, and the relationship between the literary and religio-political systems. To many Muslims *The Satanic Verses* constitutes an utterly negative representation of Islam. Moreover, this negative representation has been linked to the author's personal ideological hostility to Islam. Many Western readers have failed to understand that what appears to them an unwonted fanatical interpretation of a novel also concerns the issue of interpretation and its ideological character. Hence, the one good thing to have come out of this controversy may well be the revitalization of the debate on the "worldliness" of the literary system: the politics of textuality and representation, as well as the politics of interpretation.

This book examines the representation of Islam and Muslims in the sub-Saharan novel as well as in the critical discourse it has generated. I shall argue that the full gamut of unexamined opinion about Islam that flourished in Western Orientalist scholarship has been copied into

African(ist) europhone writings. These attitudes not only reflect a failure to account for the full complexity and heterogeneity of Islam and its history in sub-Saharan Africa, but they also lead to misreadings of novels with an Islamic subtext. The ideological character of the textualization of Islam in the novels and of the criticism the novels have generated forms the central thesis of my study.

African novelists have almost always defined their role as that of ideologues, of social visionaries with a clear vision of alternatives for the socio-economic and political rehabilitation of their peoples. Hence the novels, as I shall demonstrate, express at once the novelist's interpretation (representation) of social reality and articulate the writer's various alternatives for the overall reform of society. This paramountly important aspect of African poetics is what warrants the sociological framework of my book. How are the writers' politics articulated in their texts? And at what cost?

It is mainly in critical writing that one sees what may be termed an Africanist version of Orientalism. The body of criticism I examine here displays many of the stereotypes, clichés, and unexamined opinions about Islam that Edward Said (1979) has shown to characterize Western Orientalist discourse. These opinions are principally demonstrated in the way critics explain the nature of the conflicts and tensions in novels with an Islamic subtext.

It is the practice of much traditional criticism to explain these conflicts by "othering" Islam, by opposing it, for example, with African traditional wisdom or with materialist Marxism. Sometimes the conflict itself is overemphasized in a Manichean manner. I demonstrate that such explanations fail to contextualize the tensions or situate the questions discussed within an Islamic paradigm. This can be substantially explained by a failure or refusal to recognize the diversity in unity of Islam and the myriad voices that Islam can accommodate, and hence the possibility of conflict emanating from varying emphases and interpretations.

Moreover, such concepts as "Sufi Islam," "orthodox Islam," "revolutionary Islam," "Asharism," and "Mu'talizism" are used to provide explanation for attitudes and actions taken by characters in different social and historical contexts. This mode of analysis is problematical. Instead of situating Muslims and Muslim groups within particular socio-economic and historical contexts, cross-cultural categories are used as stable categories of analysis based on their implied ahistorical consistency. This is greatly responsible for the misrepresentative readings of novels with an Islamic subtext. My study is a call for more context-specific, differentiated analysis of such novels. There are, however, many obvious traits of hostile ideology in critical writing on sub-Saharan African novels of the Islamic tradition. In his analysis of Sembène Ousmane's *O pays, mon beau peuple!* (1957), for example, Martin Bestman spends much time accusing Sembène Ousmane of being blind to the positive contribution of Christianity to Africa. He calls this *tricher avec le réel* (tampering with the facts). Some of the things Bestman would have very much liked to see Ousmane talk about in his novels include the Christian church's fight against slavery, witchcraft, and ritual human sacrifice. Bestman exhibits ignorance of Islamic morality by conceding that the Koran and the Bible teach people *à tendre l'autre joue*. When he comes to the subject of Islam proper, Bestman wholeheartedly agrees with what he perceives to be Ousmane's attitude toward Islam: that it is the greatest impediment to social progress.[1] Bestman's take exemplifies the ignorance of and ideological hostility to Islam in much traditional criticism in the African novel. One of the major tasks of my study is to unmask this critical practice and illustrate its attendant misrepresentation of Islam and misinterpretation of novels with an Islamic inspiration.

No single study that focuses on the imaginative responses to Islam by black African novelists has been done before. There have been articles on specific authors or a limited corpus of novels. Interestingly enough it is my reading of such studies, which in general display considerable ignorance about Islam and as such misrepresent it and provide misreadings of sub-Saharan African novels of the Islamic tradition, that awakened my interest in this field. I hope that my study will set the record straight and provide scholars with useful information regarding the history and sociology of Islam in sub-Saharan Africa and a methodological framework for the study of African novels of an Islamic orientation. My study seeks to challenge some of the unexamined opinions about Islam that are carried over from Orientalism to African and Africanist literary and critical discourse, but my ambition is less to present the "truth" about Islam than to analyze in this discourse the rhetorical strategies of ideology hostile to Islam.

That the task of the study of the Islamic presence in Africa and in the African novel has fallen mainly into the hands of non-Muslims and non-Africans is not an inert factor. I am by no means arguing here for an insider's perspective. Such a perspective does not carry with it the guarantee of objectivity, and even some Muslim scholars produce very reductive studies of the kind produced by their non-Muslim colleagues. One must remember that beyond being a Muslim, the scholar has to earn a livelihood by publishing in Western languages, in Western periodicals, for Western readers. (It must also be noted that there have been non-Muslim Western scholars who have provided much needed, if piecemeal, revisionist studies in this area.) I will examine all the manipulative messages that I can in literary and critical discourse so that I may expose in them traces of distorting ideological hostility.

The method of analysis used in this study fits the mold of approaches to literature and criticism that seek to restore the study of literature within the bounds of human affairs. I certainly understand Edward Said's doubts about the possibility of nonpolitical knowledge in the area of cultural studies: knowledge that is scholarly, impartial, and above partisan belief.[2] But the assumption of this study is that there is the possibility for scholarship that pays adequate attention to its object without transforming or deforming the object in the process. In short, I believe in scholarship that is sensitive to the complexity of its object.

My methodology is a hybrid. It draws on Edward Said's studies on Orientalism in general and Orientalism's Islamic component in particular. His theoretical observations on the relationship between the world, the text, and the critic are useful as well. So are recent revisionist studies on anthropological and cross-cultural discourse. Of special relevance are Gayatri Spivak's "politics of interpretation" (1987) and Tapalde Mohanty's insights (1984) on the use of cross-cultural concepts like "women" as a category of cross-cultural analysis. Mohanty's study is quite central to my discussion of the concept of the "Muslim woman." It will also be useful in my bid to debunk the use of such cross-cultural concepts as "Sufi Islam," "orthodox Islam," "militant Islam," and "passivist Islam" as models of reference in the explanation of attitudes and actions of people in different social and historical contexts. I also draw on Chantal Zabus's interesting analysis (1991) of linguistic differentiation in African fiction.

The corpus of novels to be analyzed includes Cheikh Hamidou Kane (1961), selections from the works of Sembène Ousmane and Aminata Sow Fall, Ahmadou Kourouma (1968), and Ibrahim Tahir (1984). Major critical works on these novels include Mohamadou Kane (1982) and Debra Boyd-Buggs (1986).

Sub-Saharan Africans are still largely Euro-illiterate and very few among the Euro-literate minority are actually interested in reading novels, so one can still legitimately ask the Sartre question: For whom does the African novelist write? To whose taste must the writer cater if there is a desire to be published and read at all? How do these variables affect the way Islam is packaged in these novels? These questions are especially critical in my analysis of linguistic differentiation in Aminata Sow Fall's narratives.

Chapter 2 establishes the link between Western Orientalist scholarship on Islamic societies in the Near and Middle East, and Western colonial scholarship on Islam and Muslim societies in sub-Saharan Africa. The features of Orientalism as they are analyzed by Edward Said (1979) apply also to colonial scholarship on Islam in sub-Saharan Africa. Such scholarship has grossly distorted Islam because it was generally hostile to Islam, was politically motivated, ahistorical, and essentialist, analyzing Islam from a logic that was deliberately external to it. The inconsistencies in the image of Islam and of Muslims in this Africanist Orientalism are explained by the fact that European colonial perceptions of Islam had hardly anything to do with Islam as a system of beliefs but rather as a focus of resistance to European cultural and political hegemony. Beyond establishing a link between Orientalism and colonial scholarship on Muslim black Africa, the second chapter of this book anticipates the third chapter by demonstrating that the tenured distortions of Islam in contemporary European writing on Africa, especially in the criticism that pertains to sub-Saharan African novels of the Islamic tradition, have their origins in hostile colonial writings on Islam and African Muslims. Critics and writers, having in general no access to Islam except through colonialist writings, have simply copied their script from such writings.

Chapter 3 documents and analyzes the pattern of denial and ideological hostility to Islam in current European writing on Africa and in literary criticism on sub-Saharan African novels with an Islamic subtext. The writings of Wole Soyinka, Debra Boyd-Buggs, Pierrette Herzberger-Fofanah, and many other critics are analyzed to present the ideological hostility to Islam in their works, as well as their ignorance about the fundamentals of Islam and the history and sociology of Islam in sub-Saharan Africa. Debra Boyd-Buggs (1986) is selected for detailed scrutiny to assess the extent to which her ignorance about Islam has led to a misinterpretation of Islamic references in West African fiction, notably in Cheikh Hamidou Kane's *L'Aventure ambiguë*. The general features of traditional criticism of African novels by authors of the Muslim tradition are also examined. These features include hostility to Islam, essentialism, and an inadequate familiarity with the Islamic framework. The recurring stereotypes about Islam and Islamic history in black Africa that flourish in colonial and contemporary European writing are revisited in light of recent revisionist studies on the subject such as those of René-Luc Moreau, Mervyn Hiskett, and Christopher Harrison. Chapter 3 concludes by acknowledging that there are a few recent critical articles that adopt mature, informed, and context-specific approaches to the study of the roles of Islam in contemporary African societies as these roles are put into text by African Muslim writers.

Sembène Ousmane, one of Africa's leading writers and film makers, is probably also one of Africa's most misunderstood artists. Chapter 4 examines some of the manifestations of the reasons for these misreadings of his works. It has been suggested, for example, that his Marxist ideological orientation is incompatible with Islam's alleged fatalistic ethos. Critics have thus been led by the assumption that Islam preaches resignation in the face of adversity to cast Ousmane, a proponent of personal and social responsibility, as an apostate. According to this approach, Ousmane consistently identifies Muslim characters in his fiction with the forces of reaction and defeatism. Chapter 4 illustrates by a thorough analysis of four of Sembène Ousmane's most studied novels that the approach defined above is reductive and does much violence to his complex narratives. Ousmane does not consistently identify Islam with fatalistic resignation, and in fact many of the positive characters in his fiction are shown to derive their progressive attitudes from their Islamic sensibilities. Critics who come up with the opposite conclusion, such as Patrick Corcoran, Martin Bestman, and Wole Soyinka, betray their ideological hostility to Islam in their discourse, a hostility that prevents them from seeing anything in African novels approximating a vindication of Islam's contributions to African culture. Chapter 4 is particularly interesting in that it shows how Soyinka's attitudes toward Islam, as they are analyzed in the preceding chapter, spill over into his critical writings.

Having examined the origins, varied manifestations, and consequences of the prejudices toward Islam in traditional African(ist) criticism, the last two major chapters of this book focus on examining how two Muslim African writers relate textually to their Islamic heritage. The fifth chapter, which is on Aminata Sow Fall, highlights the ambiguities of the African Muslim writers who see as part of their artistic vocation a European language articulation of the integrity of their culture in the European literary language.

Traditional criticism has unanimously cast Aminata Sow Fall as a promoter of Islam. An analysis of three of Sow Fall's novels illustrates that, on the contrary, there is a tendency in her fiction to present her ethnic heritage, while singularly muting the Islamic component of her culture. She does this by refusing to translate into French culturally bound Wolof objects and events, while she readily translates into French those aspects of Senegalese culture that are connected to the wider world of Islam. This wholesale "translation" of Islam has given misleading clues to critics in their interpretation of the concept of charity that motivates the plot, and constitutes the central theme of *La Grève des Bàttu*. It is also shown that the muting of Islam in the linguistic texture of Sow Fall's narratives is part of a general tendency to glorify *cosaan* (pre-Islamic Senegalese culture). This hardly squares with the conventional view that Sow Fall promotes Islam in her narratives.

If Aminata Sow Fall extols pre-Islamic African culture, Ibrahim Tahir, the northern Nigerian writer, is what one might call a literary Islamic fundamentalist. Chapter 6 examines his first and as yet only novel, *The Last Imam*. There is no place in this novel for the celebration of non-Islamic culture. In fact the words "Nigeria" and "Africa" are never mentioned in the entire novel. There is only one cursory reference to Nigeria's colonial history. Tahir's novel is the articulation of a nostalgia for the Sokoto Islamic state created in the early nineteenth century through the *jihad* of Usman Dan Fodio. The narrative perspective is unambiguously Islamic, and the narrative reads like a fictionalized exposition of Islamic doctrine and practice. Whereas a syncretistic ethos dominates in the works of Sow Fall, the accommodation to non-Islamic Fulani-Hausa cultural beliefs constitutes the major source of tension and conflict in Ibrahim Tahir's novel. The ideal is in a return not to ancestral practices, but to the strict observance of Islamic law, the *sharia*. I have dedicated a full chapter to *The Last Imam* not only because virtually no study has been done of it to date, but also because of what it tells us about the West African *tajdid* tradition and current religious conflicts in Nigeria. The quest for orthodoxy in *The Last Imam* also exposes the fallacy of one of the assumptions of the proponents of "Islam noir," which is that Islam as it is practiced in sub-Saharan Africa is comfortably accommodationist.

The concluding chapter summarizes the major questions raised in the study. There is a summary recapitulation of some of the more obvious distortions of Islam in the novels studied and the criticism that pertains to them. Based on the nature of these distortions, methodological guidelines are proposed for further study of sub-Saharan African novels of the Islamic tradition. As well, other areas of research along the lines of this work are suggested.

## Notes

1. Martin Bestman, *Sembène Ousmane et L'Esthétique du roman négro-africain* (Sherbrooke, Canada: Naaman, 1981), 42.
2. Edward Said, *Orientalism* (New York: Vintage Books, 1979), 10.

# 2

# Africa, Islam, and the Legacies of Colonialism

> It is our duty to study the Muslim society of our colonies in the minutest details. . . . It presupposes special studies of Islam which *the great Orientalists of France and of Europe* have now virtually succeeded in establishing. . . . [The study] will seem very attractive to many because of the scientific interest attached to it. But above all it is interesting for *political* and administrative reasons. It is almost impossible to administer an Islamic people wisely, if one does not understand its religious faith, its judicial system and its social organisation which are all intimately connected and are strongly influenced by the Coran and the prophetic tradition. It is this understanding of native society which, alone, will enable a peaceful and profound action on the minds of the people. It is, therefore, in this study . . . that we will find the surest bases and the most suitable directions for our Muslim policy.[1] (emphasis added)

Edward Said has written the most virulent attack to date on Western scholarship on the Muslim Orient.[2] However, it maintains an almost exclusive focus on the Near and Middle East, having virtually nothing to say about the reductive and essentialist portrayal of Muslim societies in sub-Saharan Africa elaborated in Western scholarship, notably in the colonial period (1860–1960). Moreover, since the appearance of Said's disquisition on the biases of European studies of Islam, scholars in the West have begun to realize their prejudices on the topic. As yet, however, very little has been written on the subject of Western scholarly distortions of Islam in black Africa.[3] The policy statements of William Ponty, the French governor-general in Senegal (1907–1915), quoted at this chapter's beginning, establish a clear link between Orientalism and colonial scholarship on Islam and Muslim societies in sub-Saharan Africa.

9

Before opening a discussion of how Said's work has prepared the way for a study of Western distortions of Islam in Africa, a quick summary of Said's critique of Orientalism is in order. Albert Hourani provides a useful synopsis of Said's arguments.[4] Said's criticism is built mainly on two interrelated lines, positing that Orientalists have misunderstood the Muslim Orient either due to prejudice or the tendency to interpret it in terms of the wrong categories, and that the work of the Orientalists has been too closely linked with the political interests of their countries (Hourani: 63). As well, from a methodological point of view, Western scholarship has tended to be essentialist in using the religious category to explain all the phenomena of Muslim societies and cultures (Hourani: 57). Finally, Said contends that Orientalist thought and scholarship have created a self-perpetuating body of "truths" about Islam and Oriental Muslim societies that have very little relation to the reality of the object studied, but have gained authority in intellectual and academic life.

Said's attack on Orientalism is to a large extent applicable to colonial scholarship on Muslim societies in sub-Saharan Africa. A very significant feature of this scholarship is indeed its political motivation; it was commissioned by the colonial administrations, which required Orientalists to be the guides of policymakers. Little wonder, then, that the most influential writers on African Islam were scholar-administrators, or at least those closely linked with the administration.

For example, the writer of the apology of British occupation of Northern Nigeria, *A Tropical Dependency* (1906), was no other than Flora Shaw, the colonial correspondent for the *London Times,* and subsequently, Lady Luggard, wife of Lord Luggard, the first high commissioner of the British protectorate of Nigeria. In her book, Lady Luggard argued that African Islam had lost its initial grandeur and had betrayed its own ideals. Britain could, therefore, no longer ignore its historic responsibility to take over.[5]

Likewise, Christiaan Snouck-Hurgronje and C-H. Becker, the most respected specialists on Islam in Holland and Germany, respectively, were both employed by their governments as advisers on Islamic policy. (The writings of Becker on Islam in East and West Africa contributed in a major way to the formulation of German public opinion about Islam.) In July 1938, for example, the Belgian government commissioned ethnologists from the University of Ghent to survey Islam in the Belgian Congo and disclose its secrets so that the administration could manage it more efficiently.[6]

The French did produce by far the most prodigious scholarship on Islam in Africa. This is at least partly due to the predominance of Muslims in the areas that came under French rule. The colonial practice of the French in commissioning scholars to examine the Islam in the territories that came under French control can already be observed in the studies produced in Algeria following French occupation. Shortly after the conquest of Algeria by the French in 1830, General Bugeaud felt the need to be well informed about his Muslim subjects and the nature of the society he was in the process of "pacifying." The bureaux Arabes were intended to be centers of research into Muslim society and to advise the colonial administration on how to deal with the native population. The tract on Sufi brotherhoods, *Marabouts et Khouan: Etude sur l'Islam en Algérie* (1884), was written by Louis Rinn, the head of the Native Affairs Department. Thirteen years later, Governor General Cambon initiated an official investigation into the state of Islam in Algeria. The outcome of this investigation was the publication of the seminal work of O. Depont and Xavier Coppolani, *Les Confréries religieuses musulmanes* (1897). Depont was himself a senior colonial administrator; Coppolani was a civil servant who later became civil commissioner in Mauritania, where he died at the hands of the people he thought he thoroughly understood.

One of the first works on Islam in West Africa, *De la Sénégambie Française* (1885), was written by officials of the imperial government, Frédéric Carrère and Paul Holle. The intention of this work, writes Mervyn Hiskett, was not only "to describe the customs and institutions of the Senegambian people but also to advocate certain views as to how French possessions in Senegambia ought to be governed" (Hiskett: 212).

Similarly, Robert Arnaud was commissioned in 1905 to investigate the state of Islam throughout the West African colonies and to draw up a manual of Muslim policy. The *Précis de politique musulmane* (1906) resulted from this investigation.

An anthology of works on African Islam by colonial administrators would be truly encyclopedic. François Clozel, Maurice Delafosse, Jules Brévié, and Paul Marty, to name a few, all adapted their writings for use by the colonial establishment they served. Paul Marty was certainly the most prodigious of them all during the period of World War I. And his writings contributed much to the shaping of French perceptions of Islam. He is probably best remembered for his invention of the concept of "Islam noir" to describe an Islam that owes its distinction to the wholesale adoption of pre-Islamic African customs.

Colonial officers, European thinkers, and missionaries wrote on Islam in Africa not from a logic internal to Islam itself, but as a focus of resistance to European political and cultural designs. For instance, the political character of German colonial perceptions of Islam is especially apparent when one looks at the period of the first concrete German colonial administration, which started in 1885. There was an immediate confrontation with East African Arabs and, later, with Muslim slavers. This Muslim resistance, as Hiskett points out, was both economically and ideologically motivated. It was mounted partly to defend Muslim trading. The resistance movement was, however, also associated with Mahdism (Hiskett: 216). East African Muslims readily identified the Europeans as the followers of the great tyrant, the anti-Christ (Arabic *dajjal*) who, according to Muslim tradition, would appear as one of the major signs of the end of times.

Many factors came together to color German perceptions of and attitudes toward Islam: German experience in East Africa, the impact of the propaganda of the French churchman Cardinal Lavigerie on German Catholic opinion, and the powerful propaganda of German Protestant missions. The resulting general attitude of hostility among Germans toward Islam was, however, at odds with the stance sometimes taken by the German imperial government. During the Franco-Prussian War (1870–1871), for example, Germans enlisted the support of the Muslim Turks against the French in North Africa. Hence, for reasons of political expediency, Germany was inclined to regard the Islamic world as a strategic ally. Hiskett's concluding remarks once more emphasize the political character of colonial Germany's ambiguous attitudes toward Islam: "In general, the German attitude to Islam resembled that of other European nations, in that it was made up of a variety of different sets of moral, religious and political assumptions and attitudes, few of which had anything to do with Islam as a system of belief or a way of life" (Hiskett: 217).

France was quick to realize that Islam represented a formidable obstacle to its imperial designs. French General Louis Faideherbe had become governor of Senegal by 1854, and his policy statements would remain terms of reference for French colonial policymakers. He did not hide his views on the subject. He wrote: "Les progrès de l'islamisme chez les noirs nous sont fatals" [Islam's advances among black Africans are going to be fatal for us].[7] Eugene Mage, official explorer for the French government, was more explicit when he wrote that "most of the problems of Africa come from Islam. Neither in our present colonies, nor in those to be created later, should we encourage it under any circumstance, even when it appears to be benign, as is sometimes the case in Senegal."

French perceptions of and attitudes toward Islam were by no means monolithic. René-Luc Moreau, Christopher Harrison, and Mervyn Hiskett have analyzed the politics that informed this heterogeneity of views, especially among the French. According to Moreau, French policy was driven by the imperatives of colonial rule (Moreau: 190). There were the imperatives of conquest as well as those of administration and economics. At the time of colonial conquest political entities based on the Islamic faith were being formed in Africa. From the perspective of the colonial powers, Muslims appeared to constitute the first obstacle to be surmounted. One can recall the rhetoric of General Faideherbe backed up by the campaign against such Muslim leaders as Al-Hajj Umar, Samori Ture, and Tierno Alieu of Goumba. The administrative phase brought with it administrative and economic imperatives: courts, chieftaincies, and tax collection structures had to be established. With the profitable peanut business of the *mourides,* members of the brotherhood of the formerly exiled Amadou Bamba, the image of the *marabout* (Muslim cleric) evolved from that of the parasitic exploiter of his students to that of the entrepreneur and rich businessman that France could ill afford not to deal with.

Moreau also speaks of imperatives that were totally external to Africa and Africans. He observed, notably, the situation during the two world wars in which the French colonial establishment was very paranoid. Concern about developments in the Muslim world was enough to warrant this. With the fall of the Ottoman caliphate in Turkey, French support for the idea of sponsoring an alternative caliphate in Morocco became very strong, and it is in this light that one should understand French backing of the Moroccan sultan's claims for spiritual suzerainty in northwest Africa. As Christopher Harrison puts it, "the degree of French obsession with and suspicion of Islam that continued right up until decolonization cannot adequately be explained without reference to this fact."[8]

It is not necessary for us to fully document here the measures taken by the French in response to the perceived pan-Islamic threat, such as strict control of pilgrimages to Mecca and banning the import of most publications from the Arab world. All these measures were taken despite the numerous pledges of loyalty from many Muslim leaders in French West Africa. The situation became even more tense when, in

1954, armed rebellion against France began in Algeria. One of the more significant measures taken was the establishment by the colonial administration of files on political and religious personalities suspected of secretly speaking against French (or European) interests. An inventory of Muslim leaders was established, clearly indicating who was to be promoted, who was to be carefully watched, who was to be ignored, and who was to be discredited and destroyed (Moreau: 191–192). Moreau's paradigm of imperatives may be too tidy to adequately reflect the protean nature of French attitudes toward Muslims in the sub-Saharan colonies. What Moreau illustrates, however, is the thesis that such attitudes were only marginally informed by a logic that is internal to Islam.

Hiskett's analysis also underscores the dynamic at work, but his emphasis is on the changing ideological orientations in metropolitan France that in turn affected perceptions of and attitudes toward Islam in the colonies. The republicanism, with its unapologetic anticlericalism, of the early days of French colonial expansion was such that colonial policymakers did not judge non-Christian religions unfavorably. Hiskett cites Napoleon Bonaparte's flirtations with Islam in Egypt. As well, Gaspard Théodore Mocher, who explored Gambia in 1818, was similarly open-minded, showing uncritical approval for what he perceived as Islam's revolutionary republicanism. Speaking of the movement of Abd al-Qadir in Futa Toro, he wrote:

> Towards the end of the eighteenth century, Abdoul [Abd al-Qadir], a simple mahometan priest, raised the standard of revolt: the enthusiasm for liberty and religious fanaticism made his little band invincible, he gained the victory and made the *amatore* prisoner, exposed him for a whole day to the heat of the sun, then stripped him publicly of all marks of royalty and caused him to return to the condition of a simple subject. (Hiskett: 211)

One may be shocked by what Hiskett refers to as an "uncritical approval for republicanism—including its brutalities" (Hiskett: 211). Nevertheless, the point should not be missed. In many ways Islam has functioned as a myth to be used in support of such divergent ideologies as republicanism, communism, and capitalism. We should, therefore, see it as perfectly normal that, in this instance, the ideological orientation of Mocher predisposed him to interpret this specific historical incident as an illustration of the revolutionary spirit. Anything that will distract from this particular interpretation is simply ignored.

The attitude of René Caillé, the monarchist who traveled across

Sudan from Senegal to Timbuktu, and then across the Sahara to Morocco, is predictably different from Mocher's. As a supporter of the monarchist cause of France, writes Hiskett, Caillé, "when he mentions Islam, it is usually to comment peevishly on Muslim fanaticism or scornfully on what he considers to be the laziness and lack of hygiene in the Muslim communities through which he travelled" (Hiskett: 211).

Hiskett further argues that anti-Islamic attitudes became more pronounced with the setting up of the Second Empire under Napoleon III, who depended on the middle class and the Catholic Church for support. It was during his reign that France entered the scramble for Africa "in the conviction that France had a mission and a duty to spread French Catholic culture and civilization." The attitudes of Carrère and Holle, Hiskett suggests, are typical of this period. The two colonial administrators referred to the *ulama,* as "preachers of a doctrine of which the effect is to maintain or throw back the Blacks into barbarism, by rendering them deaf to the teachings of a divine religion which will infallibly bring about their intellectual and moral transformation" (Hiskett: 212–213).

To further illustrate that French perceptions of Islam had much to do with the ideological orientations in metropolitan France, Hiskett refers to the work of Henri Duveyrier, *Les Touareg du Nord* (1864). Unlike Carrère and Holle, Duveyrier does not condemn Muslims outright. He maintains that there are tolerant and cooperative Muslims with whom France could work and others (fanatics) who must be dealt with as enemies. Hiskett adds that this view of Islam that sees it simply in terms of how it fitted or failed to fit in with French imperial ambitions became that of the early colonial administration in French West Africa (Hiskett: 213).

My discussion of the politically motivated scholarship on Islam in Africa would be incomplete without a mention of the role played by European Christian missionaries. Islam had been perceived as a threat to Christian Europe ever since it had appeared in the seventh century. I do not wish to duplicate here the discussion of Europe's canonical hostility to Islam. Of immediate importance are the features of missionary perceptions of Islam and how they contributed to shaping certain views on Islam that one still finds in contemporary African literary scholarship.

In 1454, Pope Nicholas V declared in his papal bull, *Romanus Pontifex,* the right of the Portuguese to the "peaceful" occupation of all the lands of the unbelievers that might be discovered along the west coast of Africa. Accordingly, since the fifteenth century, the Portuguese and the Spanish justified their conquests by the need to fight against Islam and to win souls to the true faith. In the course of that century, writes Latour Da Veiga Pinto Françoise: "L'un des buts des expéditions maritimes portugaises fut de découvrir un hypothétique passage fluvial sur la côte occidentale de l'Afrique qui menerait au royaume du fabuleux 'Prêtre Jean,' roi Chrétien puissant, dont l'alliance permettrait de prendre à revers les Musulmans." [One of the objectives of Portuguese maritime expeditions was to discover a rumored river passage on the western coast of Africa leading to the kingdom of the legendary "Prester John," a powerful Christian king. An alliance with him would facilitate a surprise attack against the Muslims.][9]

Regardless of any bases in reality of the legendary personage, there is ample evidence to illustrate Hiskett's argument that regardless of their varying motivations, Europeans in the wake of the colonial era shared similar attitudes toward Islam, which were the assumptions of Christians of their day: "That the world was divided into Christian believers and the rest who were misbelievers or downright infidels. . . . One has only to read Ca Da Mosto, Diogo Gomes, Joao de Barros and other travellers to the Atlantic coast in those early times, to become aware of the automatic assumption of superiority over both Muslims and adherents of traditional African religions" (Hiskett: 205).

It was in the nineteenth century that the Christian missionaries were finally able to establish themselves in black Africa. This lasting penetration coincided with European colonial expansion. As more Muslim lands came under European control, missionary interest in Islam was aroused. The importance of the fall of India is well underlined by Canon C. H. Robinson; he indicated that Queen Victoria of England now had more Muslim subjects than the sultan of Turkey: "This alone is sufficient to justify the most careful attention that can be paid to the present and future prospect of Islam."[10]

Since missionaries were now able to penetrate the Muslim world under the protection of the imperial administration, they began to elaborate their individual ideological attitudes toward Islam. As Britain, for example, became a colonizing power, the British felt the need to preach the Gospel to non-Christians, and this required some sort of knowledge about the religions of the colonized peoples and how Christianity stood in relation to them. The titles of the books written by Christian missionaries in this period are indicative of their programmatic thrust. Among these, one finds C. H. Robinson's *Muhammedanism: Has It Any Future?* (1897) and S. W. Zwemer's *Mohammed or Christ?* (1916). Walter Miller wrote copiously on Islam in Nigeria, and his writings represent a paradigm for many missionary scholars of Islam. One of his more memorable quotes reads: "This lack of all homelife; the utter prostitution of virtues; the total disregard of morals, all these have made West Africa a seething sink of gross iniquity. . . . Boys and girls grow up in the densest atmosphere of sin, where there is hardly a redeeming feature, and all this under the strictest adherence to the outward laws of Islam."[11]

It is easy to understand why the missionaries waged an anti-Islamic crusade, because Islam was a focus of resistance to their proselytizing. We must not, however, assume that the relationship between the missionaries and the colonial administration was always healthy. Although one always hears of a conniving between the missions and the civil colonial authorities, the reality was much more complex.

For example, as Christopher Harrison observes, the "charitable" activities of Cardinal Lavigerie in Algeria may have fitted well with France's rhetoric of the civilizing mission of colonialism, but the Algerian colonial administration was, nevertheless, forced to restrain the cardinal in his zeal to use Algeria as a base to spread the Christian faith throughout Africa. These restraining measures were dictated by political prudence (Harrison: 18).

One also recalls the controversy over the bid to apply France's 1901 secularization laws to Islamic education in French West Africa. The colonial Catholic clergy was infuriated by the colonial authorities' decision not to impose the laws on the Muslims. The church establishment accused the administration of Islamophilia. Monsignor Bazin, the head of the White Fathers in French West Africa in 1908, warned that Islam was the sin of Europe in Africa, a sin for which Europe would have to pay a high price (Harrison: 60).

Although the decision not to apply the secularization laws to the Muslims was clearly dictated by political expediency, it is a fact that some administrators were atheists or at least anti-clerical and were, therefore, not warm to the idea of spreading Christianity in the colonies. There may be some truth after all to the suggestion that some administrators occasionally supported the Muslims "just to annoy the priests."

It is also wrong to assume that missionaries' attitudes to Islam were all of a kind. The attitudes of R. Bosworth-Smith toward Islam were remarkably different from those of evangelicals like C. H. Robinson and Miller. While Bosworth-Smith, like others, desired the ultimate victory of Christianity over Islam in Africa, he also believed that the best way to achieve this was to cooperate with Islam. He argued that, though less beneficial than Christianity, Islam did put an end to, among others, drunkenness, human sacrifice, and polytheism: "The main part of the continent [of Africa], if it cannot become Christian, will become what is next best to it, Mohammedan."[12]

The notion that Islam's role in Africa should be welcomed as preparing the way to a higher truth—Christianity—may not have been widely held by missionaries, but the notion's echoes can be found in the writings of Edward Blyden, the West Indies–born missionary, who spent a great part of his life in Sierra Leone and Liberia in the late nineteenth and early twentieth centuries.

Blyden's admiration of Islam and Muslims sets him apart from nineteenth-century missionary scholars of Islam. He saluted Islam's universalism and its ethos of racial equality.[13] He also had great admiration for the simple but effective methods used by Muslim missionaries to spread the faith in Africa. A careful reading of Blyden's works will, however, reveal that his attitudes toward Islam are at best ambiguous.

To use V. Y. Mudimbe's words, Blyden had "faith in the practical superiority of Islam over Christianity."[14] But it must be stressed that such faith never led to the questioning of Christianity's theological superiority as a revealed religion over Islam. His interest in Islam was motivated by his attachment to his vision of what Christianity could have been, freed, as it were, from its cultural accretions. Another interest that inspired his admiration for Islam was pan-Africanism. He clearly believed that Islam had a salutary impact on African society: "Mohammedanism in Africa has left the native master of himself and of his home; but wherever Christianity has been able to establish itself, with the exception of Liberia, foreigners have taken possession of the country, and, in some places, ruled the natives with oppressive rigour" (Blyden: 309).

On the specific subject of Islam's impact on Africa, Blyden wrote that "all careful and candid observers agree that the influence of Islam in Central and West Africa has been, upon the whole, of a most salutary character. As an eliminatory and subversive agency, it has displaced or unsettled nothing as good as itself" (Blyden: 174).

Clearly Blyden, the missionary, welcomed Islam's displacement of pre-Islamic African beliefs and practices. Would he, however, have welcomed Islam's displacement of Christianity? He proposed a problematic syncretism in the following passage: "Where the light from the Cross ceases to stream upon the gloom, there the beams of the Crescent will give illumination; and, as the glorious orb of Christianity rises, the twilight of Islam will be lost in the greater light of the sun of Righteousness. Then Isaac and Ishmael will be united" (Blyden: 233).

Blyden's radiant metaphors should not obscure one fact: his belief that Islam came to prepare the Africans for the dawn of a higher truth, that of Christianity. The derivativeness of Islam is suggested by the symbolism of the Crescent's beams compared with the light from the Cross. Moreover, anyone familiar with biblical imagery will readily read "the sun of Righteousness" as "the Son of Righteousness," Jesus Christ. Isaac (Christianity) and Ishmael (Islam) will not come together in an honorable union, Ishmael will simply be lost in the majesty of his brother, Isaac. Blyden's view that Islam was a man-made religion that should be tolerated to the extent that it prepares the Africans to receive the sublime truth of Christianity becomes unambiguously clear in other passages.

Blyden considered Islam to be a creed of "purely human origin" (Blyden: 6) that should be tolerated because, though inferior to Christianity, it fulfills albeit imperfectly the mission of the latter: "We ought not to grudge the African the glimpses of truth which they catch from the Koran; for knowledge of parts is better than ignorance of the whole" (Blyden: 20).

That Blyden's interest in Islam was transitive, that is to say mediated by his ultimate concern, the triumph of Christianity in Africa, becomes quite clear in the following passage: "There will be nothing to prevent Christianity from spreading among the pagan tribes, and from eventually uprooting the imperfect Muhammedanism which so extensively prevails" (Blyden: 20).

I have sought, in my analysis of Blyden's pronouncements on Islam, to detect what Spivak calls the sovereign subject as it "operates an imperfectly hidden agenda."[15] It is the text itself that betrays its politics. The approach to Islam so far delineated, which involved studying it not from a logic internal to it but from the point of view of its ecology within colonial or evangelical designs, is bound not only to distort Islam but to produce contradictory images of Islam and Muslims.

An examination of colonial writings on Islam underscores this heterogeneity of attitudes and perceptions. Allegedly, Islam allows a handful of corrupt and scheming clerics (*marabouts*) to enrich themselves at the expense of the poor.[16] Allegedly, Islam is a rather humble religion that uses what little money it does have for the benefit of the needy.[17] Allegedly, Islam inculcates in its adherents fatalistic and resigned attitudes to life.[18] Allegedly, Islam is a communist ideology. Allegedly, it is a militant and revolutionary creed.[19] And, allegedly, African women are better off under Islam than in traditional pre-Islamic society.[20]

All these views about Islam and Muslims may very well have been born out of the different experiences of colonial officers with Muslim populations and their varying ideological relationships to Islam. These contradictory distortions are, therefore, partly the result of the essentialist approach that Said decries in his study. The behavior and actions of Muslims in different historical and sociopolitical contexts are always explained by the single unchanging fact that they are Muslim. Therefore, "any political, historical and scholarly account of Muslims must begin and end with the fact that Muslims are Muslims" (Said: 315).

What is more regrettable is that these "ideological fictions" about Islam and the African Muslim have continued to inform the perceptions of contemporary commentators on Africa's experience with Islam. More specifically, Africanists and African literary critics of African literature, as well as some African writers, continue to make generalizations about Islam and Islamic history in sub-Saharan Africa based on ideas borrowed from politically overdetermined European Orientalist sources. In the next chapter, I will assess the extent to which the survival of colonial perceptions and attitudes toward Islam contributes to outright misreadings of sub-Saharan African fiction of the Islamic tradition.

## Notes

1. William Ponty, cited in Christopher Harrison, *France and Islam in West Africa, 1860–1960* (Cambridge: Cambridge University Press, 1988), 107. Ponty's original statements were made in August 1913. Further references to Harrison's work will be indicated parenthetically in the text.

2. Edward Said, *Orientalism* (New York: Vintage Books, 1979). All subsequent references to this work will be indicated parenthetically in the text.

3. The first important examination of Said's work and its importance for the study of African literature is George Lang's "Through a Prism Darkly: 'Orientalism' in European-Language African Writing," in Kenneth Harrow, ed., *Faces of Islam in African Literature* (London, Portsmouth: Heinemann, 1991). While Lang's notion of an Africanist strain of Orientalism is useful to us, we will not focus, as he does, on Orientalist reductions of the complexity of Islam to a monolith. Of immediate relevance to us is the political character of Western scholarship on Islam in sub-Saharan Africa elaborated during the colonial period. We will return to Lang in our discussion of African(ist) literary criticism.

4. Albert Hourani, *Islam in European Thought* (Cambridge: Cambridge University Press, 1991). Further references to Hourani's book will be indicated parenthetically in the text.

5. Mervyn Hiskett, *The Development of Islam in West Africa* (New York: Longman, 1984), 209. Subsequent references to this work will be indicated parenthetically in the text.

6. Adnan Haddad, *L'Arabe et le Swahili dans la République du Zaïre: Etudes islamiques, histoire et linguistique* (Paris: Sedes, 1983), 86. All subsequent references to this work will be indicated parenthetically in the text.

7. Cited in René-Luc Moreau, *Africains musulmans: Des communautés en mouvement* (Paris: Présence Africaine, 1982), 187. All subsequent references to René-Luc Moreau's study will be indicated parenthetically in the text.

8. Christopher Harrison, *France and Islam in West Africa, 1860–1960* (Cambridge: Cambridge University Press, 1988), 107. Further references to Harrison's work will be indicated parenthetically in the text.

9. Françoise Latour Da Veiga Pinto, *Le Portugal et le Congo au XIXe siècle* (Paris: Presse Universitaire de France, 1972), 43.

10. C. H. Robinson, *Mohammedanism: Has It Any Future?* (London: Gardener, Darton, 1897), 50.

11. S. M. Zwemer, ed., *The Mohammedan World of Today* (New York: F. H. Revell, 1906), 48–49.

12. R. Bosworth-Smith, *Mohammed and Mohammedanism* (Lahore: Sind Sagan Academy, 1974), 40.

13. Edward Blyden, *Christianity, Islam and the Negro Race* (orig. 1887) (Edinburgh: Edinburgh University Press), 15–17, 175.

14. V. Y. Mudimbe, *The Invention of Africa: Gnosis, Philosophy, and the Order of Knowledge* (Bloomington: Indiana University Press, 1988), 126. All subsequent references to this study will be indicated parenthetically in the text.

15. Gayatri Chakravorty Spivak, "The Politics of Interpretation," in *In Other Worlds: Essays in Cultural Politics* (New York, London: Routledge and Kegan Paul, 1988), 118.

16. Ponty, disappointed at not receiving a satisfactory number of files on *marabouts,* reissued a circular in December 1911 that had this to say about them: "MARABOUTIC PROPAGANDA—The hypocritical façade behind which are sheltered the selfish hopes of the former privileged groups and the last obstacle in the way of the complete triumph of our civilising work. . . ." Cited in Harrison: 55.

17. The lieutenant–governor general of Senegal argued against the application of the secularization laws regarding the financing of confessional schools to Islam in the following terms: "The Muslim cult does not have any clergy. . . . The pecuniary resources of the Muslim cult in Senegal are almost nil; they are made up of offerings by the faithful and are used for the benfit of the needy amongst their fellow Muslims." Cited in Harrison: 60.

18. See Harrison: 72–73.

19. Armand Abel, *Les musulmans noirs du Maniema,* a publication of the Center for the Study of the Problems of the Contemporary Muslim World (Bruxelles: Centre pour l'étude des problèmes du monde musulman contemporain, 1960), 32.

20. Paul Marty argues that "the situation of women is certainly better amongst the Islamized population of the Niger valley than amongst the fetishist societies. Islam gives her a certain personality, thanks to which she can acquire, possess and sell [material goods] . . . to a certain extent govern her own life

and, above all else, she may pray. The fetishist woman, similar to the woman of pagan antiquity, takes no part in religion . . . and if she is reasonably free physically to come and go as she pleases she is not by any means her own mistress." Cited in Harrison: 132.

# 3

# Islam and Africanist Literary Criticism

*The twenty-first century man or woman cannot be a creature of medieval fantasies and dogmatic superstition. What follows now is, I know, a highly unlikely proposition, but who knows? . . . And so to the proposition—if the United Nations, or more probably UNESCO, has not yet found a theme for the closing decade of this century, what about declaring it a Decade for Secular Options?*
—Wole Soyinka, "Religion and Human Rights," *Index on Censorship*

There is a deeply ingrained pattern of prejudice toward and denial of Islam in European writing on Africa. While this denial and ideological hostility occurs in many realms including the political, of more immediate interest to me are the perceptions of and attitudes to Islam in contemporary African(ist) literary criticism. Wole Soyinka,[1] therefore, is of interest to the extent that a discussion of his systematic "othering" of Islam in his nonliterary pronouncements will be an effective way of bringing my discussions to the realm of African literature and its criticism.

The scholarly exchanges between Ali Mazrui and Wole Soyinka in the new *Transition* pertain to the debate on ideology and cultural politics in literature and the human sciences in general, and more specifically to the question of African authenticity and the Islamic factor.[2] Mazrui wrote the article, "Wole Soyinka as a Television Critic: A Parable of Deception," in response to Soyinka's negative critique of Mazrui's television series, *The Africans: A Triple Heritage*, in *Index to Censorship*. In his article, Soyinka accuses Mazrui of denigrating indigenous African culture in the series. Perhaps more significantly, he alludes to the fact that Mazrui is not only culturally Arabized, he is also by both blood and vocal identification part Arab. He considers it relevant to refer to this fact especially as in the exchanges Mazrui insists that the TV series regards Western enslavement as more extensive and more brutal than that of the Arab slave trade. The series, argues Soyinka, is clearly a form of Islamic propaganda and that Mazrui is, like Gaddafi, an alienated African. The only response Soyinka deems suitable to the series is the production of a new series on the (real) African done "from a black African perspective."

In his turn, Mazrui defends his series against Soyinka's charges of denigrating indigenous African culture and accuses Soyinka of identifying the threat to Africa's authenticity primarily in religious terms. Linguistic alienation, in Mazrui's view, is far more destructive. He also accuses Soyinka of not having watched the entire series, otherwise he would never have made his charges. He also considers Soyinka's dismissal of him as an Arab as a manifestation of his ethnosectarian prejudices and his anti-Northern (Nigerian) and anti-Islamic proclivities. Moreover, Soyinka is accused of practicing political eugenics, of being the latest champion of racial blood quantification: "Why is Soyinka taking us down this fascist path of racial quantification and genetic explanation?" asks Mazrui.

Some of the issues of this debate are potently relevant to a study of Islam in African literature and the scholarship that pertains to it. Although Soyinka denies it, his major charge against Mazrui's series is that the documentary is a work of pro-Islamic propaganda. Although only one of the nine segments of the series directly deals with religion, Soyinka casts the theme of the series in unmistakably religious terms:

> The explicit thesis of his [Mazrui's] series was the contest for the African soul by the two religious superpowers—Christianity and Islam. In the process, a subtle act of denigration of African authentic spirituality becomes apparent. Even though as a scholar Mazrui pays lip service to African deities which existed from before the advent of Islam and Christianity, such religions to him lacked substance, depth or relevance to contemporary society. ("Religion and Human Rights," 83)

Elsewhere, Soyinka expresses what were to him the ostensible and the real intentions of the series: "A series which was dedicated to redressing the appalling ignorance and misrepresentations of a vast continent ended up being just another expensive propaganda for the racial-religious superiority of *seductive superstition* imported into or forced down the throat of the African continent" ("Religion and Human Rights," 85, emphasis added).

What is this "seductive superstition" that has been imported to or "forced down the throat of Africa?" If the references to Islam still remain veiled, they become transparent when Soyinka writes: "Let those who wish to retain or evaluate religion as a twenty-first century project feel free to do so, but let it not be done as a continuation of the game of denigration against the African spiritual heritage as in a recent television series perpetrated by Islam's born again revisionist of history, Professor Ali Mazrui" ("Religion and Human Rights," 85).

The above statements deserve commentary. It is significant to note that not much is made so far of Mazrui's ethnic identity. Instead, there is concentrated focus on his religious identity: he is a Muslim. And Soyinka has made sweeping statements about Islam itself as a religion: it is a "superstition." He also generalizes about the history of Islam in Africa: it is alien to Africa, it does not belong there; moreover, it was mainly spread through violence and force. What is especially striking here is Soyinka's rhetoric of violence, the tropes of ideological hostility.

By the sound of it, Mazrui has committed a violent crime by *perpetrating* the series. He is not only a Muslim, he belongs to Islam; he is owned and moved to action by the seductive forces of this superstition. He is a born again, a fanatic, a religious crusader, perhaps a dangerous professor. Soyinka, the authentic African visionary, is clearly surprised that there are still individuals who hold that religion, Islam especially, has any relevance to a new vision of Africa as this continent faces the challenges of the twenty-first century. Islam may after all not only be alien to Africa, it is also alien to our era. It is not only an imported superstition, it is also an antiquated superstition, a tale that is full of fury and violence but signifying nothing.

In his defense, Mazrui contends that his television series, contrary to Soyinka's accusations, is a celebration of indigenous African culture. Responding to Soyinka's charges that the documentary denies African culture any relevance to Africa's future, Mazrui argues that the series articulates the relevance of the culture for two of the most important concerns of our age, the concern for the environment and the concern for gender equality ("Wole Soyinka as Television Critic," 166). The documentary, contends Mazrui, salutes African indigenous values as more protective of the environment than either Islamic or European-Christian mores ("Wole Soyinka as Television Critic," 167). An excerpt from the documentary reads:

> In traditional Africa, animals had souls and could be either good or evil, holy or profane. There was a time when African springs and val-

leys could be sacred and mountains could touch gods. The forces of creation and the things created were part of the same reality. Christianity and Islam brought a god who was separate from the creation, enthroned in heaven while man was made King over the animals below. The animal world was now a servant of man, rather than a partner. Theories of evolution had taught Westerners [recently] that animals were their brothers; Africans had known that for centuries. ("Wole Soyinka as Television Critic," 167)

Mazrui suggests in the series that both Islam and Christianity have played havoc with African religious paradigms. The series, argues Mazrui, salutes African culture for giving women more central roles than did either Christianity or Islam:

The African woman under Western influence has been relegated to less fundamental roles in society. . . . Secretarial work is less basic than cultivation, typing is less basic for human survival than cultivation, typing is less fundamental than drawing water, office work less central to the human condition than firewood and energy. ("Wole Soyinka as Television Critic," 171–172)

Mazrui further affirms in his article that in parts of Africa Islam has marginalized women even more ("Wole Soyinka as Television Critic," 177).

Although Mazrui's arguments cited above constitute a strong defense in response to Soyinka's charges against the series, it is interesting to question their probity from a slightly different perspective. First of all, regarding the gender question, the distinction between fundamental and nonfundamental roles that Mazrui tediously reiterates is at best spurious. If one were to follow this paradigm then slaves should have nothing to complain about: their work is certainly more fundamental than that of their masters, who are quite content being employed as consumers of their slaves' services. What Mazrui neglects is the whole question of real social value attached to the work performed in a given society. Talpalde Mohanty has addressed this question in her article, "Under Western Eyes: Feminist Scholarship and Colonial Discourse." Quoting Rosaldo Michelle, she writes that "a woman's place in human social life is not in any direct sense a product of the things she does (or even less, a function of what biologically, she is) but the meaning her activities acquire through concrete social interactions."[3]

It is therefore crucial to make a distinction between, for example, the act of mothering (which is very fundamental indeed) and the status a given culture at a given time confers upon it. Social roles are not in themselves necessarily prestigious or marginalizing. They can only be contextually analyzed. Coming from Africa himself, Mazrui should know that women working in offices as clerks, typists, or receptionists generally perceive themselves—and are perceived by others—as being more fortunate than the women who perform (more fundamental?) tasks such as farming the land or cutting and carrying firewood. Needless to say that, apart from being a generalization, the view that African women were better off in pre-Islamic African society than in African Muslim societies is one that many scholars do not share.

In response to Soyinka's charge that the series denied indigenous African culture "relevance to contemporary society" and that the documentary dismisses African culture and promotes Islam, Mazrui quotes from his series: "In any fruitful union of our triple heritage, the indigenous legacy must surely be the real foundation" ("Wole Soyinka as Television Critic," 169).

Mazrui's defense is arguably strong. But some of its weaknesses need to be highlighted. To start with, Mazrui's evidence to show that his series celebrates indigenous African culture is inconclusive.

First of all, the series is audio-visual in form. Therefore, frozen excerpts from a documentary do not suffice to prove Mazrui's case. After all, the series relied not only on an oral commentary but also on the synchronization of voice and image, the selection of sequences and their strategic syntactic disposition, techniques of telescoping, and other narrative techniques. All of these devices could have been used to promote Islam in the series regardless of the content of the oral commentary that Mazrui quotes.

One also senses in Mazrui's arguments an eagerness to please, a desire to be considered as one of the promoters of African culture. One can with reason doubt the good faith of Mazrui when he states, in defense of his stance on the Rushdie affair, that he, Mazrui, (a self-proclaimed Muslim) is categorically against all forms of capital punishment. One can also be unconvinced by Mazrui's call for the establishment of holidays in African countries to commemorate African deities. Muslim readers in particular may find it bizarre that one who declares daily that "there is no god but Allah" should call for the honoring of pre-Islamic African deities. Whether this is vintage Mazrui, as Soyinka suggests, or genuine concern for Africa's cultural authenticity is a matter of interpretation. I, however, see traces of ideological ambiguity at work here. Mazrui may very well have unwittingly accepted what I surmise to be Soyinka's definition of the true Africans as those who are critical of alien ideologies that historically brought havoc to a forged ahistorical monolith called African culture. The question that remains to be answered is this: Can one be a committed Muslim, or for that matter a committed Christian, and still remain a "true" African? While Mazrui's answer will be fraught with ambiguity, Soyinka's will tend to be in the negative.

Soyinka formulated his response to Mazrui's defense in the article "Triple Tropes of Trickery." Here Soyinka emphasizes the necessity of redoing the series from a "black African's perspective." Apparently Mazrui is not qualified to do the job: not only is he culturally Arabized but "he is by both blood and vocal identification part Arab," and also proudly speaks of his Arab lineage. Mazrui is not exempt from "interested" charges of the kind that could be made against the Buddhist who tells the Hindu that Buddhism is more compatible for Indians than Christianity or Islam ("Triple Tropes," 181). Soyinka further affirms that although some conversions to Islam in Africa took place through persuasion and dialogue, Islam "was mostly imposed through violence, coercion and conquest" ("Triple Tropes," 181).

The monadism implied in Soyinka's argument with its attendant racialism is one that is obviously problematic. I will not endeavor here to define who the true Africans are, nor to know what Soyinka means by a "black perspective." It is, however, obvious that Soyinka is malevolently preoccupied with Islam. In his exchanges with Mazrui, he rehearses some of the negative opinions about Islam that one finds in colonial writings. Islam is a seductive superstition that was imposed on the Africans through the sword. Perhaps the most disturbing aspect in Soyinka's posture in the debate is the move to discredit an African scholar's interpretation of African history on the bases that the scholar is a Muslim and has allegedly Arab-Islamic sympathies.

Also significant is the fact that Soyinka's only evidence that Islam was spread through violence is not from historical scholarship, but from a work of fiction, Sembène Ousmane's *Ceddo* ("Triple Tropes," 181). Soyinka automatically erodes the boundaries between history and fiction. Moreover, even if one were to take *Ceddo* as a faithful reflection of historical fact, one could legitimately ask whether the conversion of the Ceddos of Senegal constitutes a paradigm for all conversions in Africa. The fact is that *Ceddo* neither reflects historical reality, nor does it as a consequence tell us much about the complex modes of conversion to Islam in Africa.

Moreover, Soyinka claims that he treats Islam seriously. His special reference for this claim is his treatment of the subject in his book *Myth, Literature and the African World* (1979).[4] But what exactly does

Soyinka mean by the expression "treating Islam seriously"? It is admittedly to Soyinka's credit that he signals an oversight in traditional criticism of African literature. Due to the background of the majority of the better known (sub-Saharan?) African writers, he argues that

> it is often forgotten that there is also an important proportion of the literary output whose inspiration derives from a non-Christian worldview, most notably that of Islam. Either in self-contained forms, that is springing entirely from and resolved within an Islamic frame of reference . . . or, as a reaction against the Christian presence . . . the Islamic vision has played a fertile role in the literary creations of the last century. (*Myth*, 76)

Shortly after acknowledging the Islamic tradition as an important source of inspiration, Soyinka proceeds to sketch the different trends in the literature of Islamic inspiration. He singles out the work of Amadou Hampaté Bâ, *Vie et enseignement de Tierno Bokar, le sage de Bandiagara,* as belonging to the tradition of direct proselytizing (*Myth*, 81). One of the features of *L'Aventure ambiguë* (*The Ambiguous Adventure*) of Cheikh Hamidou Kane is that in it "the *superstitions* of Islamic religion are given a philosophical glow" (*Myth*, 86, emphasis added). Soyinka then speaks of a different school of iconoclasm, one bent on secularizing "old deities." Of course, to Soyinka, this is a welcome ("organic") step forward: "The gods themselves, unlike the gods of Islam and Christianity are already prone to secularism; they cannot escape their history" (*Myth*, 86).

No special analytical skills are required to see that Soyinka's secularist vision informs his attitudes toward religion in general and Islam in particular. Has he not written the history (read nondestiny) of the "gods of Islam and Christianity," these superstitions of the past that Africa must now go beyond? How should anybody expect Soyinka to react to the specter of a fellow African intellectual perceived as wishing to "retain or evaluate religion as a twenty-first-century project"? Soyinka thus creates a neat new school of African writers to which Sembène Ousmane belongs: "The works of this latter group reveal the current trend in African writing, a trend which is likely to become more and more dominant as the intelligentsia of the continent propose ideological solutions that are *truly divorced* from the *superstitious accretions of our alien encounters*" (*Myth*, 86, emphasis added).

That Soyinka is hostile to Islam needs no further illustration. What is of immediate relevance to us is the extent to which this ideological hostility to Islam leads him to misinterpret African novels with an

Islamic subtext. Having already conveniently put Ousmane in the camp of those with an assertive secular vision totally devoid of the superstitions of Islam, how will Soyinka deal with positively depicted Muslim characters in Ousmane's fictional world? The answer is simple: he will secularize them. This will be seen in the chapter on Sembène Ousmane. It must, however, be emphasized at this point that Soyinka, the secularist, is not a promoter of Christianity either. I have only analyzed his response to Islam because it falls within the purview of this study. As well, Soyinka is only one of several African critics who are malevolently preoccupied with Islam.

For example, Martin Bestman and Patrick Corcoran betray in their critical writing attitudes to Islam similar to those of Soyinka. They both agree with Ousmane's alleged portrayal of Islam as the greatest impediment to self-determination and progress. I will examine these critics and more in the chapter on Sembène Ousmane. I wish, however, to single out one critic, Debra Boyd-Buggs, for immediate analysis. She has dedicated a book-length study to one of the most notorious character types in Senegalese fiction.

Clearly Boyd-Buggs's dissertation must be applauded for being one of the first works to concretely acknowledge the historical role played by Islam in African society and to recognize Islam as a fertile source of inspiration for many West African writers of fiction.[5] Having said that, however, I also recognize the need to highlight some of the misconceptions and misinformed opinions about Islam in her work.

Boyd-Buggs's study starts with a very interesting distinction between "maraboutism" and "maraboutage": "Maraboutism refers to the existence in the Muslim world of religious personnel who serve as intermediaries between God and men: maraboutic interventions that involve the syncretism of Islamic practices with elements of traditional African religion are called maraboutage" (Boyd-Buggs: 1).

One can gather from this definition that maraboutism, characterized by the existence of religious intermediaries, exists in the entire Islamic world, but maraboutage, involving syncretism between Islamic and non-Islamic practices, is an African monopoly. The author further restricts the phenomenon of maraboutism itself to African and Arab countries "where it is practised" (Boyd-Buggs: 4). It is easy to anticipate the author's thesis regarding the peculiar character of the Islam that is practiced in black Africa, one that is defined by its ontological impurity. Reference is made here to the infamous concept of "black Islam," which the author clearly subscribes to: "In Senegal, as in other parts of *Black Africa,* Islam involves the syncretism of two world views: animism and the fundamental beliefs and duties of Islam. The coming together of these two cultural currents has resulted in a phenomenon that certain islamologues and sociologists refer to as Black Islam" (Boyd-Buggs: 9).

I do not wish to anticipate my discussion of this erroneous and condescending concept of "*Islam noir.*" Of immediate importance to us is Boyd-Buggs's use of this concept as it relates to her notions of Senegalese conversion to Islam and the role of the marabouts in this conversion.

The author emphasizes the view that the Senegalese were able to accept Islam because the brand of Islam preached to them was custom-tailored to meet their capabilities. This work of simplifying Islam "for the believers most of whom were illiterate" was carried out by the marabouts (Boyd-Buggs: 10). The simplification in turn was accompanied by the deforming adaptation of Islam to the special character of the Senegalese. "The islamization of the Senegalese people was accomplished by the marabouts or Muslim spiritual guides who were able to adapt successfully the Muslim religion to the cultural style of the country" (Boyd-Buggs: 9).

The view that Muslims in black Africa are particularly given to syncretic religious practices and that the Africans' conversion to Islam is superficial and incomplete are ideas that were developed in the politically motivated colonial scholarship on Islam. Recent scholarship on the subject has proved that such views are at best highly simplistic and condescending (an issue I shall return to in my concluding discussion of the general misconceptions and errors in European-language writing on Islam and Islamic history in Africa). A fundamental question needs to be asked: does this critic have the fundamental knowledge of Islam that would enable her to discuss the Islamic framework in the novels she interprets?

Boyd-Buggs's study, which required a lengthy stay among the Muslims of Senegal, is typical of the kind of analysis that invites a rebuttal. Boyd-Buggs's thesis regarding polygamy is that a proper reading of Islamic sources indicates that Islam favors monogamy over polygamy:

> Actually *the Prophet's words about polygamy in the Koran* do not entitle a man to four wives: "*Si vous craignez d'être injustes envers les orphelins*, n'épousez que peu de femmes, *deux, trois ou quatre parmi celles qui vous auront plu. Si vous craignez d'être injustes*, n'en épousez qu'une seule *ou une esclave. Cette conduite vous aidera plus facilement à être justes.*" [If you fear that you will be unjust to the

orphans, *then marry only a few women* of your choice: two, three, four, or a slave. This action will help you to become just more easily.] This passage from the Koran clearly states that if, and only if a man has the financial means to equally love and provide for more than one wife, polygamy is permissible. In one sense, these words of the Prophet suggest that most men should restrict themselves to a single wife, since few men, if any, can love several women on an equal basis. They will almost always prefer one over the others. (Boyd-Buggs: 226, emphasis added)[6]

Anyone with knowledge of Arabic will immediately detect Kasimirski's tendentious interpretation, in French, of the Koranic verse. Nowhere in the original verse does the phrase *peu de femmes* figure. That and the translator, Kasimircki's, use of the restrictive French form *ne . . . que* (only, as in "marry only a few women") are interpolations intended to support the thesis of the Koran's favoring of monogamy. Therefore, any argument based exclusively on this "translation" is doomed to be flawed.

Problematically, Boyd-Buggs appears to be unaware of the fundamental distinction between the Koran, which Muslims consider literally as the Word of Allah, and the *ahadith* as the teachings of the Prophet. One does not have to be a Muslim to acknowledge the distinction. Moreover, what does one make of the statement that "only if a man has the financial means to equally love and provide for more than one wife. . . ."? Certainly financial means are required to provide for one's spouse materially, but what has a man's "ability" to love a woman got to do with money?

It is also not clear how Boyd-Buggs makes the link between the Koranic emphasis on *adl* (fairness or equity), which she herself interprets as the equal treatment of the wives, and the necessity to *love* the wives equally. The French translation makes no mention of love. Is the writer not in effect perhaps unconsciously interpreting a Koranic verse with a Euro-Christian frame of reference?

In another verse from the same *sura* (chapter) the Koran acknowledges a man's inability to love equally his wives: "You are never able to be fair and just as between women, even if it is your ardent desire: but turn not away (from a woman) altogether so as to leave her (as it were) hanging (in the air)" (Koran, 4: 129).

This acknowledgement coincides with Boyd-Buggs's view, although she is not as categorical as the Koran. It is significant to note, however, that such a scriptural acknowledgement does not lead to Boyd-Buggs's conclusion that Islam favors monogamy over polygamy.

My brief analysis has illustrated that Boyd-Buggs's knowledge of the object of her study is significantly limited. It is of interest to show how this factor negatively affects her ability to interpret the Islamic references in the novels she studies. I will limit my analysis, for now, to her critique of Cheikh Hamidou Kane's novel, *The Ambiguous Adventure*. One of the distorting features in Boyd-Buggs's study is her conception of the ideal Muslim as he is portrayed in Senegalese fiction. Moussa Tine in Mamadou Dia Mbaye's *Au delà de la vertu* is just one such archetype of the ideal Muslim (Boyd-Buggs: 66). The most outstanding trait of this paradigmatic Muslim is that he is "a true ascetic, he separates himself from the world" (Boyd-Buggs: 65). Similarly, Maître Thierno in Kane's *The Ambiguous Adventure* is a "model mystic whose life is exemplary of Islamic virtues" (Boyd-Buggs: 70); he "is one of the most flawless examples of Islamic virtues" (Boyd-Buggs: 64). The principal attribute of this flawless Muslim is his monasticism—he separates himself from the world: this notion clearly echoes one of the areas of polemic against Islam, its alleged exclusive concern with spiritual matters. One of his other outstanding Islamic virtues is that he is an "extremely rigid individual who never laughs" (Boyd-Buggs: 70). This concept of the ideal Muslim as one who is exclusively preoccupied with spiritual concerns informs Boyd-Buggs's problematic interpretations of the nature of the conflict dramatized in Kane's work.

Boyd-Buggs clearly sees an opposition between the otherworldly preoccupations of the model Muslim, the ascetic Maître Thierno, and the pragmatic concerns of la grande royale, the Diallobé princess. The central question posed by the novel is clear. In the wake of colonial conquest should the Diallobé send their children to the French school to learn the ways of the conqueror or not? Going to the French school will, in the eyes of the supporters of the school, improve the material lot of the Diallobé. According to Boyd-Buggs, the maître, who is preoccupied "with the spiritual and not with the physical" (Boyd-Buggs: 71), is the spokesman for tradition and the partisan of Muslim conservatism (Boyd-Buggs: 134). He, therefore, dismisses the earthly concerns of his people: "The question which arises from this conflict involves the possibility that Thierno's teaching really did not deal with the whole man. The Grande Royale contends that man is not all spirit. At this point, the theme of equilibrium comes to play. Thierno's teaching over-emphasizes the spiritual while ignoring the physical needs of the Diallobé people" (Boyd-Buggs: 138).

I have already come across this view of Islam in colonial scholarship, the view of Islam as a reactionary religion, one that is unsympathetic to any changes aimed at improving earthly society. It is a similar view that informs Kenneth Harrow's study, "Camara Laye, Cheikh Hamidou Kane, and Tayeb Salih: Three Sufi Authors."

According to Harrow's analysis, the maître represents the Sufi guide, the spiritual leader whose exclusively spiritual concerns are in direct conflict with the sociopolitical preoccupations of la grande royale, the embodiment of the prince. Harrow's study thus reduces the complex issues at stake to the struggle between the prince and the spiritual leader. I wish to argue that the text seeks to subvert precisely this kind of dichotomy.

The issue at stake is well spelled out: the Diallobé want to know from their maître whether or not he is in favor of Diallobé children going to school. This question could be broken down to simpler ones. Is "secular" education incompatible with Islamic values? Is the quest for material felicity irreconcilable with the Islamic ethos? Are God and work antinomies? And last, is Kane's novel suggesting an opposition in Islam between spiritual and temporal powers?

Harrow's interpretation is unequivocal about the irreconcilable conflict between power and religion: "An opposition signalled symbolically in terms of day versus night, female versus male, robustness and great style versus fragility and physical debility, life versus death, fructification versus debility—in short, between worldly values and spiritual ones."[7]

The parallels between these observations and Boyd-Buggs's are unmistakable. Both critics base their analyses on the thesis of an opposition between spirituality and practical human action aimed at solving concrete human problems.

However, the very first page of the novel presents the maître, the alleged ascetic or model Muslim who is exclusively concerned with spiritual matters, as a man who recognizes the necessity of work: "Two occupations filled his life: the work of the spirit and the work of the field" (*The Ambiguous Adventure,* 7). Moreover, instead of expressing opposition to the French school, the maître acknowledges its necessity. Interestingly enough, it is the chief (the real prince) and the "school headmaster" who are openly opposed to it.

The maître has heard rumors that in the Western world God and socio-economic justice, God and the fight against human injustice, are seen in oppositional terms. Hence, in that context (and here he is probably alluding to communist revolutions, or even specifically to the French Revolution): "The revolt against poverty and misery is not distinguished from the revolt against God" (*The Ambiguous Adventure*, 11).[8]

The maître blames so-called men of religion, who ruled unjustly in the past, for this unhappy equation. Much like Bakary and Bakayoko, the activists in Sembène Ousmane's *Les Bouts de bois de Dieu,* the maître is of the opinion that material misery breeds spiritual apathy. Hence education that may prevent material misery is in effect a way of saving religion.

On the first meeting with the prince, the maître finally makes a very important remark concerning the historical complementarity between spiritual and temporal power in Diallobé governance: "And the masters of the Diallobé were also the masters whom one-third of the continent chose as guides in the way of God, as well as in human affairs" (*The Ambiguous Adventure*, 12). The maître clearly did not see his vocation as being directly in opposition to that of the prince?

It is worth noting that the maître's attitude thus delineated in the first part of the novel remains basically the same throughout. In a second encounter with the "temporal head" of the Diallobé, the maître, in response to the latter's misgivings concerning "secular" education in the French school, reiterates the argument that the fight against misery, that is, the quest for material felicity through education, is in the interest of religion: "Extreme poverty is, down here, the principal enemy of God." (*The Ambiguous Adventure*, 34).

Boyd-Buggs states that the maître "is one of those who want to save God at all costs" (Boyd-Buggs: 70). This observation is hardly supported by the fact that in a letter to Samba Diallo in France, the chief recounts the discussions during his last meetings with the maître. Here again the chief construes his opposition to foreign education as an act in defense of God. The maître's reply is at once unequivocal and decisive. God needs no man to defend him: "But, I ask you, can God be defended from man? Who can do that? Who has the right? To whom does God belong? Who has not the right to love Him or to scoff at Him? Think it over, chief of the Diallobé: the freedom to love God or hate Him is God's ultimate gift, which no one can take from man" (*The Ambiguous Adventure*, 125).

This remark is significant in many respects. First of all God cannot be seen as an obstacle to human happiness. Second, contrary to the fool who later kills Samba Diallo for refusing to pray under pressure, the maître is a proponent of freedom of conscience. This reading is at variance with Boyd-Buggs's view upon reading Kane's novel that "Islam might be viewed as an obstacle to individual freedom of conscience" (Boyd-Buggs: 133).

In fact the maître's remarks are in line with the Koranic principle that states: "Let there be no compulsion in religion." Finally, the maître's remark is a cryptic allusion to some self-styled Islamic states that selectively apply Islamic law (*sharia*) in the name of the promotion of religious values. The maître's explanation for this is truly refreshing in light of contemporary pseudo-theocratic systems in the Muslim world:

> The truth is, O God, that there are always cunning men to make use of Thee. Offering Thee and refusing Thee, as if Thou hast belonged to them, with the aim of keeping other men in obedience to them! Chief of the Diallobé, reflect that the revolt of the multitude aginst these shysters may take on the significance of a revolt against God—when on the contrary it is the most holy of holy wars! (*The Ambiguous Adventure*, 126)

All this goes to show that the maître is very lucid regarding the theological concept of the interconnectedness of the temporal and the spiritual, worldly and otherworldly concerns, and unequivocally recognizes the need for "secular" education and humans' involvement in the affairs of the world.

The problems in the critical approaches to Kane's novel are typical of critical approaches to Islamic content in general. The problems are mostly due to a failure to situate the conflict dramatized in the novel within an Islamic paradigm. This is a consequence of the ignorance of that framework coupled with uncritical adoptions of tenured notions of Islam's exclusive concerns with spiritual instead of temporal concerns. The ignorance exhibited by traditional criticism regarding the history and sociology of Islam in sub-Saharan Africa is matched by a general ignorance of Islam itself. Many Africanist scholars and African writers, including Soyinka, have acknowledged the Islamic tradition as a major source of inspiration for many of Africa's best writers. Accordingly, the need to understand the Islamic framework has been felt. I contend, however, that ignorance of Islam as a religion still characterizes many of the studies on the Islamic content of sub-Saharan African novels.

One of the popular approaches to sub-Saharan African novels of the Muslim tradition involves the identification of the representatives of Islam or the Islamic voices in a given fictional work. This identification is in turn used to determine the author's attitudes toward Islam. I do not consider this approach invalid in itself. What is questionable, however, are the criteria used for such a selection. It is not so difficult in real life to determine who represents Islam: I simply see whether the person's stance is in conformity with the stance of the Koran and the Sunna on specific issues. To discern the Islamic voice in a novel can be much more complicated, even though an omniscient narrator sometimes makes it unequivocally clear whose voice represents Islam.

It might also be esthetically relevant to find out the criteria used by the narrative to characterize the Islamic voice. The narrator, or even the author, might be using the wrong criteria due to ignorance of the characteristics of a Muslim. The possibility that Islam is associated with the least Islamic character for ironic reasons is one that the critic still has to bear in mind. What about the critic's own criteria? What are the critic's definitions of a Muslim? Are they informed by Islam's basic definition of a Muslim, or are they gleaned from the haphazard observation of Muslims? Are the critics' sources about Muslim works of the imagination including the one that is the subject of critical interpretation? I wish to argue that in general traditional criticism of the sub-Saharan novel tends to use more or less responsibly all these sources except the Islamic one.

Just as Soyinka, to prove his point regarding the violent propagation of Islam in Africa, simply refers to a fictional source (Ousmane's *Ceddo*), Martin Lemotieu, in order to illustrate the centrality of the institution of begging in Islam, has no other source except Kane's *The Ambiguous Adventure*.[9] Some critics simply have their private criteria for selecting the Islamic voice in a novel; this electoral practice is obvious with Boyd-Buggs.

It is significant that critics do differ considerably over who represents Islam in a given novel. It is interesting, for example, to see the amazing diversity of opinion about which character represents the Islamic voice in Aminata Sow Fall's *La Grève des Bàttu*. There are divergent views about which character best represents the values of Islam, especially on the subject of charity.

Boyd-Buggs, without any hesitation, identifies the marabout, Birama, as the ideal Muslim in the novel: "Birama stands for the ideals of Islam and Sow Fall uses him as the expositor of the authentic meaning of the *zakat*. Described as unselfish, wise, and full of knowledge, he is obviously a man worthy of respect, a practising believer who not only teaches (he is a Koranic schoolmaster), but who prays and reads the Koran faithfully" (Boyd-Buggs: 84).

I am not interested at this point in showing the errors in these statements. Attention should, however, be drawn to the fact that the critic has made no reference to Islamic sources in her attempt at defining the authentic meaning of *zakat* and at identifying the ideal Muslim. More significantly, to promote her thesis she has had to do considerable violence to Sow Fall's text: nowhere in the novel, for example, are we told that Birama is unselfish or that he reads the Koran faithfully. Indeed, one wonders from where Boyd-Buggs gets her definition of the ideal Muslim. It is certainly not from Sow Fall's text, nor for that matter from Islamic sources. Furthermore, she sees the other marabout in the novel, Kifi Bokoul, as the antithesis of Birama: "Kifi Bokoul is an alms deviant in that he urges Mour to make sacrifices to the poor solely for the purpose of bringing of certain desires to fruition" (Boyd-Buggs: 88). (The dishonesty of Seringe Birama encourages sacrilege, because out of opportunism, he cannot stop the deviations of Mour, who provides his food.)

It is significant to note that Jacqueline Boni-Sierra's assessment of the two characters is diametrically opposed to Boyd-Buggs's. For Boni-Sierra, Birama is little more than a charlatan: "L'imposture de Seringe Birama favorise le sacrilège car, par opportunisme, il ne peut entraver les déviations de Mour qui le nourrit."[10]

For Boni-Sierra, Kifi Bokoul, Boyd-Buggs's deviant, not only represents the power of God on earth, he is actually God incarnate: "L'intrigue nous met en sa présence. . . . Comment Dieu nous apparaît-il dans l'intrigue? . . . La fiction littéraire permet à l'auteur de le personnifier dans Kifi Boukoul, 'cet homme qui n'est pas un homme,' cet homme sans visage ni forme humaine précise." [The plot brings us to his presence. . . . How does God appear in the plot? . . . Literary fiction allows the author to present him in the person of Kifi Boukoul, "this man who is not a man," this man whose face and form are not human, as Boni-Sierra observes.] (Boni-Sierra: 82)

Such a diversity in views is due, to a very large extent, to the critics' interpretation of Islamic references from a logic that is external to Islam. I will illustrate in my analysis of Sow Fall's work how this Orientalist predilection accounts for many of the misreadings of Sow Fall's novels.

The emphasis I have placed on the necessity to understand the Islamic framework in order to interpret correctly the Islamic references in imaginative texts must not blind us to the attendant danger of essentialism. I am referring to the danger of subordinating discrete circumstances of Muslims in diverse socio-economic contexts to what Edward Said calls the sheer unadorned and persistent fact of their being

Muslims. Said spares no words in condemning Orientalist essentialism for assuming that "any political, historical and scholarly account of Muslims must begin and end with the fact that Muslims are Muslims" (Said: 315).

The essentialist approach to the study of Islam and Muslim societies involves what Said calls radical typing, the tendency to obliterate the distinctions between the type, which in this case is "the Muslim," and ordinary human society (Said: 231). In other words, an absolute coincidence is posited between the definition of the type and reality. "Thus in trying to illuminate a prototypical and primitive linguistic type, as well as a cultural, psychological and human one, there was also an attempt to define a primary human potential out of which completely specific instances of behavior uniformly derived" (Said: 233).

I define the primary human quality to be the fact of being a Muslim. Essentialism can thus be observed in traditional criticism in its tendency to use the Islamic identity of certain characters to explain all their actions, especially those deemed negative. This systematic assumption of rigid religious determinism informs many studies that seek to interpret the Islamic content of sub-Saharan fictional works. In fact, some critics read novels as though they were explicit theological tracts.

For John Davidson, Bakri in *Seasons of Migration to the North* represents "the religious rigor of Islam," that is to say the oppression inherent in the culture of Islam.[11] The novel, according to this reading, explicitly deals with the origins of the oppression and subjugation of women. Predictably, the origin is the "misogynistic mastery of Islam" (Davidson: 397). All the negative attitudes toward women displayed by characters in the novel are ascribed to such characters being Muslim. Similarly, Sonia Ghattas-Soliman builds her analysis of the same novel on the premise that "the Sharia (the laws of Islam), the Quran and the Hadiths (the teachings and sayings of the Prophet Muhammad) are the foundations of the legal system in the Sudan and in the Middle East in general."[12] And she adds that "since local customs and practice have their root in the Quran and in the Hadiths, they will serve as a basis for our [study]" (Ghattas-Soliman: 91).

I am not concerned with the fact that these statements are false generalizations. What is significant to me is that they form the premises for explaining the oppression of women in Tayeb Salih's novel.

Lemotieu similarly sees Islam as the principal explanatory category in his analysis of the attitudes of Muslim characters in the sub-Saharan African novel:

> Comment en effet saisir la psychologie de Fama, celle de Tahirou, de Samba Diallo ou d'Ibrahima Dieng sans faire référence à ce moule religieux dans lequel ils ont été formés? (Lemotieu: 51)

> Indeed, how can one understand the psychology of Fama, or that of Tahirou, Samba Diallo, or Ibrahim Dieng without making reference to this religious mold in which they have been shaped?

I do not deny the relevance of the religious orientation of the characters. What is problematic is seeing it as the determining factor for all the actions undertaken by the characters as Lemotieu's analysis suggests. The ideological character of the essentialist approach becomes obvious when one realizes that rarely is Islam used to explain the positive stance taken by a Muslim character in a novel.

To conclude this review of problematic criticism of the sub-Saharan African novel with an Islamic subtext, I turn to a study that may be considered paradigmatic of the translation of Orientalist attitudes and approaches to African literary criticism: Pierrette Herzberger-Fofana's article, "Les Influences religieuses dans la littérature féminine d'Afrique Noire."[13]

The following ideas can be extracted from Herzberger-Fofana's study: Islam was invented by Muhammad; Islam is a fatalistic, reactionary, and misogynistic creed. Moreover, the critic rehashes the concept of "Islam noir," and her study is informed by the essentialist approach. Perhaps the more interesting aspects of this work are the suspect strategies deployed by the critic to attenuate her rhetoric against Islam.

The expressions *religion d'origine orientale, préceptes de Muhamed*, and *la religion de Mahomet* evoke the concept of "Mohammedanism" used by some non-Muslims to designate what to them is a religion invented by Mohammad. I have observed one of the consequences of this ideological stance in Boyd-Buggs when she practically collapsed the fundamental frontiers between *ahadith* (the teachings of the Prophet) and the Koran, literally considered by Muslims to be the Word of Allah.

Herzberger-Fofana's text betrays the origin of her ideas, French Orientalist discourse. The inconsistency in her spelling of the Prophet's name provides the clue. The name "Mahomet" conjures up the image of the false prophet—but then the critic reverts elsewhere to the more standard name, "Mohamed." This inconsistency is open to interpretation. I, however, choose to read this as the "palimpsest effect." Herzberger-Fofana's script is superimposed on an earlier script (Orientalist discourse), which it seeks to perpetuate but under a new label of objective scholarship. The older script is simply clawing at the new text to tear away the mystifying veil of scholarly objectivity.

According to the older script, Islam is a fatalistic creed, the opiate of the people. That is precisely Herzberger-Fofana's reading of Aminata Sow Fall's novel, *La Grève des Bàttu:*

> "Opium du peuple," la religion est une drogue qui d'une part permet au peuple d'oublier sa misère, de se satisfaire dans la médiocrité et d'accepter son sort. (Herzberger-Fofana: 196)

> As "opium of the people," religion is a drug that on the one hand enables the people to forget their misery, to be content in mediocrity, and to accept their fate.

That religion in general is referred to in this text only thinly disguises the fact that the critic's particular focus is Islam. Moreover, in a move to give her statements the aura of objectivity, Herzberger-Fofana adds somewhat paradoxically:

> D'autre part la religion est une force. Les mendiants puisent leur énergie dans leurs convictions religieuses pour se soulever contre le pouvoir. (Herzberger-Fofana: 196)

> On the other hand, religion is power. The beggars derive their energy from their religious convictions in order to rise against the state.

The rhetorical strategies deployed by Herzberger-Fofana could be likened, to use Soyinka's felicitous metaphor, to "the (fabled) habit of the African rodent that blows soothing air on the wound in the flesh of its human victim after every bite" ("Triple Tropes," 180).

The same technique is used in her interpretation of the subjugation of women in the novels she analyzes. One of the most repugnant scenes in Sow Fall's *Le Revenant* recounts Ousseye's ruthless beating of his wife because she did not do his laundry, and he further demands an apology. True to the essentialist approach, Herzberger-Fofana uses Islam to explain this scene of domestic violence: "Une telle subordination de la femme s'inscrit dans la conception musulmane." [Such subordination of women is in conformity with Muslim principles.] (Herzberger-Fofana: 198)

Again, the critic moves quickly to add a rather interesting concession: "La religion Chrétienne contient des préceptes d'autorités qui peuvent aisément rivaliser avec la religion de Mahomet." [Christianity contains principles of authority that can easily rival the religion of Mahomet.] (Herzberger-Fofana: 198)

Another feature of Herzberger-Fofana's study is its subscription to the concept of "Islam noir":

> Religion d'origine orientale, l'Islam se fondant avec les rites traditionnels a donné naissance à un culte spécifique: "l'Islam noir" qui diffère quelque peu des préceptes de Mohamed. (Herzberger-Fofana: 192)

> Islam, a religion of Oriental origins, when it fuses with traditional beliefs, gives rise to a distinct religion: "black Islam," which differs somewhat from the teachings of Mohamed.

It must be further emphasized that for none of the assertions the critic makes about Islam does she present any evidence. Perhaps, more significantly, Herzberger-Fofana's ideas about Islam negatively affect her exegesis of the works of women writers in sub-Saharan Africa, a point I will address in my chapter on Aminata Sow Fall. Suffice it to indicate here that her erroneous view of *La Grève des Bàttu* as the most caustic criticism of the influence of Islam in Senegalese society (Herzberger-Fofana: 194) is a direct consequence of her inability to interpret correctly the Islamic references in this novel.

The analysis in chapter 1 of this book focused on the often contradictory perceptions of Islam in colonial scholarship. The subsequent analysis of Soyinka, Boyd-Buggs, and other contemporary critics of African literature illustrates the survival in contemporary scholarship of some of misconceptions about Islam. It is now time to revisit a few of these ideas both in light of recent scholarship on the subjects they evoke and, where applicable, from a logic that is internal to Islam.

While African writers like Wole Soyinka, Sembène Ousmane, and Ayi Kwei Armah promote the view that Islam was spread in Africa through violence, there are other writers and commentators who curiously allude to Islam's preparedness "to accept a humble role as a catalyst and a wide range of levels of commitment; 'it does not nag excessively those who lie towards the pagan end of the continuum.'"[14]

At the other extreme it has been suggested that Africans' conversion to Islam is only superficial. In other words, the ethical and social codes of Islam are too austere for the psyche of the African. This notion is not unrelated to Boyd-Buggs's view of the role of the marabouts as Muslim proselytizers who simplified Islam to suit the ethos of the

Senegalese. This construction of the assimilation of Islam in black Africa has given rise to the notion of "Islam noir," black Islam.

The view that Islam was spread by the sword is a very old one; it is not my intention to document its history. What is more immediately significant is that African writers like Ousmane and Soyinka continue to subscribe to this generalization. I have already mentioned Soyinka's comments in his exchanges with Mazrui. Ousmane is definitely less tempered in his views. Concerning the spreaders of Islam in Africa, he wrote:

> Then, later, Islam was introduced to West Africa by Mohammed's spiritual heirs. From the beginning, they opposed feudalism but their presence, because of their scholarship, was tolerated by the Africans. In Mali, fetishists and Muslims were living together. The mosques were respected and nobody came to desecrate them. However, when the Muslims became more powerful, they decided to suppress all the other religions. They did the same thing in Ghana and Timbuctu. The Gao empire was destroyed by the Muslims.[15]

The spread of Islam in Africa is a subject that has continued to interest many contemporary scholars and historians. Perhaps the better known among them are Mervyn Hiskett, René-Luc Moreau, Thomas Hale, and Nehemia Levtzion. Such scholars have benefited from research facilities that were not available to their predecessors; more historical, literary, and sociological sources in non-European languages have become available. This is of course aided by the imperatives of more rigorous, context-specific scholarship. The result has been a significant revision of many stereotypical and ahistorical views about African history and society in general and African Islamic history and sociology in particular.

On the subject of African conversion to Islam, Hiskett writes:

> The process of conversion to Islam from a traditional African religion—whether animism or polytheism—began as soon as the first Sudani started to copy certain of the habits of his Muslim acquaintances, and to interest himself in their ideas. It has continued ever since. Under what circumstances did this process begin? What course did it then take? What were its end results? (Hiskett: 302)

For analytical purposes, Hiskett distinguishes between two principal modes through which Islam was spread in Africa—military conquest and peaceful persuasion. He highlights the significance of conquest in the sixteenth-century conversions in the Volta region. Likewise, conquest enjoyed brief success in Wahabu under the nineteenth-century jihadist Al-Hajj Mahmud, as well as in the territories of the Alimamy Samory (a Sembène Ousmane hero) during his career as a jihadist. Hiskett, however, questions the effectiveness of the imposition of Islam by conquest:

> Such conversion, by force of arms rather than by the persuasion of argument and example, tended to bring clans and yet larger political and social groups nominally to Islam. This happened all together and all at once because at the stroke of the sword, Islamic institutions and the government of the Sharia are imposed upon them. However, while this may have compelled some of the people to conform to Islamic law and behavior to some extent, no one can say how many of them really accepted Islam in their hearts. (Hiskett: 302)

Hiskett asserts a second method of conversion, that of peaceful persuasion carried out by Muslims who lived in non-Muslim societies in which they lived and worked. The conversions of Gao, Tamdakkat, and the other cities in the western Sudan before the eleventh century, writes Hiskett, were thus effected, although the history of such conversions also included violent interludes. Contrary to widely held opinion, Hiskett suggests that ancient Ghana might after all have been converted peacefully and not through violence. The violent political rivalry between Sumanguru and Sunjata apart, it was peaceful penetration that brought Islam to ancient Mali. Wandering Sunjata, Kunti shaykhs, and their Marka followers succeeded in bringing Islam to the Bambaras and the northern Mossis. The nineteenth-century jihads, however, proved more compelling in enforcing Islamic observance.

Hiskett's analysis must warn us at once from making undiscriminating generalizations about the spread of Islam in Africa and from creating neat dichotomies between conversion by peaceful means and conversion through conquest. Hiskett suggests that peaceful conversion is not really an alternative to forceful conversion. Instead, "conversion is better seen as a continuum, a single line, that runs through peace and violence according to the circumstances of place and time" (Hiskett: 303).

Scrupulous scholars must therefore be context-specific in their analysis. They must ascertain when and where a particular mode of conversion played a more significant role in the spread of Islam. Slogans such as "Islam was spread by the sword" or "Islam was forced down the throat of the Africans" are not only paternalistic to Africans, both Muslim and non-Muslim, but they also grossly distort a much more complex historical reality. Such slogans ignore, for example, the effectiveness of people directly or indirectly involved with trade as spreaders of Islam in black Africa, just as was the case in Indonesia and Malaysia, for instance. Of course, sometimes trade provides only the context for the spread of the new ideas. Patrick Ryan has argued that *ulama* (Islamic scholars), who were not traders themselves, may have significantly contributed by bringing Islam to the Yoruba capital of Old Oyo in the sixteenth century. He also emphasizes the role played by Muslim Hausa slaves of non-Muslim Yoruba in the spreading of Islam in Yoruba land (Hiskett: 303–304). Levtzion has also emphasized the simplicity and rationality and scholarship of Islam as explanations for Islam's attractiveness in West Africa.[16]

It must be added that the continued growth of Islam in Africa, especially during and since the colonial period, makes it necessary to deemphasize the role of conquest in the spread of Islam in black Africa. Peter Clarke's statistical data in this regard are significant: he observes that Islam has made the most rapid progress in West Africa in recent times. At the beginning of the twentieth century, Burkina Faso (formerly Upper Volta) and the Ivory Coast were regarded as non-Muslim by the colonial administration. In the 1960s, a random sample of people in Burkina Faso argued that Islam had been making progress and that the trend would continue. "Among the reasons given were Islam's effective use of radio, the feeling that it was an 'African' religion, and that it was easier to become, for example, a Muslim than a Catholic" (Clarke: 134).

The notion that Islam's success is due to its being an "easier" religion relative to Christianity is one that I will contend with later. What is relevant to note here, however, is that Islam continues to make steady gains in Africa. The trend observed in Burkina Faso is also observable in many other parts of the African continent. For example, the southern part of the Ivory Coast was categorized as non-Muslim by the colonial administration, but by the beginning of World War II a historian made the significant if exaggerated prediction that "an Islamic Ivory Coast was a reality." The percentage of Muslims in the Ivory Coast rose from 7 percent in 1921 to 22 percent in 1960 (Clarke: 135).

The explanations given above for the success of Islam in Burkina Faso betray a certain view about the fit of Islam to the African psyche—in other words, the belief that Islam was more appealing to the Africans because it was less ethically exacting. Islam's admission of polygamy is often cited as an example. It is, indeed, interesting to note that while some detractors of Islam emphasize violence as the means by which Islam was spread in Africa, others underline the facility of Islam as a reason for its appeal. Mary Kingsley argues that conscience, when conditioned by Christianity, is an extremely difficult thing for an African trader to manage successfully for himself, for he would be forced constantly to make compromises. And "the man who is always making compromises gets either sick of the thing that keeps on nagging at him about them or he becomes merely gaseous minded all round." By contrast, she continues, Islam gave a clearer "line of rectitude under African conditions" (Clarke: 139).

Christianity, according to this analysis, contains more austere metaphysical truths and more exacting moral codes than Islam. Africans are thus attracted to Islam because it demands much less of them, a total break with the past is not required, and up to four wives are allowed. The paternalism of these views requires no commentary. Moreover, they fail to explain recent trends in conversion to Islam in many parts of Africa.

In this regard, Peter Clarke argues that the supposed fit is suspect because recent research in western Nigeria shows that due to economic pressures, to education, and to Christianity, polygamy "will soon be a 'rarity' of the past. This does not appear to have influenced Islam's progress in the region" (Clarke: 140).

I do not necessarily agree with the prediction of the demise of polygamy among African Muslims, or for that matter among Muslims in general. The worldwide Muslim trend toward monogamy (I would say serial polygamy) is unmistakable. But such trends informed by economic and demographic factors as much as by national government policies may be reversed at any time when the above conditions are altered. The point the research illustrates is nonetheless clear: The appeal of Islam in Africa cannot be explained in terms of its alleged moral laxity. Such a myth is in fact contradicted by yet another, that Islam's socio-ethical code is too austere and rigid for the African mind.

Indeed, Boyd-Buggs's thesis that Islam was simplified through syncretism by the marabouts who spread it in Senegal is not a new idea. It can be traced back to colonial perceptions of the African Islamic reality. In fact, her comments echo with incredible faithfulness François Clozel's views when he wrote that "the fetishist convert in uttering the ritual formula does not acquire the mentality of the Arab or the Berber. . . . Sudanic Islam seems to be profoundly stained with fetishism. It is a mixed religion, the product of two original beliefs" (Harrison: 99).

Much has been written about the zeal with which Europhone Africanists have documented the originalities of Islamic practice in sub-

Saharan Africa. So original is African Islam that it had to be recognized as a separate and distinct Islam, a black Islam.

The concept of black Islam is informed by nineteenth-century racialist theories. Blacks are (genetically?) incapable of understanding or living by the sublime metaphysical precepts of the Koran. Colonial administrator-scholars like Paul Marty were not content to document what were to them peculiarities of Islam in sub-Saharan Africa, they also subscribed to racial determinism. About the Senegalese *mourides,* Marty wrote that "the black mentality is completely incapable of bearing the metaphysical concepts of the Oriental semites and the ecstatic digressions of the Soufis" (Harrison: 116).

Elsewhere, he expanded the category of the races that are incapable of understanding the metaphysical concepts of Islam to include the Malaysian and the Chinese. He did not, however, relinquish the idea of racial determinism. "As Islam distances itself from its cradle . . . it becomes increasingly deformed. Islamic confessions be they Malaysian or Chinese, Berber or Negro are no more than contrefaçons of the religion and state of the sublime Coran" (Harrison: 116).

Africans who choose to may find comfort in the fact that this time they have not been singled out as the only race incapable of assimilating sublime concepts. Of course, for the proponents of black Islam, Marty's comments call for the recognition of more Islams, e.g., Malaysian, Chinese. However, recent scholarship has become increasingly critical of the concept of black Islam.

René-Luc Moreau is probably one of the first Western scholars to examine critically the concept of black Islam. He does not deny that there are elements of pre-Islamic culture in Islamic practices in sub-Saharan Africa, but he rejects the approach of Jean-Claude Froelich and even dismisses the concept of syncretism. In his view, syncretism is frozen and ahistorical and thus fails to describe the dynamic dialogue between the present and the past that one observes in Islamic practices in Africa:

> Mais on ne peut guère, ici non plus, parler de syncrétisme, il s'agit du jeu normal du dialogue et des échanges culturels, conforme aux lois de l'adaptation et de l'adoption, dans un mouvement aux rythmes et aux phases diversement modulés. (Moreau: 234)

> Even here, one can hardly speak of syncretism. It is about the usual dynamic of dialogue and cultural exchanges, which are informed by the laws of adaptation and adoption, in a movement whose rhythms and phases vary.

According to this view then, if there is at anytime a society (Arab or non-Arab) in which the Islamic ideal can be observed, such an ideal is what it is, historical and relative. Hence adds Moreau:

> Chez certains peuples, il y eut peut-être un dynamisme rectiligne vers l'Islam, progressif et continu, mais ceci fut sans doute rare; le plus souvent il y eut des ruptures, des retours en arrière et des reprises. (Moreau: 234)

> In some societies, there might have been a rectilinear movement towards Islam, one that is progressive and continuous. But this was certainly rare. More often there were discontinuities, regressions, and repetitions.

The past dies very hard and even when it does, it has the ability to reincarnate itself in the present and cohabit with it. As Adnan Haddad puts it,

> A vrai dire, les traditions et les moeurs auxquelles se heurtent toute nouvelle religion, ne sont pas pour leurs peuples respectifs comme un chapeau que ceux-ci n'auraient qu'à ôter, au contraire elles marquent tout, elles pénètrent tout, elles imbibent tout, elles cristalisent tout. (Haddad: 130)

> In reality, the traditions and mores that any new religion confronts are not, for those who practice them, like a hat that the people can simply take off. On the contrary, they stamp everything, penetrate everything, and bind everything together.

Hence, there is the Islamic concept of *tajdid* (renewal), which emphasizes the need for Islamic reform aimed at bringing the Muslims back to purer Islamic practices whenever the circumstances call for that. Islamic history is replete with such *tajdid* movements. One readily recalls the eighteenth-century reform movement of Mohammad Ibn Abd al-Wahab in the Hijaz, the heartland of Islam, about which Moreau writes:

> Les Wahabites ont voulu passer aux actes en luttant à la fois contre les grands schismes—le Kharijisme et le Chisme—et au sein du Sunnisme, contre les divisions d'écoles et de confréries, en proscrivant tout culte des saints, le prophète y compris, et toutes les superstitions populaires déclarées d'origine païenne. (Moreau: 259)

The Wahabis, who decided to take action, fought at once against the great schisms—Kharijism and Shism—and within Sunnism iself, against divisions along the lines of brotherhoods and schools of thought by prohibiting all worship of saints including the Prophet, and all popular beliefs deemed to be of pagan origin.

The *tajdid* process undertaken by the nineteenth-century West African jihadist Usman Dan Fodio also sought to combat mixed Islam among the Hausa. Hence, from West Africa to the Hijaz (today's Saudi Arabia) the phenomenon of mixed Islam sometimes characterized by the inordinate reverence for holy men is the concern of Islamic purists. This conclusion certainly undermines the definition of African Islam, an Islam that is characterized by the belief in saints who act as mediators between God and humans. These beliefs have existed and continue to exist in different parts of the Muslim world. I will end my discussion of the issue of mixing and the more specific concept of black Islam by quickly mentioning the contributions of Moreau and George Lang to scholarship on this subject.

Following Moreau, Lang has insisted on the universality of the phenomenon of mixing and diversity of approach. So-called African Islam marked by the survival of pre-Islamic practices is not an anomaly in the Muslim world. In other words, diversity and variety of approach are not an African monopoly (Lang: 305). Part of the problem is that Africanists writing about Islam fail to look beyond the African continent to the wider Islamic world for parallels in trends.

Countless examples can be adduced to illustrate the parochial and/or ideologically burdened representation of Islam and Muslims in African(ist) criticism. The issues so far raised deal more directly with the interpretation of the Islamic subtext in West African novels. The images of Islam that emerge from critical literature indicate a translation of colonial perceptions of Islam as a primitive and regressive superstition, either imposed by force or else singularly deformed to suit the defective ethical standards of the Africans.

As in the case of colonial perceptions, the views about Islam in literary criticism lack consistency. At one end of the spectrum, there is the view that Islam's hold on the African mind is at best tenuous. At the other end, the essentialist approach posits a rigid religious determinism that explains the actions and thoughts of Muslims by relating them to the unchanging, ahistorical, and all-determining fact of their being Muslims. The issues raised so far and many more relating to the shortcomings of traditional criticism will be presented in the course of my revisionist study of a selected body of sub-Saharan African novels of Islamic tradition.

My survey of the critical literature would, however, be partial if I failed to indicate some purple patches on the critical canvas. It has now become a fact that the study of much African fiction is impossible without reference to the Islamic tradition. Thus, three books have been published, all of which are collections of essays dealing directly with interpreting the Islamic subtext in African fiction. I am referring to the *Nouvelles du sud* special issue, *Islam et littératures africaines* (1987), *Faces of Islam in African Literature* (1991), and *The Marabout and the Muse: New Approaches to Islam in African Literature* (1996). It is obvious from my analysis that some of the studies in these books still exhibit problems in the treatment of their Islamic subject. Some studies should, nevertheless, be singled out for proposing a new kind of approach to the study of Islam in the African novel.

Edris Makward's essay, "Women, Tradition and Religion in Sembène Ousmane's Work," is truly refreshing. The study acknowledges a new shift in the African novel from a linguistic (English-French) to a religious polarity based on writers' attitudes toward Islam. The thought was impressed upon him by an address given in 1979 by Wole Soyinka:

> In his address, Soyinka started by eloquently praising Sembène Ousmane for his sharp criticism of Islam and Islamic influence in Senegal in his novel, *Les Bouts de bois de Dieu* (1960), while denying Cheikh Hamidou Kane the merit of authenticity because of his positive treatment of Islam in *L'Aventure ambiguë* (1961), as an integral part of his people's heritage rather than an alien religion imposed through the sword, and through intensive social and political pressure.[17]

Soyinka's address must have sounded like a rehearsal of his showdown with another unapologetic promoter, Ali Mazrui. Soyinka, the high priest of secularism and African authenticity occasionally rises to the occasion to excommunicate the unrepentant cultural apostates of Africa.

Makward's analysis of the attitudes of Armah and Yambo Ouologuem within the context of the emerging religious polarity is very interesting for its attention to details and scrupulousness. His identification of Ouologuem as an apostate seems, however, anachronistic in view of the Malian writer's recently reported new intensive Islamic spirituality.[18] Notwithstanding, Makward's study has many merits, not the least of which is the questioning of the widely held opinion that Ousmane is an apostate.

Anny Claire-Jaccard's study, "Les Visages de L'Islam chez Mariama Bâ et chez Aminata Sow Fall," is in my estimation one of the more serious attempts at analyzing the imaginative responses to Islam by African writers.[19] The study's competent use of Islamic sources (e.g., the Koran) sets it apart from such studies as Ghattas-Soliman's. The study's greatest merit, however, is its context-specific analysis of the conflicts dramatized in the novels of the two writers. Her knowledge of Islam enables her to detect when a character's actions are motivated by genuine Islamic feeling and when they contradict Islam despite the character's declared motives. Most refreshing is her analysis of the causes of oppression of women in the works of the two writers.

Claire-Jaccard's mature use of Islamic sources recalls the study of Morita Knicker, "Le Coran comme modèle littéraire dans *L'Aventure ambiguë* de Cheikh Hamidou Kane."[20] Only an intimate knowledge of the Koran could have enabled Morita Knicker to decipher the subtle use of Koranic verses in Kane's novel. The intertextual study demonstrates that African novels of the Muslim tradition do not only relate to the Islamic framework from a purely thematic perspective. One of the many merits of Knicker's study is that it enhances my appreciation of the interface between two textual traditions, the Islamic and the Europhone.

Before ending this global summary of the traces of Western Orientalist opinion on Islam in Africanist writing, I must acknowledge my debt to George Lang's article, "Through a Prism Darkly: 'Orientalism' in European-Language African Writing." Lang's study documents the features of Europhone writings on Islam in sub-Saharan Africa and the carrying over of what has historically been the European dogmatic view of Islam into Europhone Africanist writing and thought. The manifold effects of the often unconscious reduction of Islam's prismatic complexity upon Africanist writing, even to some extent among writers of Islamic tradition, constitute Lang's primary concern. One of the consequences of the denial of the complexity of Islam, writes Lang, is that it impedes the understanding not just of Islam but of Africa, and diminishes the "full spectrum of its variety to a single murky hue." In the realm of literary criticism, "very often one or other facet of Islam is either missed by Western critics or cast out of context." Lang's study is a significant contribution to the discussions on the Islamic texture of the sub-Saharan African novel. Without it I would still have produced this chapter, but not with the same conviction and confidence.

A more balanced and more tolerant image of Islam is emerging in African(ist) literary criticism. Studies in the recently published *The Marabout and the Muse: New Approaches to Islam in African Literature,* edited by Kenneth Harrow, (1996) represent a significant development in this direction. The volume, which is a sequel to *Faces of Islam,* underscores Islam's pluralist heritage in the Maghreb and sub-Saharan Africa.

Moreover, the process of replacing tenured stereotypes with informed ideas based on exacting scholarship is a painful and slow one. In as much as I salute some of the work that has been recently done on the subject of Islam and the sub-Saharan African novel, I must state that such studies are still piecemeal, and call for more integrated approaches to the subject.

In the following chapters, I will look at specific novels to analyze the problems with traditional criticism of these texts as well as to see the specific ways that Islam is textualized in them. Of particular interest is the task of determining the authors' textual relationships to Islam, and of highlighting the failure of traditional criticism to understand these sometimes complex relationships.

## Notes

1. The attitudes of Patrice Lumumba, one of Africa's revolutionary legends, readily come to mind. Lumumba's party, Mouvement National Congolais-Lumumba (MNC/L), was born and developed in the heartland of Congolese Islam (Batela-Bakusu of Maniema and of Sunkuru). It is noteworthy that the word "Islam" is never cited, neither in the writings nor in the speeches of Emery Patrice Lumumba. One commentator observes that the resolutions adopted by the MNC/L made no mention of the concerns voiced by the Muslims (Haddad: 91).

2. The debate is in four articles. The first one, Mazrui's "Wole Soyinka as a Television Critic: A Parable of Deception," *Transition* 54 (1991): 165–177, is Mazrui's response to Soyinka's "Religion and Human Rights," *Index on Censorship* 17, no. 5 (1988): 82–85, in which Soyinka critiques Mazrui's 1986 PBS and BBC Television series, "The Africans: A Triple Heritage." Soyinka's rejoinder, "Triple Tropes of Trickery," *Transition* 54 (1991): 178–183, provoked yet another counterattack from Mazrui in "The Dual Memory: Genetic and Factual," *Transition* 57 (1992): 134–146. "Footnote to a Satanic Trilogy," *Transition* 57 (1992): 148–149, is Soyinka's (*Transition*'s chief editor's) way of imposing a truce.

3. Tapalde Chyandra Mohanty, "Under Western Eyes: Feminist

Scholarship and Colonial Discourse," *Boundary* 2, nos. 12.3 and 13.1 (Spring/Fall 1984): 333–358.

4. Wole Soyinka, *Myth Literature and the African World* (Cambridge: Cambridge University Press, 1976). All references to this study will be indicated parenthetically in the text under the abbreviation, *Myth*.

5. Debra Boyd-Buggs, "Baraka: Maraboutism and Maraboutage in the Francophone Senegalese Novel," Ph.D. thesis, Ohio State University, *Dissertation Abstract* 47: 899A, 86. All subsequent references to this study will be indicated parenthetically in the text as Boyd-Buggs.

6. Boyd-Buggs cites from the translation by Kasimirski. The most standard English translation of the Koran is Yusuf Ali's, in which the verse reads:

> If ye fear that ye shall not
> Be able to deal justly
> With the orphans
> Marry women of your choice,
> Two, or three, or four,
> But if ye fear that ye shall not
> Be able to deal justly (with them)
> Then only one, or (a captive)
> That your right hands possess (4: 3)

*The Meaning of the Holy Qur'an,* new edition (Brentwood: Amana Corporation, 1991). All subsequent references to the Koran will be indicated parenthetically in the text.

7. Kenneth Harrow, "Camara Laye, Cheikh Hamidou Kane, and Tayeb Salih: Three Sufi Authors," in Kenneth Harrow, ed., *Faces of Islam in African Literature* (London, Portsmouth: Heinemann, 1991), 290.

8. I have used the translation by Katherine Woods, Heinemann, 1972.

9. Martin Lemotieu, "Interférence de la religion musulmane sur les structures actuelles de la société négro-africaine: L'Exemple de *La Grève des Bàttu* d'Aminata Sow Fall," *Nouvelles du sud: Islam et littératures africaines* (Paris: Silex, 1987), 52. Subsequent references to this study will be indicated parenthetically in the text.

10. Jacqueline Boni-Sierra, "Littérature et société: Etude critique de *La Grève des Bàttu* d'Aminata Sow Fall," *Revue de littérature et d'esthétique négro-africaines* 5 (1984): 82. Further references to this study will be indicated parenthetically in the text.

11. John E. Davidson, "In Search of a Middle Point: The Origins of Oppression in Tayeb Salih's *Season of Migration to the North*," *Nouvelles du sud: Islam et littératures africaines* (Paris: Silex, 1987), 387. Further references to this study will be indicated parenthetically in the text.

12. Sonia Ghattas-Soliman, "The Two-sided Image of Women in *Seasons of Migration to the North*," *Research in African Literatures* 20, no. 3 (Fall 1989): 91. Subsequent references to this study will be indicated parenthetically in the text.

13. Pierette Herzberger-Fofana, "Les influences religieuses dans la littérature féminine d'Afrique noire," *Nouvelles du sud: Islam et littératures*

*africaines* (Paris: Silex, 1987), 191–199. Subsequent references to this study will be indicated parenthetically in the text.

14. Such is the view of R. Hurton. Cited in Peter B. Clarke's "Islam, Development and African Identity: The Case of West Africa," in Kirsten Holst Petersen, ed., *Religion, Development and African Identity* (Uppsala: Nordiska Afrikaninstitutet, 1987), 137. All subsequent references to Clarke's study will be indicated parenthetically in the text.

15. Excerpt from a lecture delivered by Sembène Ousmane at Howard University, Washington, D.C., 19 February 1978. Cited in Françoise Pfaff, *The Cinema of Ousmane Sembène: A Pioneer of African Film* (Westport, Conn.: Greenwood Press, 1984), 168.

16. Nehemia Levtzion, *Islam in West Africa: Religion, Society and Politics to 1800* (Great Yarmouth: Galliard Printers, 1994), 208.

17. Edris Makward, "Women, Tradition and Religion in Sembène Ousmane's Work," in Kenneth Harrow, ed., *Faces of Islam in African Literature* (London, Portsmouth: Heinemann, 1991), 187.

18. Thomas Hale, *Scribe, Griot, and Novelist: Narrative Interpreters of the Songhay Empire* (Gainesville: University of Florida Press, 1990), 169.

19. Anny Claire-Jaccard, "Les visages de l'Islam chez Mariama Bâ et chez Aminata Sow Fall," *Nouvelles du sud: Islam et littératures africaines* (Paris: Silex, 1987), 171–182.

20. Morita Knicker, "Le Coran comme modèle littéraire dans *L'Aventure ambiguë* de Cheikh Hamidou Kane," *Nouvelles du sud: Islam et littératures africaines* (Paris: Silex, 1987), 183–190.

# 4

# Critical (Mis)Readings of Sembène Ousmane

*And why should ye not fight in the cause of God and of those who, being weak, are ill-treated and oppressed?* (Koran, 5: 75)

For them (the Muslims), life is nothing; all that matters are religious acts; their existence is only a hyphen between birth and death.
—Sembène Ousmane, *O pays, mon beau peuple!*[1]

Many of Sembène Ousmane's commentators have decided rather hastily and somewhat unfairly that the novelist totally rejects Islam as a nonprogressive ideology in his fiction. I wish to argue here that such misreadings of Ousmane's work also constitute misrepresentations of Islam that can be attributed to the critics' ignorance of and or prejudice toward Islam.

My analysis involves a reexamination of the arguments put forward by some Sembène Ousmane commentators—Mbye Cham, Martin Bestman, Patrick Corcoran, Louis Obielo-Okpala—who all argue in favour of the thesis that Ousmane's ideology, as it is expressed in his works, implicitly rejects Islam. I shall single out the most frequently used argument, which asserts that Ousmane's materialistic philosophy is diametrically opposed to and irreconcilable with Islam's allegedly reactionary concept of predestination, which only makes for apathy and resignation in times of socio-economic crisis.

The three novels, *Les Bouts de bois de Dieu*,[2] *O pays, mon beau peuple!*[3] and *Véhi-Ciosane ou Blanche-Genèse*,[4] relate most specifically to this theme, but in them, Ousmane's imaginative response to Islam is more complex than traditional criticism has made it out to be. Ousmane does not categorically reject the notion of the will of Allah, nor for that matter of Islam as a divine creed. All he does is present Muslims in dialogue, who debate the concept of predestination. The dialogic structure of the novels effectively debunks a fatalistic and, hence, reactionary interpretation of the concept in order to replace it with a progressive interpretation, one that reconciles the idea of the will of Allah with social activism.

In his article "Islam in Senegalese Literature and Film," Mbye Cham discusses the three artistic responses to Islam as a dominant religious force in Senegal.[5] These responses by Senegalese writers range from vigorous embrace and advocacy of Islam as the only legitimate and most effective means of achieving social cohesion and well-being, to expressions of a fundamentally materialistic ideology that sees in Islam the greatest impediment to self-determination and progress of which Sembène Ousmane is the most prominent example. That a predominantly Muslim society could produce only one literary genius to belong to the extreme pole of Islamic rejection, at least according to Mbye Cham, is of little surprise. It is still interesting to raise the question as to whether the ideological stance that Sembène Ousmane takes in his novels warrants his being labeled as an apostate. This is a legitimate question to ask because Ousmane's feeling of closeness to his people's cultural heritage is unquestionable. Moreover, Sembène Ousmane not only espouses a realist aesthetics:

> Il y a une relation entre la réalité et ce que j'écris.
>
> There is a relationship between reality and what I write.

but also assumes the role of secretary of his society:

> Lorsque j'écris, je m'adresse à mon peuple pour dire voilà comment nous sommes.[6]
>
> When I write, I am addressing my people to tell them that this is the way we are.

That such a writer could categorically reject one of the major forces that unite the Senegalese people and give them the sense of a common cultural heritage is accordingly a subject that warrants investigation.

What, in Cham's opinion, distinguishes the apostate Sembène Ousmane from the more conciliatory critics of religious holy men and charlatans is that he goes beyond "the misdeeds of the individual to project and ultimately reject Islam" (Cham: 178). According to Cham's analysis, many of the short stories in *Voltaïque,* such as "Communauté" and "Mahmoud Fall," create oppositions in which Islam is portrayed as being on the side of oppression. In some ways *Borrom Sarret* is similar to *O pays, mon beau peuple!* and *Les Bouts de bois de Dieu.* It represents two opposing reactions to socio-economic challenges. The one that Ousmane clearly endorses is represented by the cart owner's wife, who places a premium on concrete human actions to solve problems, while her husband, representing the negative response, focuses on Allah and the "*grands marabouts.*" The cart owner's attitude, according to Cham, is ascribable to his "profound sense of religious piety" (Cham: 180). This view, which postulates that Ousmane consistently and systematically identifies the representatives of Islam with negative attitudes to progress, informs the studies done by Martin Bestman, Patrick Corcoran, Wole Soyinka, and Louis Obielo-Okpala on *Les Bouts de bois de Dieu, O pays, mon beau peuple!,* and *Véhi-Ciosane.*

Martin Bestman defines the negative impact of Islam on its followers in Ousmane's work in the following terms:

> En apprenant aux croyants à subir leur malheur sans mot dire, elle (la religion musulmane) semble opposée à toute initiative personnelle et à toute innovation.[7]
>
> By teaching believers to accept suffering silently, it (the Muslim religion) seems to reject all personal initiative, and all innovation.

This belief in fatalism is, in Bestman's opinion, an impediment to progress. Moreover, it also enhances exploitation of man by man. Hence, Ousmane's positive characters categorically reject

> la bonté de la providence et opposent un refus catégorique à la religion révélée. (Bestman: 46)
>
> the benevolence of providence, and call for an outright rejection of revealed religion.

This equally explains their opposition to the "fervents," whom religion has taught resignation to the "*hasards de la vie*" (Bestman: 47). Similarly, Patrick Corcoran asserts that Faye's opposition to his father and the other reactionaries (Muslims, of course) in *O pays, mon beau peuple!* is due to their exclusive quest for spiritual transcendence, which "squares badly with Faye's attitude to the social injustice he sees around him."[8] Similarly, Louis Obielo-Okpala situates Sembène Ousmane's work in the corpus of anticlerical works by such sub-Saharan writers as Birago Diop, Mongo Beti, and Ferdinand Oyono.[9] The critic argues that Ousmane's general antagonism to religion is informed by his ideology of activism. Sembène Ousmane's assumed indictment of Islam is, therefore, part of his battle against ideologies he deems inimical to the total liberation of his people. In total agreement with Martin Bestman, whom he quotes, Obielo-Okpala observes that

> l'image de l'Islam que Sembène Ousmane nous offre dans ses écrits est celle d'une drogue qui enivre l'individu et détourne son attention de la dure réalité de sa vie. (Obielo-Okpala: 15)

> the image of Islam that Sembène Ousmane offers us is that of a drug that intoxicates the individual and prevents him from facing the stark realities of his life.

To support his thesis, the critic divides Ousmane's Muslim protagonists into three categories: the fanatics, the hypocrites, and the humanists. The fanatics are those who interpret Islamic doctrines literally and model their lives accordingly. Predictably, one of the worst consequences of the influence of Islam on such characters is their fatalistic approach to life:

> Ce fatalisme se manifeste comme une sorte d'échappatoire pour les fidèles, puisqu'ils interprètent tous les événements qu'ils ne savent pas expliquer comme les manifestations de la volonté de Dieu, et cela détruit toute initiative de même que la volonté d'agir puisque les événements sont considérés comme prédéterminés par Dieu. Les fatalistes chez Sembène Ousmane proposent la volonté de Dieu comme réponse à la question de l'existence et du destin de l'homme. Au lieu de lutter contre les obstacles de la vie et de trouver une réponse rationnelle à leur problème, ils se résignent et considèrent tout effort comme vain et comme une opposition à la volonté de Dieu. (Obielo-Okpala: 17)

> This fatalism acts like an escape mechanism for the faithful, as they interpret all events that they cannot explain as manifestations of the will of God, and this destroys at once all initiative and the will to act since these events are considered predetermined by God. The fatalists in Sembène's (literary) world use the will of God as a response to the question of existence and the destiny of man. Instead of fighting to surmount the difficulties of life, and seeking rational solutions to their problems, they are resigned and consider any effort to be vain and a challenge to God's will.

Obielo-Okpala's approach to the subject of Islam and fatalism in Ousmane's works is admittedly more nuanced than the works of the other commentators reviewed here. He recognizes a multiplicity of Muslim voices and attitudes in Ousmane's fiction. It is, however, curious that Obielo-Okpala elects to infer Ousmane's imaginative response to Islam not from the writer's positive portrayal of the "humanist Muslims," or perhaps more equitably from the varying portrayals of Muslims in Ousmane's work. In other words, in spite of the apparent sophistication of his approach, the fanatics and the hypocrites are fated to be the representatives of Islam in Ousmane's work. As well, Wole Soyinka sees an indictment of Islam in *Les Bouts de bois de Dieu* where, in his interpretation, the "Islamic voice in the community is shown to be treacherous and reactionary."[10]

The commentaries of Charm, Corcoran, Soyinka, Bestman, and Obielo-Okpala, therefore, have one thing in common. They all posit a fundamental irreconcilability between Ousmane's supposedly Marxist ideology of progress with its exclusive attention to material goals and the spiritual transcendence sought by Muslims. Could this interpretation withstand a thorough analysis of the three novels?

Admittedly, many characters in *Les Bouts de bois de Dieu* justify a resigned attitude to the plight of the African railway workers by invoking the belief in the submission to the will of God. El Hadji Mabigué, who equates fighting the injustice and exploitation perpetrated by the whites with rebelling against the will of God, is a case in point. Likewise, Séringe N'Dakourou, the imam, is furiously opposed to the strike. He too, like Mabigué, sees the presence of whites as a blessing from God and white privileges as ordained by God. Hence, rebelling against the white employers amounts to a rebellion against the Almighty—the ultimate act of heresy!

It is worth indicating, however, that not all opposition to the strike is given a religious justification. The character Bachirou, for example, presents different reasons for his stance:

> Notre syndicat n'est pas encore très solide pour se lancer dans une grève dont nous n'avons peut-être pas mesurée toutes les conséquences. (*Bouts*, 38)
>
> Our trade union is not yet strong enough to get involved in a strike whose consequences we have not yet thought through.

But, of course, as the character Samba suggests, this is just an ostensible reason for Bachirou's refusal to take part in the strike. The real one being that Bachirou thinks of himself as a *"metropolitain,"* a "cadre," whose self-interest will not be served by the strike action.

Moreover, one may ask whether the characters opposed to the strike on allegedly religious grounds could justifiably be considered as representatives of Islamic thought and conduct even within the context of the novel. This question is fundamental, since it is the basis on which the identification of Islam with reactionary thought is made. First of all, I have every reason to believe in Ramatoulaye's accusations against her brother, Mabigué. The latter is a fornicator and a thief. It is revealing that his only reply to these accusations is his resentment at not being addressed as el Hadji. The case of the imam brought from Dakar by the white authorities to pacify the strikers is not more edifying.

There is everything to suggest that the imam has been bought. His ostentatious mannerisms that go against the Islamic concept of *zuhd* (modesty) only serve to indicate that his invocation of the belief in God's will only thinly hides the "worldly" motivations of his stance. This may explain why his litany is ineffective. I cannot help considering Mabigué and the Séringe as mere Tartuffes. They do not represent an Islamic voice in the novel. That critics should interpret their negative portrayal by Sembène Ousmane as an indictment of Islamic morality is hardly warranted.

None of the progressively minded characters in the novel—those who support the strike—categorically rejects the concept of the will of God or for that matter Islam itself as a creed. The most devout Muslim in the novel, Fa Keita, is in favor of the strike. I need not, however, capitalize on this outstanding example. What the progressive protagonists provide in general is not a categorical rejection of the concept of "the will of God," but an interpretation of it that reconciles the concept with human responsibility, the religious obligation of Muslims to take positive action aimed at self- and collective improvement—the only belief that makes human accountability meaningful. Bakar cautions Sounkaré not to use religion as a justification for passivity:

> "Ne mêle pas la religion à ça. Peut-être bien que c'est la volonté de Dieu, mais nous devons vivre. N'est-il pas écrit: 'Aide-toi, je t'aiderai'?" (*Bouts,* 43)

> "Do not bring religion into this. Perhaps, it is the will of God, but we need to live. Is it not written: 'Help yourself, and I will help you'?"

The argument used here against resignation is of a deeply religious character; and in fact the book alluded to here is the Koran, in which it is written: "God will not change the condition of a People until they themselves show a readiness to change it" (Koran, 9: 11).

Along the same lines Bakar raises another issue that apparently escaped the attention of some Sembène Ousmane commentators. This issue concerns the classification of Ousmane's characters into two groups. The first group, the progressives, emphasizes man's obligation to strive for material felicity, for the needs of the body, while the other one, constituted by fervent Muslims, focuses exclusively on spiritual concerns.

However, it is with the same idea of the inextricable unity of the spiritual and the material that Bakayoko dismisses the Séringe's position:

> "Ne sait-il donc pas que ceux qui ont faim et soif désertent le chemin qui mène aux Mosquées?" (*Bouts,* 336)

> "Doesn't he know that those who are hungry and thirsty abandon the roads leading to mosques?"

In short, the strike is not only sanctioned by Islam, but it is necessary to the continued observance of Islamic worship.

It is also significant to note that the progressive characters in the novel use Islam as a frame of reference to justify their actions. Ramatoulaye begs Hadramé to grant her a loan of rice "pour la gloire de Dieu" and warns her lying brother Mabigué that "Dieu n'aime que la vérité!" Likewise, Mame Sofi asked the water vendor to grant her a loan of water for the thirsty children, only after the vendor, on being asked, asserted that he was a believer. His refusal to let the children drink after this profession of faith inspires Mame Sofi's revulsion and subsequent use of force: "Tu dis être croyant et tu laisses ces enfants mourir de soif!" (*Bouts,* 98).

The "femme au cure-dents" interprets Ramatoulaye's killing of Mabigué's bull as an act of divine intervention intended to provide the hungry with meat. Ramatoulaye does not refute this providential interpretation, she only gives it further confirmation:

> "La providence est grande mais chacun doit prendre sa part. . . . Je savais que Dieu était de mon côté et je sais aussi que l'on peut mourir de faim. . . . Dieu sait tout cela lui aussi." (*Bouts,* 116)

"Providence is great, but we must all play our part. . . . I knew that God was on my side, but I also knew that one can die of hunger. . . . God knows all this himself."

The narrator himself seems to subscribe to the notion of divine providence. The strikers, no longer content with simply spending their days idly, decide to organize war dances. This decision, suggests the narrator, has Allah's unconditional approval:

> Dieu lui-même s'était mis de la partie, il avait balayé ses parterres, son ciel n'avait plus un nuage; au-dessus des toits, des arbres, des montagnes il n'y avait plus qu'un immense vide bleu. . . . On ne voyait même plus onduler les minces fumées qui d'habitude encrassaient l'air. (*Bouts*, 126)

> God himself had taken sides. He had swept the grounds, his sky no longer had clouds; on top of the roofs, the trees and the mountains, there only remained a blue expanse. . . . One could no longer even see the fine waves of smoke which usually fouled the air.

It is also significant that the dances executed are those of the nineteenth-century Muslim activist El Mami Samori Touré, a legacy of the "jours anciens oubliés depuis des temps immémoriaux." Ousmane is creating here a mythical revolutionary past out of a historical reality that is much more recent than the narrative suggests. This play with time must make us guard against imagining that when Ousmane proudly talks about a glorious traditional past in his novels he means pre-Islamic times.

The situation in *O pays, mon beau peuple!* is very much like the one in the novel just discussed. Ousmane's spokesman, Faye, espouses a combative attitude in the face of white exploitation and a natural catastrophe. "The crux of the problem for Faye," writes Patrick Corcoran, "lies in his rejection of the Muslims' attitude to free will" (Corcoran: 37). There is, however, nothing in this novel to suggest Muslim opposition to the formation of cooperatives or to human initiative aimed at eradicating the pest. On the other hand, Papa Gomise's Christian education makes him skeptical about the appropriateness of Faye's activism:

> L'éducation reçue des missionaires avait habitué Gomis à se confier à la Providence. (*O pays*, 241)

The education he received from the missionaries had given Gomis the habit of putting trust in providence.

Elsewhere it is traditional African beliefs that provide a religious explanation for a natural catastrophe:

> "Cette année . . . nous n'avons pas sorti d'offrande. Si nous sommes punis c'est à cause de cela. Sortons le Cangourang." (*O pays,* 166)
>
> "This year . . . we have made no ritual sacrifices. If we are punished, this is why. Let us bring out Cangourang."

Obviously, Faye, unwilling to subscribe to this kind of remedy, advocates burning the larvae. It is, however, significant that at the same time he tells the people to go along with their ritual since they believe in it. There are admittedly negative statements about Islam in this novel. However, such statements beg for justification within the context of the novel and can by no means be taken as Ousmane's definitive attitude toward Islam. Doctor Abgo, for example, speaks of the conflicts within the African community, such as tensions between the illiterate and the barely literate. He tries to explain the nature of these differences and ends up making the following out-of-context statement about Muslims that has so often been quoted by critics fishing for evidence of apostasy:

> "Ceux qui retardent le plus ce sont les adeptes de Mohammed." (*O pays,* 164)
>
> "The most backward thinking are the followers of Mohammed."

No attempt is made by the speaker to justify this assertion; the truncated nature of the utterance underscores its inconclusiveness. There is another statement made by the narrator in which Patrick Corcoran finds ample illustration of the reactionary nature of Islam:

> Pour eux (les Musulmans) la vie n'est rien; seuls les actes religieux ont une valeur; leur existence n'est qu'un trait d'union entre la naissance et la mort. (Corcoran: 88)
>
> For them (the Muslims) life is nothing; only religious acts have value. Their existence is only a hyphen between birth and death.

Should this statement be valid, all of Sembène Ousmane's novels, short stories, and films dealing with the subject of marabouts and imams who spend all their time in worldly pursuits and trying to enrich themselves at the expense of their more gullible coreligionists, will not make sense at all.

The only relatively serious discussion of Islam in the novel is in the context of Moussa and his wife's attempts to bring back their son, Faye, to the observance of such religious duties as prayers. If, however, we are to take Faye's attitude toward Islam as Sembène Ousmane's, my attempts at defining the author's concrete response to that religion will be met with frustration. First of all, it is not so clear that Faye's relationship with his father is strained because of his refusal to perform ritual prayers at the mosque. Faye himself is the first to deny this explanation in a candid discussion he has with his uncle and friend, Amadou:

> "Si mon père ne veut pas me parler ce n'est pas parce que je ne vais pas à la prière, pas plus que je ne vais à la maison." (*O pays,* 120)

> "If my father does not wish to talk to me it is not because I don't go to the prayers, nor for that matter because I don't go to his house."

During the same discussion he admits his belief in God but adds that he is certainly not a "crédule" because: "Croire . . . et être empoisonné font deux" [To believe and to allow oneself to be poisoned are two different things] (*O pays,* 233). Moreover, Faye is very reluctant to really discuss his faith, which he considers to be personal. When confronted on another occasion by his mother on the same subject of prayer, Faye skilfully evades the issue by asking:

> "Qui t'a dit que je ne priais pas?" (*O pays,* 139)

> "Who told you that I do not pray?"

And when in an intimate moment, his wife shows her readiness to learn about Islam with the aim of eventual conversion, again Faye evades the subject by trivializing it:

> "J'aurai droit à quatre femmes." (*O pays,* 139)

> "I will have the right to marry four wives."

On the same occasion he reveals his disbelief in the effectiveness of prayers but adds:

> "Gardons nous seulement du mal et que Dieu nous aide à l'extraire de nos esprits." (*O pays*, 140)

> "Let us simply stay away from evil, and may God assist us in removing it from our hearts."

Finally, in a memorable encounter with his father he justifies his decision never to perform pilgrimage from a theological viewpoint! "Dieu se trouve partout" [God is everywhere] (*O Pays*, 232). Perhaps more significantly he admits:

> "Je crois en Dieu et le crains. Lorsque je suis seul quelque chose de grand me préoccupe l'esprit. Je sais que Dieu doit exister quelque part." (*O pays*, 233)

> "I believe in God, and fear him. When I am alone, big questions haunt my mind. I know that God must exist somewhere."

In spite of all these declarations of faith in Allah, another passage is often cited as the final expression of Faye's atheism. Probably out of spite for his father's narrow vision of religion, Faye tells his father that should he (his father) enter paradise, he is welcome to shut the doors behind him. We should, however, bear in mind that Islamic history is replete with examples of devout Muslims who frown upon the attitudes of their coreligionists who see worship not as an act of absolute adoration of the Creator but simply as the heavy price to pay for the coveted bliss of paradise. The Sufi poetess Rabia al Adawiya provides an interesting definition of worship: "O, Lord! If I worship thee from fear of hell, cast me into hell. If I worship thee from a desire for paradise deny me paradise."[11]

This definition of worship places Allah as the "object" of desire and not only as the mediator of another desire, the "lust" for paradise. Faye's attitudes to worship may arguably belong to a certain Sufi tradition that frowns upon ritual prayer as a thing meant only for the vulgar. This Sufi vision would admittedly not be accepted by all Muslims as completely orthodox, precisely since it tends to make prayer more a state of mind than a practice. Nonetheless, the reverence in worship it calls for combined with a sensitivity to attitude is altogether Islamic.

All this aside, *O pays, mon beau peuple!* as a whole does not provide us with concrete information as to Faye's attitude toward Islam. One would have liked to know the concrete response to Islam of the character whose progressive views Ousmane endorses. This frustration is even more acute after reading the résumé in Mbye Cham's article, which asserts that

> l'extrême gauche de l'évantail se distingue, quant à elle, par les romans et les films d'Ousmane Sembène dont la réponse à l'Islam souffre aussi peu d'équivoque que celle des promoteurs traditionnels.[12]

> the extreme left of the spectrum is represented distinctly by the novels and films of Sembène Ousmane, whose response to Islam is as unnuanced as that of the promoters of Islam.

My readings of *Les Bouts de bois de Dieu* and *O pays, mon beau peuple!* clearly show that this is not the case. In fact the only unequivocal truth one gathers from the two novels is that the inhibiting effects of the belief in fatalism cannot be ascribed to Islamic influence. It is precisely Islamic wisdom, not "secular" or Marxist thought, that is used to combat this negative interpretation of the concept of the will of God. Faye's desire that his father should perform the pilgrimage is motivated by the hope that such an experience will debunk the notion that Islam advocates passivity:

> "Regarde tous les pays que tu traverseras, observe bien les gens que Dieu mettra sur ton chemin. N'oublie pas . . . de lever la tête pour contempler les maisons et les mosquées. . . . Toutes ces choses ont été faites par la main de l'homme. Un grand toubab a dit "L'homme c'est la conscience de Dieu," et je trouve qu'il a raison." (*O pays*, 233)

> "Look at all the countries you shall traverse; observe carefully the people whom God will put on your path. Do not . . . forget to raise your head to contemplate the houses and the mosques. . . . All those things were made by the hands of man. A great white man has said, 'Man is the conscience of God,' and I think that he is right."

To speak in more general terms, the narrator in *O pays, mon beau peuple!* constantly draws attention to the sense of community that Islam provides for its followers, a sense of charity expressed in the observance of *sadaqat*, and the general sense of equality and communal spirit that the following passage expresses so well:

> Comme dans un enchantement venait la nuit. Dans la pénombre, la masse en prière ne se distinguait plus que par la clarté des pagnes. Enfin chaque femme regagna sa demeure, mais avant de se séparer, elles joignaient les mains dans un geste fraternel d'amour envers Dieu en portant l'index à leur visage. (*O pays,* 89)

> As if by magic, the night fell. In the semi-darkness, the people in the prayer could now only be distinguished through the brilliance of each person's dress. Finally, each woman returned to her home, but before parting, they all joined their hands together and pointed the forefinger toward the face as a sign of brotherly love for God.

So much for the thesis that Ousmane's works present Islam as "the obstacle to the true integration of individual and society in Senegal!" (Cham: 178)

The closing paragraph of this novel, a highly poetic tribute to Faye the martyr, is full of religious symbolism:

> Oumar Faye, lui, était bien mort et gisait dans la terre . . . ce n'était pas la tombe qui était sa demeure, c'était le coeur de tous les hommes et de toutes les femmes. (*O pays,* 256)

> Oumar Faye lay on the ground, completely dead. . . . His abode was not the grave; it was in the hearts of all the men and the women.

This passage may very well have been written by the great thirteenth-century Sufi Jalalud din Rumi whose thoughts on eternity Idries Shah eloquently sums up as follows: "When we are dead, seek not our tomb in the earth, but find it in the heart of man."[13] A study of the Sufi inspiration in Ousmane's work has yet to be done. The structure of social crisis and the attendant polyphony of reactions by Muslim characters to such situations as obtain in *Les Bouts de bois de Dieu* and *O pays, mon beau Peuple!* could be discerned in *Véhi-Ciosane*. *Véhi-Ciosane* relates the story of the disintegration of a Senegalese rural community, Santhiu Niaye, in the wake of the mass exodus of its inhabitants to the city in search of a better life. But the village had known its days of glory: indeed, the narrative posits a fallen epic world. Santhiu Niaye was once a prosperous community. The narrator speaks of the *sakne,* the granary that gave testimony to the affluence of the community. The romantic songs composed and sung by women complete the idyllic canvas. But by the time the story actually begins, it is obvious that the community has lost its original vitality. The women are no longer capable of composing new songs; instead they used the old songs that their mothers used to sing in the prime of their youth, and now these lively songs only underscore their anxiety (*Ciosane*, 24).

The anxiety of the women is due to the fact that the young men of the community are moving to the city in search of a better life. Clearly, the community is facing a major crisis. However, the most tragic fact of this situation is that nothing is being done to deal with the crisis. The fatalistic worldview of the villagers simply inhibits any desire to take concrete measures to redress the situation. Apart from this general social crisis, the narrative relates a domestic drama, which is not unrelated to the social crisis, and which itself inevitably becomes a public drama.

Ngone War Thiandum, the faithful and devoted wife of Guibril Guedj Diob, is severely shaken. She starts losing faith in the tradition that has governed her life when she learns that her husband has impregnated their daughter. What Ngone finds particularly unbearable is the fact that her husband is given social rank and prestige by tradition, not only because of his apparent religious piety but also and especially because he belongs to a noble caste. That tradition that confers unwarranted privileges to a group of people, and that has taught her unconditional submission to her husband, is what the present crisis leads her to put into question. Much of the narrative relates the different opinions regarding the appropriate penalty Guibril must be made to pay for his abominable crime.

The two plot strands of the novel converge in the fact that tradition or a certain worldview is shown to be responsible for the fatalism that is destroying the community, as well as for Guibril's crime and the varying responses it elicits. Traditional criticism has readily identified Islam as the factor that Ousmane indicts in this novel. Louis Obielo-Okpala's study is paradigmatic of this critical approach.

According to Obielo-Okpala,

> L'auteur de ce roman s'élève contre l'influence de l'Islam sur la vie sociale à Santhin Niaye [*sic*]. Il essaie de montrer que la doctrine du paradis et la volonté de Dieu sont les sources principales de l'aliénation et du retard qui caractérisent ce hameau. L'auteur attribue l'esprit rétrograde et le malheur qui menacent les habitants de cette communauté à la forte emprise de l'Islam sur eux. Au lieu de combattre l'environnement qui devient de plus en plus hostile, ils se croisent les bras et préfèrent attendre une vie meilleure dans le Paradis d'Allah. (*Ciosane*, 17)

> The author of this novel condemns the influence of Islam on the social life in Santhin Niaye [*sic*]. He tries to show that the doctrines of para-

dise and the will of God are the main causes of the alienation and backwardness that characterize this hamlet. The author attributes the backward spirit and the suffering that threaten the members of this community to the strong grip Islam has on them. Instead of combating the environment, which is becoming progressively hostile, they prefer to cross their arms and wait for a better life in the paradise of Allah.

Admittedly, the narrator of *Véhi-Ciosane* attributes the crisis bedeviling Santhiu Niaye to the fatalistic disposition of its inhabitants. It is apathy that blinds their minds, that makes them incapable of taking initiatives of daring to sacrifice for the future of their children. (*Ciosane,* 23–24). It is very tempting to consider Islam as the ideology responsible for the fatalistic world view of the Muslims of Santhiu Niaye, but a careful reading of the novel gives a slightly more variegated picture.

One passage is often used by critics to support the thesis that Ousmane attributes the fatalistic attitudes in the novel to Islamic influence. The text reads thus:

> Les pères de famille, les visages tannés par l'excessif soleil, les énergies dépensées en vain, se repliaient sur leur instinct de conservation avec une virulence inconsciente: une prescience d'un avenir qui les terrorisait déjà. . . . Ils se nourrissaient du *adda* . . . (coutume, tradition) et de la promesse hypothétique. Le Paradis d'Allah, comme un clou planté au centre de leur cerveau, pierre angulaire de *toute leur activité* au jour le jour, amoindrissait, ébréchait la vive imagination pour l'avenir. Ils en étaient à cet état où ils ne sentaient plus le désir et où ils s'enfermaient dans le vieil adage: "La vie n'est rien." (*Ciosane,* 23, emphasis added)

> Fathers whose skins were tanned by the hot sun and whose energies were spent, barricaded themselves in their conservative instincts with a foolhardy virulence. They had a premonition of a future that already terrorized them. . . . They nourished themselves with *adda* . . . (custom, tradition) and with the hypothetical promise. The Paradise of Allah, like a nail planted in the center of their brains, the cornerstone of *all their activities,* from day to day reduced and chipped away at their image of the future. They had arrived at the point where they no longer felt the desire for it. They were trapped in the old saying: "Life is nothing."

"La vie n'est rien"; this formula could be found in many of Ousmane's narratives. We have already come across it in *O pays, mon beau Peuple!* There, as in *Véhi-Ciosane,* it aptly summarizes the apathy that Sembène Ousmane combats in his social fiction. The cited passage suggests an essentialist identification of Islam as the ideology determining the fatalistic outlook of the inhabitants of Santhiu Niaye. The lust after Allah's paradise is said to motivate all the activities of these villagers. Nothing can divert their attention from this goal, not their material misery, not the necessity to strive to build a better future for their progeny. However, to interpret this text thus is to interpret it only partially.

First of all it is significant to note that the narrative posits two—not one—cultural frameworks informing the worldview of the characters in this narrative. The elders subsisted not only on the hypothetical promise of Allah's paradise, but also on the *adda*. That the latter is glossed and given syntactic priority may not be entirely fortuitous. The narrator wants to make the distinction between the *adda* and Islamic beliefs very clear. There is much evidence in the novel to suggest that the *adda*, perhaps more so than Islamic belief, informs the worldview of the inhabitants of Santhiu Niaye.

The debate over the trial of Guibril is centered on the issue of the cultural framework to be applied. Should he be judged according to the Koran or according to the *adda?* Medoune Diob, the brother of the accused, is eager to succeed the latter as chief of Santhiu Niaye. He, therefore, tendentiously invokes the Koran. His brother should receive the death penalty (68). Massar's argument, however, underscores the tenuous hold of Islam in Senegal:

> "Donc, chez-nous . . . les Ecritures sont lettre morte. Car jamais dans ce village, dans tout le Sénégal où pourtant prolifèrent les mosquées, pas une fois les peines que nous dictent les saintes Ecritures ne sont appliquées. Allez voir les autorités! L'estime que nous avons, que nous nourissons à leur égard, nous suffit. Il nous reste donc notre *adda*, l'héritage de nos pères." (*Ciosane*, 71)

> "So with us . . . the Scriptures are dead. Because, never in this village, nor in all of Senegal where mosques nonetheless abound, not at anytime are the legal sanctions prescribed by the Holy Scriptures applied. Go talk to the authorities! The reverence we have for them [the Scriptures], which we nurture, is enough for us. So all that remains for us is the *adda*, the culture of our ancestors."

Baye Yamar's opinion is even more categorical:

> "Notre *adda* a été la règle première de la vie de nos pères. Tout manquement à cette règle mérite ou la mort ou l'exclusion de la communauté." (*Ciosane*, 68)

"Our *adda* was the guiding principle for our fathers. Any transgression commited against its laws calls for death or banishment."

On the other hand, many characters invoke Islam to justify resignation in the face of crisis. It is nonetheless significant to note that such readings of Islam are almost always contested from within an Islamic perspective. Gnagna Guissé, for example, attempts to console her friend, Ngone, by saying that the incest is a manifestation of Allah's will:

"Nul ne peut échapper à son destin. S'il est vrai comme on le dit qu'il est écrit que tout acte était écrit avant notre naissance, que nous ne sommes que des acteurs, alors tu dois faire confiance à Yallah. Yallah voit tout. Il est le seul juge. Le seul qualifié pour juger chacun." (*Ciosane*, 36)

"No one can escape his destiny. If what is said is true, that it is written that all our actions have been predestined, that we are only actors, then you have to trust Yallah. Yallah sees everything. He is the only judge. The only one qualified to judge each person."

To counter this fatalistic theology, Ngone makes reference to the Islamic concept of personal moral responsibility and the attendant principle of accountability:

"S'il est vrai que tout était décidé par Yallah, pourquoi la morale? Pourquoi exalter le bien et flétrir le mal: ces principes servent-ils à quelque chose?" (*Ciosane*, 36–37)

"If everything is already decided by Yallah, why is there morality? Why commend goodness and condemn evil?"

Sembène Ousmane is broaching here the intractable philosophical debate on predestination and moral responsibility. It is not within the province of this analysis to resolve a problem that Ousmane himself is content to simply mention. Suffice it to say that the exchange underscores the structure of debate on the issue of Islam and fatalism in this novel. The narrative relates a similar debate between the imam of the village and Déthyè Law, the *bilal* of the mosque. The imam tells Amath, who is about to leave for the city, that the bad situation of the village is due to Allah's will (*Ciosane*, 83). Moreover, the imam accuses Déthyè Law of blasphemy when the latter protests by saying:

> "Laissons Yallah là où il est. On parlera de lui à son heure." (*Ciosane*, 83)

> "Let's leave Yallah out of this. We shall talk about him at the appropriate time."

Déthyè Law responds to the charge of blasphemy by arguing:

> "Je pense, moi, le contraire. Yallah n'aime pas les esprits recroquevillés. C'est comme l'eau qui ne coule pas, croupit. Elle devient infecte, malgré son apparence de propreté ronge la terre qui la loge. D'où la stérilité de la terre et de l'esprit de l'homme." (*Ciosane*, 83–84)

> "I believe the contrary to be true. Yallah does not love closed minds. It is just like water that does not flow; it stagnates. It becomes bad. In spite of its appearance of purity it destroys the earth that holds it. This explains the sterility of the earth and the mind of the human being."

It does not require much analytical skill to know that Déthyè Law is linking the aridity of the land of Santhiu Niaye to the mental aridity of its inhabitants. The apathy of the villagers, which is destroying the village, in Law's view, Islam clearly disapproves of.

Déthyè Law's stance in the novel is particularly significant, because, like Oumar Faye, he is often cited by critics as a mouthpiece for Ousmane's secular (anti-Islamic?) ideology. As in the case of Faye, the role and stance of Déthyè Law are fraught with ambiguity. He belongs to the millenial caste of *griots,* praise singers, bards, and custodians of cultural history. His role is, therefore, squarely situated within the framework of pre-Islamic culture, the adda. On the other hand, he is also the *bilal,* the one who summons the faithful to prayer. Thus situated midway between the two cultural frameworks, the adda and Islam, he may express himself from either perspective. It is, thus, significant that he is careful to identify the perspective from which he speaks during Guibril's trial. His frame of reference is the adda, not Islam: "Je parle donc pour le adda, car je suis le seul griot ici" [I, therefore, speak on behalf of the adda, since I am the only griot here] (*Ciosane*, 72).

It is tempting to see in this statement a subtle indictment of Islam as a faith that cannot provide solutions to a community in a period of crisis. But apart from the fact that Déthyè Law is the only representative of the *griot* voice, the reason not to speak from an Islamic perspective relates to the *griot's* avowed lack of Islamic knowledge:

> "Je confesse ici que ma connaissance des lettres arabes est très limitée. J'en pleure toutes les nuits." (*Ciosane*, 71)

"I admit here that my knowledge of Arabic scholarship is very limited. This makes me cry day and night."

Déthyè Law indeed is the voice of truth in the novel. He is outraged by the selective use of the moral code. Swift (in)justice was meted out to a man of lower caste when he was suspected of having impregnated Guibril's daughter. His property was confiscated and he was chased out of the village. Law cannot understand the endless bickering now that a member of a high caste is found to be guilty of incest. In the end Guibril is murdered by his deranged son. Medoune, who is eager to succeed his brother, is behind the murder, and the imam is aware of the plot. Therefore, Law's outrage at the imam's complicity should not be interpreted as an indictment of Islam: in fact the very last episode of the novel that is set in the village shows the *bilal,* reaffirming his devotion to Islam by making the ancient call to prayer. The villagers in unison dramatically desert the imam's congregation to respond to Déthyè Law's call. In spite of some evidence to the contrary, the novel ends up affirming the vitality of Islam and the readiness of the faithful to fight against those who wish to interpret Islam tendentiously. The narrative leaves us to speculate that the Islamic establishment in Santhiu Niaye will never be the same again. The *bilal* is ushering in a period of change marked by an unqualified adherence to truth.

After these discussions it seems legitimate to ask again whether Ousmane's artistic response to Islam is one of unequivocal rejection. Some commentators, as I have shown, strongly believe so. The truth of the matter is that some of these critics are probably too hostile to Islam to see anything in Ousmane's work approximating a vindication of Islamic values or a positive portrayal of the Islamic impact on Senegalese society. One such commentator is Martin Bestman.

Bestman spends many pages accusing Ousmane of being blind to the positive contributions of Christianity to Africa. He calls this "tricher avec le réel" [manipulating reality]. Some of the things he would have very much liked to see Ousmane talk about in his novels include the Christian church's fight against slavery, witchcraft, and ritual human sacrifice. He exhibits ignorance of Islamic morality by conceding that the Koran and the Bible teach people "à tendre l'autre joue" [to turn the other cheek]. When he comes to the subject of Islam proper, he wholeheartedly agrees with what he perceives to be Sembène Ousmane's attitude to this religion:

D'après les romans de Sembène Ousmane, la religion musulmane orthodoxe semble constituer un des plus puissants obstacles au pro-

> grès social. . . . En apprenant aux croyants à subir leur malheur sans mot dire, elle semble opposée à toute initiative personnelle et à toute innovation. (Bestman: 42)
>
> According to the novels of Sembène Ousmane, orthodox Islam is one of the greatest impediments to progress. . . . By teaching the believers to endure their lot in life silently, it seems opposed to all personal initiatives and to any form of innovation.

That Martin Bestman's analysis is ideologically burdened requires no further commentary.

As well, Soyinka chose *Les Bouts de bois de Dieu* to illustrate the thesis that Islam is a reactionary superstition that has no place among the ideological solutions proposed by the new school of African literary visionaries. To prove his thesis about Islam, Soyinka will have to illustrate that the champions of the railway workers' cause in Ousmane's work do not derive their inspiration from an Islamic worldview. To be more precise, the heroes of the strike should be shown to be moved by a purely secularist vision.

Soyinka is clearly impressed by the character of Bakayoko, the strike leader:

> The remote enigmatic Bakayoko is a promethean creation, a replacement for *outworn deities* who have the misfortune to lose their relevance in a colonial world. Amoral in the mundane sense of the word, Bakayoko appears to be sculpted out of *pure intellect* and omniscience. (*Myth*, 117, emphasis added)

The critic is performing here what one might call ideological cleansing. The deities of nonsecularist ideologies have to be removed in order to create new territories to be inhabited by pure secularist deities. This leads Soyinka to perpetrate much violence against the heterogeneous composition of Ousmane's textual territory.

Bakayoko is a Muslim living in a predominantly Muslim community. There is nothing to indicate that he is an apostate. In fact, he suggests that it is un-Islamic to be opposed to the strike. He dismisses the arguments put forward by the corrupt imam of Dakar, who is opposed to the strike, precisely by asserting that extreme material deprivation can prevent believers from going to the mosques. In short, the strike is not only sanctioned by Islam, it is also deemed necessary to the continued observance of Islamic worship. Soyinka's programmatic spell makes him blind to this fact; but the traces of ideological cleansing are most visible in Soyinka's analysis of Fa Keita's character.

Having declared that "the established Islamic voice in the community is shown to be treacherous and reactionary" (*Myth*, 117), Soyinka will predictably have problems interpreting the central role played by Fa Keita. The particular context is related to Fa Keita's wise verdict in Diara's trial. The latter proposed that Diara, who betrayed the strikers, should not be killed:

> Fa Keita, who proposes that verdict, *is only incidentally a deeply religious man,* a Moslem, and the antithesis of the fat-living collaborator, El Hadji Mabigué. The proceedings are kept secular. Fa Keita's utterance borrows nothing from religious wisdom but from a shrewd psychology and a belief in the vanishing values of a traditional "framework, an *ada* that was once our own." He strikes the right chord and the community adopts his verdict. (*Myth*, 120, emphasis added)

It is not fortuitous that Soyinka elects to cite only the last part of Fa Keita's verdict speech in his analysis, the part that apparently speaks of a millennial (pre-Islamic?) tradition "that was once our own." Soyinka strategically truncates Fa Keita's full verdict, which would otherwise debunk his argument. The idea that Fa Keita's utterance borrows nothing from religious wisdom simply flies in the face of the facts. Devout Muslim that he is, he is opposed to the capital penalty on unequivocally religious terms:

> "C'est un sacrilège de tuer; oui pour des saints hommes c'est un sacrilège, et je prie Dieu qu'il ne fasse pas naître une telle pensée dans votre coeur." (*Bouts*, 154)

> It is a sacrilege to kill; yes, for saintly people, it is a sacrilege, and I pray to God that no such thought should be born in your heart.

Fa Keita even interprets Diara's betrayal as an act of divine intervention, a providential sign:

> Toi Diara, redresse la tête; tu as été l'instrument du destin; ce n'était pas toi qui étais jugé, c'étaient les propriétaires des machines. Grâce à toi, nous n'abandonnerons plus la lutte. (*Bouts*, 155)

> You, Diarra, raise your head; you have been the instrument of destiny; it was not you who were judged, rather, it was the owners of the machines. Because of you, we will never give up our struggle.

Indeed, as Wole Soyinka says, Fa Keita is the antithesis of El Hadji Mabigué. But it is not justifiable to say that in this specific episode of Diara's trial he is only incidentally Muslim. There is no instance in the novel in which the narrative shows Fa Keita as ceasing to think and act as a Muslim—not even while he is in prison. Soyinka's interpretation could be understood only in one way. Any critic fishing for evidence of an indictment of Islam in this novel is bound to have problems interpreting the central and positive role played by the most Islamic voice in the novel, Fa Keita's. Not being able to ignore the role, Soyinka decides to secularize it. This inevitably leads to a serious tampering with the facts presented by the narrative. The kind of ideological hostility to Islam that Soyinka displays in his exchanges with Mazrui have thus been shown to spill over into his critical writings.

A discussion of the perception of Islam as a fatalistic creed, one of those stereotypes copied into African(ist) writing from hostile colonial scholarship, will perhaps be incomplete without an attempt to set the records straight. I will, therefore, briefly refer to works written by both Muslims and non-Muslims on the issue of personal responsibility in Islam and the general subject of the revolutionary character of Islam from a theoretical, historical, and contemporary perspective.

In "The Revolutionary Tradition in Islam," T. Hodgkin argues persuasively that Islam, as a worldview, more so than Christianity, "has always had a particular concern with human history, its meaning, direction, possibilities and problems."[14]

He believes that Communists and Muslims have sufficiently similar social and economic ideologies to be able to work together in their common struggle for socio-economic justice and development. Broadly speaking, Marxism and Islam share these following fundamental principles: personal human responsibility, the idea of activism, the egalitarian ideal, and the idea of history as a constant struggle between the oppressed and their oppressors that promises the ultimate victory of the oppressed. Although the comparison between communism and Islam is one that many Muslims are understandably uncomfortable with, the point cannot be missed that Islam does see as part of its vocation the fight against the exploitation of man by man.

In a similar light, Yvonne Haddad discusses in "Islam, Women and Revolution in Twentieth-Century Arab Thought" the theoretical foundation of an Islamic work ethic, Islamic revolutionism: "A progressive ideology for human capabilities . . . a world-affirming vision grounded in the idea of human responsibility and perfectibility with the committed believers ultimately seeking the redemption of the world."[15]

It is interesting to note at this point that while some detractors of Islam emphasize Islam's otherworldliness, others paternalistically explain the appeal of Islam in Africa on precisely opposite grounds. This appeal is ascribable to its this-worldly character, its secular ethic as Peter Clarke explains:

> Another theory which initially appears plausible on the basis of case studies is the "market value" theory of Islamic expansion, along the lines of Tawney and Weber's treatment of protestantism. The ethic of Islam, it is claimed, is a secular, market/commerce oriented ethic, see Qur'an, Sura 198. The alliance of market and Mosque permitted Islam's phenomenal expansion in West Africa. This does not, of course, explain either why some communities unassociated with trading converted to Islam, nor why many traders and businessmen did not.[16]

On the same subject of the Islamic work ethic Ibraheem Sulaiman analyzes the ideological foundations of Caliph Muhammad Bello's economic policy defined in his *Tanbih as Sahib ala Ahkam Al-Makasib*. The caliph of Sokoto, son and successor of Shehu Usman Dan Fodio, starts his treatise with the proposition that Islam encourages economic pursuits and extols the excellence of lawful earning. He cites the Koran verse, "When the prayer is over, disperse in the land and seek Allah's bounty," and the *hadith*, "Allah likes his slaves to be gainfully employed." This work ethic requires that Muslims strike a balance between this world and the other, since the demands of the body and those of the spirit (as Bakar suggests in *Les Bouts de bois de Dieu*) are not mutually exclusive but complementary. The caliph's ideas are summed up in his belief that to be gainfully employed is "an act of worship in its own right."[17]

As far as the subject of activism and worker militancy is concerned, Clarke and Paul M. Lubeck have discerned a direct relationship between worker militancy and Islamic religious education in Northern Nigeria. Clarke writes that "strike action seems to be higher among members of the Muslim brotherhoods and among those who have received an Islamic education than among others" (Clarke: 129). So much for the "enseignement religieux stérilisant, engourdissant" [numbing and barren religious doctrine] (Bestman: 32) that Islam is said to promote!

Vincent Monteil also insists on the character of Islam as a factor of social revolution. This is in consonance with what his friend, the French Islamist Louis Massignon, calls the apocalyptic and eschatological conception of Islam: "libérateur à la fois des corps et des consciences" [a liberator of bodies and minds].[18] Vincent discusses Islamic activism in the Senegalese context. The motto of the *mourides* is that "le travail fait partie de la religion" [work is part of religion]. This work ethic leading to a kind of agricultural collectivism, not unlike the one advocated by Faye, explains why the *mourides* collectively produce a greater part of Senegal's peanuts. "Hamallisme," another Muslim brotherhood, has stood for very honorable social causes such as the emancipation of the *rimaibé* (Fulani "serfs") and the abolition of the traditional bride price (Monteil: 126).

Having insisted that activism and the struggle for social justice and material progress of the kind advocated by Sembène Ousmane can be accommodated within an Islamic frame of reference, it must equally be pointed out that there is some substance warranting a fatalistic interpretation of the Koran. There are countless verses in the Koran extolling the virtues of patience in adversity and steadfastness in faith, and emphasizing the transience of this life and the need to prepare for the next. Islamic history is replete with examples of people and movements that have stressed a fatalistic interpretation of the Koran. It is in this light that the critic Matiu Nnoruka casts the conflict in Cheikh Hamidou Kane's *L'Aventure ambiguë* in terms of the historical struggle between two rival theological schools: Asharism and Mu'talizism. In times of crisis, the fundamentalist Asharites prefer to "se contenter de la réprobation intérieure sans prendre parti extérieurement" [limit themselves to inner disapproval, without showing an outward commitment to any contending position] while the Mu'tazilites advocate the synthesis of "logos" and "praxis" because they believe that militancy is the only authentic means of liberation.[19] When discussing Islamic activism and passivism in the West African context, it is relevant to mention, among others, the influences of the North African scholar Al Maghili and the Egyptian Al-Suyuti among West African scholars. The former emphasizes militancy, the necessity for Muslims to act, if necessary, through force for both the spiritual and material reform of society, while the latter advocates quietism, "the acceptance of the situation as it is or trying to change it by only peaceful means."[20]

These perennial theological debates resurfaced in more recent times in Senegal in the wake of colonial occupation. Questions similar to those raised in *O pays, mon beau Peuple!* and *Les Bouts de bois de Dieu* were raised. What must the Muslims do in face of political and cultural tyranny? The answers varied from one religious leader to the other. Some advocated resignation, and some accommodation, while others advocated militant opposition and paid the price.[21] That all these opinions sought justification in the Koran is very significant. The concrete social context and idiosyncrasies of religious leaders have much to do with the choice of Koranic verses used in support of preferred modes of action in given historical circumstances. The religious leaders' interpretations of the historical circumstances are the other factor.

The facts and studies so far mentioned in this analysis need no further commentary. In my discussion of the subject of Sembène Ousmane's imaginative response to Islam, reference to his nonliterary pronouncements on the subject of Islam was avoided. This is in keeping with my limited objective of demonstrating through an analysis of three of his works that Ousmane does not categorically reject the notion of the will of God. What he does is debunk a fatalistic and reactionary interpretation of this concept in order to replace it with a progressive interpretation, one that reconciles the idea of the will of God with social activism, a definition that is truer to Islam's acknowledged revolutionary character.

## Notes

1. Sembène Ousmane, *O pays, mon beau peuple!* (London: Methuen, 1985), 88. This citation is of a minor character in the novel. This is the edition carrying the critical introduction by Patrick Corcoran.

2. Sembène Ousmane, *Les Bouts de bois de Dieu* (Paris: Presses Pocket, 1957). All subsequent references to this text will be indicated parenthetically in the text.

3. Sembène Ousmane, *O pays, mon beau peuple!* (Paris: Presses Pocket, 1957). All subsequent references to this text will be indicated parenthetically in the text.

4. Sembène Ousmane, *Véhi-Ciosane ou Blanche-Genèse* (Paris: Présence Africaine, 1966). All subsequent references to this text will be indicated parenthetically in the text.

5. Mbye Cham, "Islam in Senegalese Literature and Film," in Kenneth Harrow, ed., *Faces of Islam in African Literature* (London, Portsmouth: Heinemann, 1991), 163–186. All subsequent references to this article will be indicated parenthetically in the text.

6. Interview with Sembène Ousmane conducted by Pierette Herzberger-Fofana, "Ousmane, forgéron de caractères," *Komparatistische Hefte* 8 (1983): 59, 62.

7. Martin Bestman, *Sembène Ousmane et l'esthétique du roman négro-africain* (Sherbrooke, Canada: Naaman, 1981), 42. All subsequent references to this study will be indicated parenthetically in the text.

8. In Patrick Corcoran's "Critical Introduction" to *O pays, mon beau*

*peuple!*, 37. All subsequent references to this introduction will be indicated parenthetically in the text.

9. Louis Obielo-Okpala, "L'Islam dans l'oeuvre de Sembène Ousmane" *L'Afrique Littéraire* 85 (1989). All subsequent references to this study will be indicated parenthetically in the text.

10. Wole Soyinka, *Myth, Literature, and the African World* (Cambridge: Cambridge University Press, 1976), 120. All subsequent references to this text will be indicated parenthetically in the text.

11. Cited by Mohamed Yahia Haschmi, "Spirituality, Science, and Psychology in the Sufi Way," in Rushbrook Williams, ed., *Sufi Studies: East and West* (New York: Dutton, 1973), 130.

12. Faithful abstract of Mbye Cham's article, 463.

13. "Spirituality, Science, and Psychology in the Sufi Way," in Rushbrook Williams, ed., *Sufi Studies: East and West* (New York: Dutton, 1973), 126.

14. T. Hodgkin, "The Revolutionary Tradition in Islam," *Race and Class* 21 (1980): 224.

15. Yvonne Haddad, "Islam, Women and Revolution in Twentieth-Century Arab Thought," *Muslim World* LXXIV (1984): 156.

16. Peter Clarke, "Islam, Development and African Identity: The Case of West Africa," in Kirsten Holst Peterson, ed., *Religion, Development and African Identity* (Västervik: Ekblad, 1987), 129.

17. Cited in Ibraheem Sulaiman's *The Islamic State and the Challenge of History: Ideals, Policies and Operations of the Sokoto Caliphate* (London: Mansell Publishing Limited, 1987), 112.

18. Vincent Monteil, "Contribution à l'étude de l'Islam en Afrique noire," in *Colloque sur les religions* (Paris: Présence Africaine, 1962), 124.

19. Matiu Nnuruka, "La Fonction idéologico-religieuse dans *L'Aventure ambiguë* de Cheikh Hamidou Kane," *Présence francophone: Revue internationale de langue et de littérature* 24 (Spring 1982): 81.

20. Mervyn Hiskett, *The Development of Islam in West Africa* (London: Longman, 1984), 37.

21. See René-Luc Moreau's discussions on "L"Islam colonial," *Africains Musulmans,* 201–209.

# 5

# Taming Islam: Aminata Sow Fall

*I'm an Ibo writer, because this is my basic culture; Nigerian, African and a writer . . . no, black first, then a writer. Each of these identities does call for a certain kind of commitment on my part.*
—Chinua Achebe

Achebe's dilemma in defining himself in this chapter's epigraph[1] is emblematic for nearly all African intellectuals in the postcolonial period. The Senegalese writer Aminata Sow Fall, for example, constantly laments the loss of cultural authenticity in her narratives.[2] But what is authenticity for her? What is her—to use Achebe's term—basic culture? And what is the basic culture of Senegal? Sow Fall is Senegalese, Muslim, black, and a woman. What commitments do these identities call for? In exploring these questions, I will see that the syncretic ambiguities of her life are reflected by her work, in which another unsuspected identity emerges, that of the *assimilée*. I will also see that her critics impose reductive identities on her that do not respect her complexity. Mbye Cham, for example, sees her as a promoter of Islam, but analysis of her themes and her lexicon refutes this.[3]

A thorough examination of Aminata Sow Fall's textual relationship with her Islamic heritage will illustrate that, contrary to what is frequently asserted by commentators, Sow Fall is not a promoter of Islam. On the contrary, there is a tendency in her works to deemphasize, dilute, and even mute the Islamic component of her Senegalese culture.

Many approaches can be taken to inquire into the significance of this observation. Here, my line of analysis will be linguistic. Drawing on the work of Chantal Zabus as a model, it will deal with the textual strategies elaborated by Sow Fall to assert the integrity of Senegalese culture. It will be argued in essence that Aminata Sow Fall textualizes cultural differentiation by conveying culturally bound Wolof-Senegalese concepts, thought patterns, and linguistic features in her narratives, thereby subverting the discursive hegemony of the colonial language and forcing the reader to be actively engaged with the horizons of Senegalese culture. A pattern is, however, discernible: concepts relating to Islamic culture are not only conveyed in French, but the translation involved follows the "annexing" as opposed to the "decentering" model.[4]

The consequences of this choice are many. First the lack of linguistic equivalence between the original Islamic concepts and their French "cognates" leads to culturally misleading translations. And this fact has led in its turn to the interpretive ambiguities of the kind I will discuss below in my analysis of *La Grève des Bàttu* (1979). "Annexing" Islamic cultural realities into French singularly subverts the authenticity and distinctness of Islamic culture. The ideological implications of this glottocultural undertaking are obvious. By translating Islam according to the exigencies of Franco-Catholic culture, Sow Fall is (unwittingly?) perpetuating the colonial politics of gallicizing Islam, of taming what historically was one of the most potent sources of resistance to French cultural imperialism in Senegal.

I will start by addressing the general subject of linguistic differentiation in the europhone African novel. Chantal Zabus's work is discussed as it deals with the textual strategies being currently used by African writers to rehabilitate African cultures. Although Zabus's study provides a useful conceptual framework, it will be indicated that it suffers from an oversight. It has failed to reckon with the hybridized nature of certain African cultures, such as those that have been profoundly influenced by Islam. The analysis of *La Grève des Bàttu* illustrates Sow Fall's tendency to translate into French concepts and practices that relate to the Islamic component of Senegalese culture. The attendant use of linguistic differentiation to underscore the distinctness and integrity of the non-Islamic component of Senegalese culture is seen as part of a more general singular tendency in Sow Fall to mute Islam in her narratives. While I cannot speculate on the writer's intentions, my study seriously challenges the widely held view that Sow Fall is a promoter of Islam.

Much has been written on the ambivalent situation of African writers engaged in giving expression to Africa's cultural authenticity using the ex-colonizers' languages. First of all, since language is the expression of culture, African writers are faced with the scriptural challenge of conveying African culture in European languages. Since the early 1960s, African writers have become painfully aware that the process of inner translation to which they were constrained did involve a considerable distortion of the African experience it was their mission to articulate and promote. There is, however, a broader glottopolitical issue at stake, which is the need felt by African writers to rescue the African languages from the glottophagic fangs of the European languages, an issue that is synecdochically linked to the program of political-cultural decolonization.

Studies devoted to this subject have tended to be simplistic or partial. While some only pay attention to the problem of finding European lexical equivalents for African concepts,[5] the more interesting studies have addressed the broader ideological implications of "translating" African culture into European languages. The latter approach, however, has the shortcoming of overlooking the linguistic and cultural heterogeneity of Africa. Moreover, that some precolonial African cultures were thoroughly multicultural is often ignored. Reference is made here particularly to cultures that have become hybridized by the thoroughgoing cultural influence of Islam. Senegalese culture, for example, hosts within it practices and attendant linguistic concepts that are directly related to the life of a Muslim. Such Islam-Arabic concepts have been integrated into and remained untranslated in Wolof, Senegal's lingua franca.

I am therefore paying attention to Sow Fall's decision not to articulate the integrity of the Islamic dimension of her Senegalese culture through linguistic differentiation. The linguistic approach adopted here warrants a preliminary examination of the work of Chantal Zabus on the subject of the "othering" of the European language in the contemporary europhone African novel.

Zabus's article, "Othering the Foreign Language in the West African Europhone Novel" (1990),[6] and her book, *The African Palimpsest: Indigenization of Language in the West African Europhone Novel* (1991),[7] are the most comprehensive studies on glottopolitics in the contemporary West African narrative in European languages. According to Zabus, the postcolonial europhone African novel is the living theater of an unfolding linguistic drama that is steeped in violence. West African creative writers have elaborated strategies in their texts to subvert the discursive hegemony of European languages by indigenizing them, and thus have scripturally waged war against those languages; this is in a bid to rehabilitate the African languages that have been marginalized by colonial language politics.

The first step of indigenization is semantic or syntactic relexification. Writers like Chinua Achebe, Ayi Kwei Armah, and Aminata Sow Fall have relexified the European exolect from Ibgo, Fanti, and Wolof, respectively (Zabus 1990: 350). Relexification, which is a decolonizing strategy, must not be confused with "calquing" resulting from poor or approximate second-language acquisition (Zabus 1991: 58). It must, however, be understood that although relexification is a subversive strategy, it is still based on the premise that the European language can be made to convey African culture. But the subterranean traces of the African tongue in the relexified text also sometimes vie with visible traces of the mother tongue: "When African words or phrases describing culturally bound objects or occurrences cannot be transparently conveyed (translated or relexified) in the European text, the writer resorts to the twin methods of 'cushioning' and 'contextualizing'" (Zabus 1990: 351).

An African word or phrase is "cushioned" when it is accompanied by an explanatory word or phrase in the target language. Chinua Achebe, for example, makes considerable use of the explanatory tag in *Things Fall Apart* (*TFA*). Hence, "*obi* or hut" or "hut, or *obi*"; "the elders, or *ndichie*" (*TFA*, 9); "*eze-agudi-nwangi,* or the teeth of an old woman" (*TFA*, 25); "the rope, or *tie-tie*" (*TFA*, 39); "*jigida,* or waist beads" (*TFA*, 49). Gerald Moore notes that the use of such expressions as "reception room" and "sitting room" instead of the Ibo concepts "invests them with a slightly false aura of the familiar, but the images those words suggest to the reader unfamiliar with Iboland are utterly misleading" (Zabus 1991: 159–160).

Together with contextualization, which is the provision of immediate areas of context to make the African concept intelligible, cushioning is therefore tied to the ideological conveying of "African culture in its ethno-linguistic specificity" (Zabus 1991: 173). A more radical strategy in the bid to "other" the European languages of the African novel is the refusal to gloss, cushion, or contextualize. The reader is then forced, as it were, to be actively engaged with the cultural horizons of the text if he or she is to make sense of the novel at all. This radical strategy can be readily contrasted with the "0 degree" of othering described by the authors of *The Empire Writes Back* as "being the colonialist acceptance of the European language as it is found in its 'ancestral home,' to adapt Achebe's words, that is, not 'in communion with its African surroundings'" (Zabus 1990: 349).

It is in reaction to such wholesale translation of African realities into the European languages, which amounted to cultural betrayal, that writers such as Gabriel Okara (1964) embarked upon hosting the traces of the African logos in the europhone discourse of the African novel.

Zabus's analysis thus illustrates the thesis that all the textual devices so far discussed are not only a response to the hermeneutic question of conveying African culture in European languages, they also constitute ideological strategies seeking at once to subvert the discursive hegemony of the colonial languages and to register the authenticity and autonomy of the respective African cultures to which the works give expression.

The probity of Zabus's studies cannot be overemphasized. There is, however, a significant oversight in her analysis that must be pointed out. Her constant use of the dichotomy "African words—European language" (Zabus 1990: 349; 1991: 157), or the use of the concept "African culture" in the singular (Zabus 1991: 44), betrays a failure to reckon with the heterogeneity and linguistic complexity of African culture(s) as well as the syncretic character of many African cultures. A case in point is her ignoring of the Islamic dimension of Senegalese culture that has led to her partial analysis of Sow Fall's uses of linguistic differentiation and the ideological implications of her textual strategies.

Indeed, Aminata Sow Fall makes extensive use of the techniques of cushioning, relexification, footnoting, and the untranslated word in *Le Revenant* (1976)[8] and *L'Appel des arènes* (1982).[9] Many culturally bound events like ceremonies and rituals, as well as instruments, clothes, tools, animals, seasons, and other formulas, are rendered in Wolof with or without the techniques of cushioning or contextualization. Such strategies are to be expected in narratives whose central theme is the encroachment of Western values and the threat they pose to the survival of *cosaan,* traditional Senegalese culture. I do not wish to duplicate here the work that has already been done elsewhere by illustrating the phenomenon of linguistic differentiation in Sow Fall's fiction. My contribution to the debate relates to the relative absence of linguistic differentiation when it comes to textualizing Islamic cultural realities.

If one finds in the works of Sembène Ousmane, who is traditionally considered an apostate, many references to the Islamic presence as well as many untranslated words and phrases dealing with Islamic realities in Senegalese culture, virtually no such references can be found in the novels of Aminata Sow Fall, the alleged promoter of Islam. Perhaps more significantly, fundamental Islamic words and concepts in French such as *Allah, Musulmans, Coran,* and *le Prophète* can hardly be found anywhere in the novels of Sow Fall under study. In fact, apart from the translation of *Allah* to the French *Dieu,* which is found in all her novels, only in *La Grève des Bàttu* can one find even the translation of *les Musulmans* to the French *les croyants* and *le Coran,* already a (decentering) translation to the transcultural *le livre saint.* There is no mention of these basic Islamic concepts even in translation in *Le Revenant* and *L'Appel des arènes.* Let us turn to those novels.

Sow Fall's first novel, *Le Revenant,* relates the story of Bakar, a young man of low caste, and Yama, his sister, whose beauty attracts the attention of a wealthy businessman, Amar Ndiaye, who marries her. This marriage considerably elevates the social status of Yama and her original family. Yama does more to enhance her newly acquired social status by spending lavishly on social occasions. It is in this vein that she spends inordinately at the wedding of Bakar with Mame Aïssa, the daughter of traditional "aristocrats" who cannot resist the lure of the money involved in this match in spite of the low caste of the suitor.

Bakar himself, an employee at the post office, is not immune to the materialistic virus that is eating into the moral fabric of society. He embezzles money at his place of work, is caught, and, despite the frantic efforts of his sister to save the family's newly acquired social recognition, is sentenced to jail. Yama will never forgive him for tarnishing her social status that had taken her so much energy, calculation, and money to construct. Bakar's in-laws are even more resentful; their daughter's marriage with a *badolo* (a man of low social status in the Senegalese caste system) has simply been a tragic mistake, and they therefore use all means necessary to force their daughter to ask for divorce. Bakar is thus abandoned by everybody except his parents and his loyal friend, Sada. Bakar comes out of jail an embittered man. Yama can no longer afford to associate with him, and it takes a decisive act on her part to communicate this fact to her brother. Bakar decides to attend one of the social evenings his sister regularly organizes, but because she cannot afford his being seen by her respectable guests, she virtually orders him to stay in the company of the children.

Utterly devastated by the insult, Bakar, in a bid to rebel against the hypocrisy of his society, indulges in alcohol and debauchery, much to the distress of his mother. But Bakar's ultimate act of vengeance takes a more sinister form: he has everybody believe that he has drowned. His entire community, including his sister, goes into a frenzy of mourning. Yama uses this occasion again to show off her status by organizing a characteristically lavish funeral. At night, as she is busy counting the money that the family received from well-wishers on the occasion of the death of her brother, Bakar, pretending to be a ghost, demands all the money. The family is petrified and Yama drops the money, fleeing for her life.

This tragicomic story deals primarily with the corrupting influence of (Western) materialism that is gnawing at the very cultural soul of the African society depicted in this narrative. A traditional way of life, *cosaan,* is threatened, and its demise is presented as ushering in an age of cultural alienation and social woes. This theme runs through the three novels of Sow Fall that I consider here.

*L'Appel des arènes* enacts a cultural conflict. Nalla, the son of a Europeanized couple, feels an irresistible attraction to one of the manifestations of traditional culture, the sound of the tom-tom summoning people to the arena for the traditional wrestling matches. This attraction is symptomatic of Nalla's longing for a traditional lifestyle he savored as a child at his grandmother's home, where he lived while his parents were studying in Europe. His parents cannot deal with his strange predilection. After all, his mother has spared nothing in her efforts to model her son on the future, on modernism, on French culture.

It is obvious that "Cosaan se meurt" (*L'Appel des arènes,* 79–80, 95), but Nalla brings meaning to his life by having clandestine relationships with people associated with the traditional lore, and more specifically with Malaw, the famous wrestler who is also the the descendant of the mythical Nar Lô. Nalla, the son of this "French" family ends up becoming the *garçon fétiche* (good luck charm) of Malaw during his bouts. The story ends on an optimistic note. Nalla's father breaks away from his wife's intransigence and decides to appreciate his son's yearning for a culturally meaningful life. As the father experiences the arena, he discovers in himself the same craving for the tom-tom he used to have in his childhood, but which has been buried beneath the debris of French acculturation. He then realizes for the first time that he and his wife have tried to give the wrong education to their son, a sterile, life-denying, alienating, and psychologically damaging education. Cultural authenticity is thus a very central theme in Sow Fall's narratives. It comes as no surprise that Sow Fall uses linguistic differentiation to construct otherness in her texts.

Indeed, Sow Fall makes an extensive use of linguistic variance to convey Senegalese cultural experience, while apparently Islamic realities are translated into French. Thus, in *Le Revenant* the word *baptême* is used to describe the naming ritual of a newborn (*Le Revenant,* 37). This word is culturally bound and its use evokes a Christian cultural context. To use Gerald Moore's terms, *baptême* invests the cultural event thus denoted with a false air of the familiar, which is utterly misleading for the reader unfamiliar with Islamic-Senegalese culture.

The use of the Catholic concept of *purgatoire* raises similar questions. Believing that Bakar died by drowning, an anonymous Muslim sage uses the concept of purgatory to relate an Islamic belief: "Mais celui qui périt dans l'eau va droit au Paradis, il ne connaîtra jamais le purgatoire" [But he who perishes in water goes directly to paradise; he will never experience purgatory] (*Le Revenant*, 117).

It is an Islamic belief that a Muslim who dies by drowning is considered a martyr and, therefore, enjoys the special dispensation of being admitted straight into paradise without going through the process of judgement. However, the concept of purgatory is totally foreign to Islamic belief. The closest Islamic approximation to it is the concept of *al-A'araf,* which literally means "the heights." According to one interpretation, "the people of the heights" are souls that, on the day of judgement, are neither decidedly on the side of sin nor on the side of merit, but are as it were suspended midway between the Companions of the Garden and the Companions of the Fire. Their story is summarily related in the seventh sura of the Koran, which is named after them:

> Between them shall be
> A veil, and on the Heights
> Will be men
> Who would know everyone
> By his marks: they will call
> Out to the Companions
> Of the Garden "Peace on you"
> They will not have entered
> But they will have
> An assurance (thereof)
> When their eyes shall be turned
> Towards the Companions
> Of the Fire, they will say:
> "Our Lord! send us not
> To the company
> Of wrongdoers." (Koran, 7: 46–47)

It must be noted that the people of the heights are destined for paradise and do not undergo expiatory suffering as do the Roman Catholic dwellers of purgatory. The use of the Catholic concept of *purgatoire* just as that of *baptême* is part of a rather peculiar tendency in Sow Fall's fiction to suggest a Catholic cultural framework for her novels. It is apparent that Sow Fall does not wish to stress the Islamic component in her first novel.

The very first page of the narrative interestingly suggests a Euro-Christian cultural framework. Sunday is religiously observed as a day of rest and Christmas is equally celebrated with great fervor. On the other hand, there is no mention of Friday as the Muslim day of weekly congregational prayers. In fact, the only reference made to Islamic practice in *Le Revenant* and *L'Appel des arènes* is related to prayer. But even these references are few, summary, and anecdotal. No actual incident of Islamic prayer is related in the narratives. If there are Muslims in Sow Fall's fictional Senegal, most of them have curiously been kept in the closet.

The first allusion to prayer in *Le Revenant* comes in the form of a metaphor describing the disposition of game cards:

> Les cartes disposées en éventail étaient serrées dans les mains jointes et levées en attitude de prière, comme un bien sacré. (*Le Revenant*, 17)

> The cards displayed in the shape of a fan were held between hands that were clasped and raised prayerfully, like sacred objects.

It is obvious and perhaps strange that the image of prayer evoked here is derived from Christian and not Islamic liturgical practice. In fact, the image that the narrator seeks to create only works within a Christian cultural framework. Elsewhere, the reference to prayer is truly ambiguous. Bakar is full of joy and anticipation as he prepares for his first day of work:

> Après sa toilette, il alluma la bougie qui était sur un tabouret, près de son lit, et attendit patiemment *l'heure de la prière*. (*Le Revenant*, 21, emphasis added)

> After taking his bath, he lit the candle that was on a stool by his bed, and waited patiently for *prayer time*.

Is Bakar actually waiting to perform his prayer or is the expression *l'heure de la prière* (prayer time) simply a time marker here? In light of the absence of any other allusion to prayer in this particular episode, the second possibility is more probable. Moreover the very cursory manner in which the narrative relates one of Islam's fundamental principles, prayer, says much about the position Islam occupies in Sow Fall's novels. In fact both the protagonist and the most positive voice in this novel, Sada, have no place for prayer in their lives. In one episode Bakar recalls with nostalgia his school days:

> C'était un jeudi, un jeudi, je me souviens très bien car nous n'avions pas classe ce jour-là. C'était l'heure de la Tisbaar quand les plus fervents se trouvaient à la mosquée et que d'autres, étendus à l' ombre de quelque arbre touffu digéraient leur dose de Ceebu. (*Le Revenant*, 61)

> It was on a Thursday, a Thursday that I remember very well, because we had no school that day. It was time for the *Tisbaar,* when the most devout were at the mosques, while others, lying under the shade of a leafy tree, savored their dose of *ceebu.*

The rest of the flashback indicates that Bakar and Sada were not among those who prayed.

The scantiness of references to Islamic practices in *Le Revenant* contrasts sharply with an abundance of references to pre-Islamic rituals. While we are not sure, for example, whether Bakar performed the morning prayers before leaving home for his first day of work, we are told in no uncertain terms that Bakar was instructed by his mother to rub a concoction before leaving for work every morning. And when Bakar is indicted for the embezzlement of public funds, his parent's recourse is to occult sciences (*Le Revenant*, 51). Finally when Bakar takes to debauchery it is related that his mother

> n'était pas restée inactive. Elle avait consulté marabouts et guérisseurs, interrogé les cauris et les cornes de bélier. (*Le Revenant*, 111)

> did not remain idle. She had consulted marabouts and healers, had done divination with cowries and ram's horns.

Of all these remedies, only one relating to the marabouts vaguely suggests an Islamic cultural context.

The questions raised in the analysis of *Le Revenant* also apply to *L'Appel des arènes.* As in the first novel the Islamic references in this one are scanty. To borrow the words of Jaccard,

> Il ne s'agit pas de *l'Islam, pratiquement absent dans ce texte,* mais du modernisme mal interprété. (*Les Visages de l'Islam*, 181, emphasis added)

> It is not about *Islam, which is practically absent in this text,* but about misinterpreted modernity.

The only reference to Islamic practice is again related to prayer. During the exodus led by his mythical ancestor, it is related that Malaw, at the end of the fortieth night in the wilderness, celebrated the birth of a new day by proclaiming: "Al akbar" (*L'Appel des arènes*, 71–72). It is also related that Malaw's ancestor would whisper some verses of protection over Yandi's (his horse's) head. The Islamic character of this gesture is immediately undercut when the narrative states that Yandi had a *collier de gris-gris* (charm necklace) around his neck (*L'Appel des arènes*, 91). The only other reference to Islam in the entire novel is when we are told that "la voix du muezzin retentit comme un trombone" [the voice of the muezzin resounded like a trombone] (*L'Appel des arènes*, 116).

The scantiness of the Islamic references is underscored by the abundance of references to non-Islamic beliefs and rituals. Sow Fall's fictional world is certainly one that is driven by the magical forces of the *gris-gris* and ancestor worship. The young protagonist with whom the narrator identifies is frequently seen savoring the ideal life in the middle of forests with his friend, Malaw, who sustains the cult of ancestor worship (*L'Appel des arènes*, 32, 69 ).

*La Grève des Bàttu* is the only one of Sow Fall's novels in which Islam seems to play an important role. Mour Ndiaye, a civil servant in an independent African country, intends to achieve his political ambition by attacking the traditional institution of charity and begging. With great zeal, he undertakes a state project involving the evacuation of all the beggars from the city, which wants to attract white tourists. Mour's action has resounding success. The reputation of the capital will no longer suffer from the presence of this human detritus, the spectacle of beggars festering in the streets and pestering decent folk, especially the white tourists. An age-old tradition of providing for the less privileged members of the society is threatened by the imperatives of progress, modernization, and tourism. Mour's action is hailed for its patriotism; he is decorated by the president of the republic.

This gesture of recognition only serves to whet Mour's ambitions, especially as the president also announces an imminent cabinet reshuffle. From that moment on Mour has only one dream, to become the next vice president. Mour's marabout guarantees him this position on condition that he offer a very precise kind of charity to beggars at specified locations in the city. Mour's fate is sealed by his inability to persuade the striking beggars to return to the city from which he himself has expelled them. Caught in his own trap, Mour misses the coveted position of vice president.

In this as in her first novel, *Le Revenant*, Sow Fall is dramatizing the cultural alienation of an African society. The traditional frame of reference, traditional culture and all its institutions that make for the spiritual and social well-being of society, is being replaced by a new set of values based on individualism and the appetite for false prestige, power, and material gain. With respect to this theme, and especially with respect to its Islamic content, *La Grève des Bàttu* has been the most misread of Sow Fall's novels. The problem centers around the cultural meaning of the forms of charity practiced in the novel. Sow Fall has characteristically refrained from highlighting Islam in this novel by not relating the tradition of charity to Islamic belief. Critics have however insisted on translating Sow Fall's French *aumône* (alms), *obole* (small cash gift), *charité* (charity), and *don* (gift) to the Islamic *zakat* and *sadaqat*. The result has been disarray in the criticism about the meaning of charity in this narrative, a disarray on which the following observations will endeavor to shed light.

Critics have duly emphasized the role that the principle of "charity" plays in the social satire elaborated in *Le Revenant*. The problem is that they have sought to identify this principle with the Muslim *zakat*, a form of tax prescribed by the Koran. This identification is unjustifiable given that Sow Fall does not use the Islamic-Senegalese words designating the different kinds of alms giving that obtain in Senegalese society. She has used instead such terms as *aumône*, *obole*, *charité*, and *don*, which are culturally misleading. It is significant to note, however, that Sow Fall has used linguistic differentiation in her textualizing of other culturally bound concepts, objects, and occurrences, a fact that has been notably discussed by Trinh Minh-ha.

Trinh Minh-ha's article, "Aminata Sow Fall et l'espace du don," highlights a progression in Sow Fall's language from zero degree of othering to an experimentation with the untranslated word:

> *Du Revenant* (Dakar-Abidjan-Lomé: NEA, 1976) à *La Grève des Bàttu* (NEA, 1979), le changement est décisif. On décèle chez Aminata Sow Fall un désir net de se dégager des conventions du roman traditionnel. Au point de vue linguistique, la recherche d'un degré parlé de l'écriture ressort de manière flagrante; elle offre une réponse possible à l'impasse dans laquelle se trouvent les écrivains africains de langues européennes lorsque se pose la question "pour qui écrire?"[10]

> From *Du Revenant* (Dakar-Abidjan-Lomé: NEA, 1976) to *La Grève des Bàttu* (NEA, 1979), the change is decisive. One notices in Aminata Sow Fall a clear desire to do away with the norms of the conventional novel. From the linguistic point of view, the search for popular speech patterns in her writing is strikingly present. She offers a possible response to the dilemma facing European language African writers when the question, "Who are we writing for?" is posed.

Trinh Minh-ha observes that Sow Fall's characters speak a "français sénégalais." She notes the repetition of clichéd expressions in the dialogues and the frequent intervention of Wolof to express realities that are foreign to French. Perhaps more significantly, Minh-ha observes that if sometimes Wolof expressions are footnoted in *Le Revenant,* the contrary pertains in *La Grève des Bàttu,* where the integrity of the Wolof logos becomes forcefully asserted:

> Sont mis en glossaire seuls les mots ou phrases dont l'explication semble être indispensable à la compréhension du récit. Le reste forme *la part intraduisible de l'expérience sénégalaise.* Tout se passe comme si le souci de se faire entendre *d'un public étranger* ne constituait plus une préoccupation essentielle. Il ne s'agit naturellement pas d'un enfermement mais d'un changement de priorité. Le choix, ambigu dans le premier roman, s'est arrêté sans équivoque dans le deuxième, sur *un public africain populaire.* (Minh-ha: 782, emphasis added)
>
> Only words or sentences whose meaning seems to be indispensable to the understanding of the text are placed in a glossary. The rest constitute *the untranslatable dimension of the Senegalese experience.* It is as if the need to be understood *by a foreign readership* no longer really mattered. This is naturally not about cultural isolation, but about a shift in priorities. The choice (of a readership), which was ambiguous in the first novel, was clearly made in the second novel in favor of a *popular African readership.*

Trinh Minh-ha, like many other commentators, has not addressed the fact that cultures such as Sow Fall's are hybridized. Eric Sellin's remarks on Camara Laye criticism are relevant to my line of investigation:

> What is frequently overlooked in essays devoted to Camara Laye is that the African component of the above-mentioned dichotomy [African-European] is itself composed of a double influence. One in which we encounter a symbiotic relationship between traditional African patterns and those more commonly associated with Islam.[11]

Therefore, when Trinh Minh-ha speaks of the untranslatable component of the Senegalese experience it is significant to specify the aspect of the hybridized Senegalese culture that is considered untranslatable.

If, as Minh-ha notes, Sow Fall refuses to translate or to gloss culturally bound concepts and occurrences, it is legitimate to ask why the Islamic-Senegalese words designating alms giving or alms neither figure in the glossary nor in the body of the text as part of the untranslatable dimension of the Islamic-Senegalese experience. Instead, the narrator and all the characters choose to use culturally bound French terms such as *aumône, charité, don,* and *obole.*

Anny Claire-Jaccard has demonstrated that no protagonist in *La Grève des Bàttu* practices charity according to the norms of the Koran.[12] As well, George Lang recently detected the unjustifiable identification of the concept of *aumône* in *La Grève des Bàttu* with the Islamic concept of charity.[13] It must be pointed out, however, that contrary to Lang's suggestion, the term "voluntary alms" does not adequately paraphrase the notion of charity that is elaborated in the text. The narrative also contains enunciations of the concept of obligatory charity, which is not, however, the equivalent of the Islamic *zakat,* but which effectively motivates the narrative of Sow Fall.

The notions of obligatory and voluntary "charity" in Islam need to be clarified here. Muhammad Hamidullah expresses the essence of the problem quite succinctly:

> The term *sadaqat* which we translate as the state tax on Muslims, and which is a synonym of *zakat,* signifies all the taxes paid by Muslims to their government, in normal times, whether on agriculture, mines, commerce, industry, pasturing herds, savings, or other heads. These exclude the provisional taxes imposed in abnormal times, the revenues levied on non-Muslims, subjects or foreigners, and also the non-obligatory contributions. Juridical literature of early Islam, and particularly the sayings of the Prophet leave no doubt that the term *sadaqat* was employed in this sense. It did not refer at all to alms, which can neither be obligatory nor determined as to the quantity and time of payment. The equivalent of alms is *infaq fi sabil Allah* [sic], expenditure in the path of God, or *tatauwu,* voluntary charity.[14]

I hasten to add that given present political circumstances, most Muslims no longer in practice pay *sadaqat* to their governments. In other words, contrary to the practice that was notable during the time of the guided califs, this tax is now rarely enforced or regulated by state authority. Instead, individuals pay their *sadaqat* to Islamic agencies for distribution or distribute it themselves. Hamidullah has, therefore, summarily broached a highly complex subject. Yet his analysis is useful to the extent that it makes a clear distinction between obligatory and voluntary "charity" in Islam. I will henceforth use the terms *zakat* and *tatauwu* respectively to designate obligatory and voluntary "charity" in Islam.

It must be further noted that the Koran clearly specifies the categories of people to receive Islamic charity. The list is long.[15] Hence the believer has many avenues for carrying out his or her charity recommendations and obligations. It then becomes evident that charity, even the charity that is obligatory, does not require the existence of poor people to receive it, let alone beggars. It is also worth noting that professional beggars are not even included in the list of people eligible to receive Islamic "charity." Contrary to what obtains in Sow Fall's fictional world, therefore, a beggars' strike is highly unlikely in any real Islamic society.

Nevertheless some critics approach Sow Fall's novel with the mistaken notion of the indispensability of beggars in Muslim society. Martin Lemotieu's analysis is paradigmatic of this approach:

> Si la mendicité dans le contexte musulman est présente ou du moins accepté comme telle, elle implique comme corollaire, le devoir de charité de la part des autres, l'obligation de faire l'aumône pour satisfaire à une loi fondamentale du Koran. L'on peut alors imaginer le sens et la portée d'une grève que déclencheraient ceux qui sont censés recevoir l'aumône.[16]

> If begging in an Islamic context is present or at least accepted as such, it implies, as a corollary, the duty of charity on the part of the others, the obligation to perform charity in accordance with a fundamental law of the Koran. One can thus imagine the meaning and scope of a strike brought about by those who are supposed to receive charity.

Such an analysis is unfortunately based on a wrong understanding of Islamic charity, which, as I have demonstrated, does not even require the existence of beggars.

It remains a fact, however, that the beggars' strike in Sow Fall's novel would have been inconceivable if the "services" offered by the beggars were not considered indispensable to the running of the Muslim society in the novel. The compelling realism of the novel is based on this very premise.

A careful reading of the novel will reveal four (not two) distinct categories of charity: "charity as a religious obligation" (*zakat?*), "voluntary charity," "contractual charity," and "marabout-prescribed charity." My typology seeks at once to problematize a monolithic conception of charity and to illustrate how the traditions of charity articulated in this novel only tenuously relate to Islamic belief. Sow Fall's text subordinates Senegalese Islamic practice to her syncretic cultural construct.

### Charity as a Religious Obligation (*Zakat?*)

Some characters in *La Grève des Bàttu* articulate the principle according to which believers must, if they can, give charity to the poor.

Nguirane, one of the beggars, most eloquently enunciates this principle:

> "Si nous mendions, c'est parce que les chances ne sont pas égales pour tous les individus, et que ceux qui sont plus nantis doivent donner aux pauvres. C'est comme ça que l'a dit *la religion;* en mendiant nous ne faisons que reclamer ce qui nous est dû." (*La Grève des Bàttu,* 82, emphasis added)

> "If we beg, it's because fortunes are not equal for everyone, and that those who are more endowed should give to the poor. This is the way that *the religion* said it; by begging, we are only demanding our due.

The use of the definite article in *la religion* only thinly veils the fact that the religion in question is not named.

Elsewhere, Nguirane evokes an era during which the institution of begging was still considered sacred. Far from being considered a curse, begging

> "était toute naturelle pour ceux qui se trouvaient dans l'obligation de mendier et pour ceux qui donnaient, elle était considérée comme *un devoir.*" (*La Grève des Bàttu,* 83, emphasis added)

> "was altogether natural for those who found themselves in the need to beg; and for those who gave, it was considered *a duty.*"

Sagar refers to this religious precept when she prophetically imagines the gravity of the problem that will be caused by an absence of beggars. It must be noted that the believer who offers this kind of charity expects nothing in return except, of course, the satisfaction of having fulfilled a commandment from his Creator. This charity is, therefore, similar to Islamic *zakat,* with the only difference that, in the novel, the presence of beggars is considered necessary to the offering of this form of charity. It is also significant to note that no character in the novel ever offers this charity.

### Voluntary Charity (*Tatauwu?*)

This charity is recommended by the Creator. Only the marabout Seringe Birama enunciates this principle of disinterested charity, which can be given any time and anywhere. It was simply good to help the less fortunate:

> "C'est bon. Il est toujours bon de faire un sacrifice. C'est une façon de remercier le Créateur qui t'a confiée ce que tu offres aux pauvres pour les aider à supporter leur misère. C'est bien que chaque fois que tu le peux il faut donner. La fortune n'a pas de domicile fixe, Dieu ne l'a pas attribuée d'une manière définitive. Il ne fait que la prêter." (*La Grève des Bàttu*, 88)

> "It is good. It is always good to give charity. It is a way of thanking the Creator who has entrusted you with what you give to the poor in order to help them bear their misery. It is good that you give whenever you can. Fortune has no fixed abode. God did not allocate it in a definitive manner. He only loans it."

As an act of worship, such charity is neither obligatory nor does it require the existence of beggars. Indeed, this charity, just like the other types already discussed, can very well eradicate the phenomenon of begging that, according to Kéba, dishonors man. Significantly, this form of charity is also not practiced in the novel.

### Contractual Charity

We have here a mercantile principle that posits a contract between the giver and the receiver of charity. The former gives charity and the latter offers for him or her prayers and wishes for happiness. The narrator defines the principle from the point of view of the beggars:

> Pour eux le contrat qui lie chaque individu à la société se résume en ceci: donner et recevoir. Eh bien, eux, ne donnent-ils pas leurs bénédictions de pauvres, leurs prières et leurs voeux? (*La Grève des Bàttu*, 30)

> For them the contract that linked each individual to the society is summed up in this: giving and receiving. Well, didn't they, as poor people, offer their blessings, prayers, and well wishes?

In this view of things, which obeys the laws of supply and demand of consumer economics, the plight of the poor does not concern those who give. Ironically, in fact, it is in the interest of the rich that there exist poor people who will continue to accept their "charity." For what really interests them are the prayers and good wishes that are said on their behalf. The act of giving is uncompromisingly self-serving. The narrative recurrently emphasizes the scorn the rich and the powerful have for the poor in spite of the great need they have of them. Those who give this type of charity have somehow arrogantly come to believe that there will always be an abundant supply of beggars. The irony is that almost everybody in the novel, excluding the beggars, seems to be practicing this form of charity, including the poor, and even the ordinary state policemen, who, by an ironic twist, are called upon to harass the beggars. Even Europeans offer this "charity"! For what reason? According to which cultural code?

### Marabout-Prescribed Charity

If, in the contractual charity discussed above, the one who receives charity matters to the extent that at least his prayers and good wishes are at a premium, marabout-prescribed charity requires only that the beggar accept the symbolic object that is offered to him as charity. For this charity is offered exactly according to the instructions of the marabout who prescribes it. The object is symbolic because its use value to the receiver does not interest the giver at all. The potential for problems is thus obvious. What will happen, for example, should a beggar refuse to accept an object that is utterly useless to him? The narrative gives us exactly this kind of scenario when poor Galaye, following the instructions of his marabout, offers a sheet of paper to an old woman who cannot invent any use for it:

> "C'est de la charité, grand'mère! Je te le donne en charité."
> "Moo doom! Que puis-je faire avec une feuille de papier, moi qui ne sais ni lire ni écrire?" (*La Grève des Bàttu*, 57)

> "It's charity, grandma! I give it to you as charity."
> "Moo doom! What can I do with a piece of paper, when I can neither read nor write?"

In this episode the old woman and Galaye have two different types of charity on their minds. The problem is only solved when Galaye gives to the old woman the type of charity she needs, his last savings, as a kind of bribe for her to accept the charity his marabout prescribed, the one that really matters to him, the sheet of paper. The irony resides in the fact that an indigent man, driven by ambition, is forced to give "charity" to one who is probably in less financial need than himself. This irony is a satiric commentary on the practice of charity in the society described by Aminata Sow Fall.

Another interesting case occurs when Mour Ndiaye, finding it impossible to offer "charity" according to the impossible instructions of his new marabout, Kifi Bokoul, comes back to his old marabout so that he might abrogate these conditions. Mour, however, wishes to conceal the fact that the charity he had to offer had been prescribed by another marabout. Ironically, Seringe Birama suggests an utterly easy solution, to offer voluntary charity:

> "Maintenant, dis-moi puisque vous avez fait fuir les mendiants pourquoi ne donnes-tu pas autrement la charité? Dans les maisons il y a surement des gens qui en ont besoin." (*La Grève des Bàttu*, 89)

> "Now, tell me since you have chased the beggars away, why don't you give charity by other means? There are surely needy people in the houses."

This tricky solution forces Mour Ndiaye to confess the truth—he had gone to see another marabout who gave him the impossible instructions. The conversion of one type of "charity" to another proves to be impossible in this case. The fate of Mour is sealed by the simple phrase of Seringe Birama: "Respecte les indications de ton marabout" [strictly follow the instructions of your marabout] (*La Grève des Bàttu,* 90). Indeed, Mour's great predicament can be situated within this framework of charity. Irony of fate has it that he is called upon to offer marabout-prescribed "charity" at the very moment he is decorated for having eliminated the factors that are indispensable to the carrying out of the "charity," the beggars. The entire narrative is a masterful preparation of this intractable irony. What is the role of Seringe Birama in this drama?

As I have indicated, Seringe Birama is the only one to enunciate the principle of voluntary charity. Paradoxically, however, he lives by and promotes the tradition of marabout-prescribed charity. He does nothing to check the ambition of Mour. On the contrary he fuels his ambition by prescribing "charity" that will help his client in his quest for power. It is also significant to note that following the ironic structure of the novel, the requirements of each of the successively prescribed "alms" get increasingly difficult. The first "charity" only requires that Mour sacrifice a ram with no other specification. The second sacrifice specifies that the ram be white all over. Moreover, Mour must slaughter it himself: "Tu feras sept tas de viande que tu donneras à des mendiants" ["You will make seven piles of meat, which you will distribute among beggars"] (*La Grève des Bàttu,* 28). The third case requires the sacrifice of a bull to be cut up into thirty-three parts to be distributed to the poor. Last details: the distribution must be done on a Friday and no member of Mour's household should taste of the meat. Evidently all these sacrifices are easy to carry out if one compares them with the one prescribed by Kifi Bokoul; the requirements are in themselves difficult to fulfill. But when one adds to that the fact that the beggars are on strike, one realizes that Mour's assignment is simply impossible.

The foregoing analysis illustrates that Sow Fall has rather meticulously avoided indicating Islam as the frame of reference for the traditions of charity that obtain in *La Grève des Bàttu*. It might be argued that she did so to stress the fact that those traditions are a deviation from and a perversion of the Islamic norm. Such a thesis would, however, fail to explain why the narrative still uses such vague terms as "sacrifice" to explicate what corresponds to the Islamic concept of *tatauwu* (88). Therefore, there is a strong case for positing that the annexing translations of the forms of charity practiced in *La Grève des Bàttu* are deliberately intended to mute the Islamic cultural context of the novel. This argument is further supported by Naïm Kattan's interesting observations on the translation of such civilizations as Islam.[17]

Islam, probably more than any other world religion, has a particular sensitivity to language. Naïm Kattan has addressed this issue in his short article, "Peut-on traduire des civilisations?" Muslims believe that the word of Allah is untranslatable. That is why Muslims, whether they are Turks or Indonesians, and regardless of whether or not they understand Koranic Arabic, pray in the language of the Koran:

> Dans ce cas précis, une civilisation, du moins dans une de ses essentielles dimensions, n'est pas traduisible. La langue, rapport primordial avec le réel est globalisante. (Kattan: 402)
>
> In this particular case, a civilization, at least in one of its essential dimensions, is not translatable. Language, as a primordial link to reality, is all pervasive.

Kattan provides an example of the possible consequences of translating fundamental Islamic concepts in European languages. The Arabic word *jihad* ("*Djihad*") has been translated throughout the centuries as "holy war." In modern times, this reductionist translation has been reinforced by the late Ayatollah Khomeini's periodic calls for *jihad,* holy war. There is, however, no notion of sacredness or war in the word *jihad.* A close translation would be "effort." One of the concepts derived from the word is *ijtihad,* which means efforts in the area of scholarship. In reality, therefore, *jihad* means holy war, but this reality is achieved through various means. The main fact is that *jihad* is a religious effort, it is effort exerted in Allah's cause. Furthermore, in the West, the distinction between the sacred and the profane is clear:

> Dans une civilisation [Islamic] où cette notion n'existe pas ou n'existe pas autant, la guerre sainte n'est qu'une extension d'un effort religieux, d'un ardent travail en faveur de Dieu. (Kattan: 402)
>
> In Islamic civilization, where this notion does not exist, or is not similarly accentuated, holy war is simply an extension of a religious effort, of a serious effort in the service of God.

The example provided by Kattan is an eloquent illustration of the potential for significant distortion when the fundamental dimensions of Islamic culture are translated. There is as well an ideological dimension to the problem. As Kattan puts it,

> accepter la traduction c'est admettre volontairement que dans le processus de transmission, il y ait perte et abandon. Une dimension de cette civilisation est oblitérée, altérée afin qu'elle soit et compréhensible et acceptable à une autre. (Kattan: 402)
>
> to accept translation is to freely accept the loss and betrayal that will occur in the process of transmission. A dimension of that civilization is obliterated, altered, in order to make it intelligible and acceptable to another civilization.

Kattan's study applied to the problem I am examining in Sow Fall's work reveals possible motives behind Sow Fall's decision to translate Islamic realities into French in her narratives. The choice is probably informed by a desire to undermine "otherness," to bridge the ideological gap between the culture of her largely non-Muslim French readership and Islamic culture. In fact Sow Fall hinted at this factor in an interview with Thomas Hammond:

> "J'écris pour tout le monde. J'écris aussi bien pour les Africains que pour les non-Africains. Je pense que l'on doit faire l'effort de nous faire accepter par les autres."[18]

"I write for everybody. I write as much for the Africans as for the non-Africans. I believe that we must strive to make ourselves acceptable to others."

This desire to be accepted and understood by the non-Muslim French/francophone "other" must substantially explain Sow Fall's decision to dilute the Islamic context of her narratives. She has negotiated a series of concessions to the "other's" ideological sensitivity. In the process, Islam has been altered, obliterated, and distorted or at least made to lose its strangeness and, hence, its cultural specificity. If Sow Fall's choice is a hermeneutic move, that is, a move to enhance cross-cultural understanding, then it is legitimate to enquire whether she achieved her goal.

The irony is that in the particular case of *La Grève des Bàttu,* Sow Fall has emasculated her own efforts to achieve cross-cultural understanding by rendering the concepts of charity in French. The strategy has simply led critics to misinterpret this novel. Lemothieu is not the only critic to have misinterpreted the concepts of charity in *La Grève des Bàttu*. Most critics, who characteristically have poor knowledge of Islam, have simply been led by Sow Fall's narrative to conclude that beggars and begging are indispensable to the life of an Islamic society. Dorothy Blair, for example, sees the central theme of the novel as "the role played by beggars in a traditional Islamic society, where to give alms is indispensable, not as an act of charity for the benefit of the recipient, but to put the donor in good odor with heaven."[19]

Likewise, Mbye Cham sees *La Grève des Bàttu* as a fictional exploration of one of the five pillars of the Muslim faith, *zakat,* at work in real life (Cham: 170).

The curious thing about these interpretations is that not once in the novel does Sow Fall use the terms *zakat, sadaqat,* or *tatauwu* to suggest that instances of alms giving that one finds in the novel derive from the Islamic tradition. But the ambiguities could still have been significantly reduced had the writer used such concepts as *l'Islam* instead of "la religion" and *le Coran* instead of "le livre saint." The use of such concepts would have unequivocally suggested that the traditions of charity in the novel derive from Islamic belief. Of course, such a choice would have ended up emphasizing Islam in the narrative, a prospect that Sow Fall is apparently not comfortable with. The fact remains that her textual strategies have not achieved the cross-cultural understanding they set out to achieve.

The broader ideological implications of Sow Fall's creative choices cannot be missed. The use of French by Muslims in colonial French West Africa was historically perceived by French colonial officers to have a "taming" effect. (To some colonial administrators Islam represented a formidable obstacle to French cultural ambitions.) In this light, Mariani, the inspector of education in French West Africa, observed in 1910 that "Muslims in general are difficult to handle, and they have a tendency to consider themselves superior even to us, simply because they were born Muslims."[20]

One of the solutions he proposed to deal with this Muslim cultural resistance was to divert some of the money spent on the Catholic clergy to the teaching of French: "The study of a living Christian language is the most effective remedy to Muslim fanaticism. . . . The Mahometan who knows French and English is less fanatical and less dangerous than co-religionists who can only speak Arabic, Berber or Turkish" (Harrison: 64).

Mariani clearly thought that the use of French by Muslims was a far more potent weapon in the fight against Islamic cultural intransigence than Catholic proselytizing. The subject of the impact of such assimilationist educational policies on early Senegalese writers is thoroughly handled by Dorothy Blair (1984). Suffice it to say that when Sow Fall uses such Christian concepts as *aumône, obole, baptême,* and *purgatoire* to describe the cultural life of her people, one cannot help but conclude that she is unwittingly perpetuating the French colonial policy of taming Islam.

## Notes

1. Chinua Achebe, cited in Kwame Appiah's "Soyinka's Myth of an African World," in Kenneth Harrow, ed., *Crisscrossing Boundaries in African Literature,* annual selected papers of the ALA (Washington, D.C.: Three Continents Press, 1986), 11.

2. This loss is frequently expressed in Sow Fall's novels by the expression: "Cosaan [Senegalese traditional culture] se meurt."

3. Mbye Cham, "Islam in Senegalese Literature and Film," in Kenneth Harrow, ed., *Faces of Islam in African Literature* (Portsmouth, London: Heinemann, 1991), 168. All subsequent references to this study will be indicated parenthetically in the text.

4. Meschonnic formulated the concepts of *décentrement* and *annexion* in the following terms:

> Le *décentrement* est un rapport entre deux textes dans deux langues-cultures jusque dans la structure linguistique de la langue, cette

structure linguistique étant valeur dans le système du texte. *L'annexion* est l'effacement de ce rapport, l'illusion du naturel, le comme-si, comme si un texte en langue de départ était écrit en langue d'arrivée, abstraction faite des différences de culture, d'époque, de structure linguistique. Un texte est à distance: on la montre, ou on la cache.

*Decentering* defines a relationship between two texts in two language-cultures that reflects the very linguistic structure of the language. This linguistic culture itself retains value (a presence) in the system of the text. *Annexation* is the erasure of that relationship, the impression of naturalness, the "as if," as if a text in a target language was actually written in its original language, by smoothing over differences of culture, and of linguistic structure. A text is at a distance; one may choose to show that distance or hide it.

Cited in Robert Larose, *Théories contemporaines de la traduction* (Sillery: Presses de l'Université du Québec, 1989), 82. Although these concepts refer primarily to textual translation from one language to another, they hold relevance for the specific questions raised in this chapter. African europhone narratives are cross-cultural. The writer may, therefore, choose to textualize the distance between the African culture depicted and the culture of the European language in which the latter is depicted or to conceal it. While Aminata Sow Fall has opted to put in the foreground the distance between Senegalese and French culture through a strategy of linguistic variance, she has tended to conceal that distance between French culture and the Islamic component of Senegalese culture.

5. An example of this kind of study is Patrick Scott's "Gabriel Okara's *The Voice:* The non-Ijo Reader and the Pragmatics of Translingualism," *Research in African Literatures* V, 21:3 (1990): 75–88.

6. Chantal Zabus, "Othering the Foreign Language in the West African Europhone Novel," *Canadian Review of Comparative Literature* 17 (September/December 1990). All references to this study will be indicated parenthetically in the text.

7. Chantal Zabus, *The African Palimpsest: Indigenization of Language in the West African Europhone Novel* (Amsterdam: Rodopi, 1991). All references to this work will be indicated parenthetically in the text.

8. Aminata Sow Fall, *Le Revenant* (Abidjan: Nouvelles Editions Africaines, 1982). All subsequent references to this novel will be indicated parenthetically in the text.

9. Aminata Sow Fall, *L'Appel des arènes* (Abidjan: Nouvelles Editions Africaines, 1982 edition). References to this novel will be indicated parenthetically in the text.

10. Trinh Minh-ha, "Aminata Sow Fall et l'espace du don," *The French Review* 55, no. 6 (May 1982): 782. Subsequent references to this study will be indicated parenthetically in the text.

11. Eric Sellin, "Islamic Elements in Camara Laye's *L'Enfant Noir,*" in Kenneth Harrow, ed., *Faces of Islam* (London: Heinemann, 1991), 227.

12. Anny Claire-Jaccard, "Les visages de l'Islam chez Mariama Bâ et chez Aminata Sow Fall," *Nouvelles du sud: Islam et littératures africaines* (Paris: Silex, 1987), 180.

13. George Lang, "Through a Prism Darkly: 'Orientalism' in European-Language African Writing," in Kenneth Harrow, ed., *Faces of Islam in African Literature* (London: Heinemann, 1991), 308.

14. Muhammad Hamidullah, *Introduction to Islam* (Lahor: Muhammad Ashraf, 1968), 143.

15. Koran, 9: 60. This verse does not include all the categories. For a complete list one has to scan the entire Koran and the Sunna. Adnan Haddad has provided a fairly comprehensive list after duly insisting that "ceux qui méritent l'aumône ne sont ni les mendiants professionnels ni les imposteurs, mais les vrais pauvres." *Pourquoi L'Islam?* (Paris: Sedes, 1987), 86.

16. Martin Lemotieu, "Interférence de la religion musulmane sur les structures actuelles de la société négro-africaine: L'Exemple de *La Grève des Bàttu* d'Aminata Sow Fall," *Nouvelles du sud: Islam et littératures africaines* (Paris: Silex, 1987), 52. Subsequent references to this study will be indicated parenthetically in the text.

17. Naïm Kattan, "Peut-on traduire les civilisations?" *Meta* 27, no. 4 (1982). All references to this study will be indicated parenthetically in the text.

18. Thomas Hammond, "Entretien avec Aminata Sow Fall," *Présence Francophone: Revue Internationale de Langue et de Littérature* 22 (Spring 1981): 192.

19. Dorothy Blair, *Senegalese Literature: A Critical History* (Boston: Twayne Publishers, 1984), 130.

20. Christopher Harrison, *France and Islam in West Africa, 1860–1960* (Cambridge: Cambridge University Press, 1988), 64. Further reference to Harrison's work will be indicated parenthetically in the text.

# 6

# The Quest for Orthodoxy in Ibrahim Tahir's *The Last Imam*

*Diamourou, the old griot, who was bothered by all this, said sometimes what he felt. An impenetrable disbeliever like Balla living in a village like Togobala, a village of Allah! A witchdoctor, a caster of evil spells, a public enemy of Allah! Well! Well!*
 —Ahmadou Kourouma, *Les Soleils des indépendencies*[1]

*This is a Muslim Kingdom and the Word of Allah must be kept.*
 —Ibrahim Tahir, *The Last Imam*[2]

We have advanced the argument in chapter two that the concept of *Islam noir* overlooks the *tajdid* tradition in the Islamic history of sub-Saharan Africa. How have sub-Saharan African writers of the Muslim tradition articulated the dynamic relationships between Islam and local African cultures? We anticipate somewhat our answer by stating that such writers as Camara Laye, Sembène Ousmane, Ahmadou Kourouma, and Ibrahim Tahir have in varying degrees illustrated a consciousness of Islamic orthodoxy in the societies they depict in their novels. Our introductory quotations underscore this consciousness. In this chapter we will examine the novel of Ibrahim Tahir, *The Last Imam,* which thematizes the intractable conflict between Islam and the pre-Islamic Fulani-Hausa cultures of Muslim Northern Nigeria. This novel is interesting not only because of its overt concerns with orthodoxy, but also because of what it reveals about renewal movements in Islam. The all-pervasiveness of the Islamic ethos in Tahir's work contrasts sharply with the syncretism in Sow Fall's fictional world. In the *Last Imam,* utopia is not in Africa's ancestral past, but in puritanical Islam that sees as its vocation the erasure of that very past.

We will first examine Lemuel Johnson's study on Islamic orthodoxy in the West African novel. It will be argued that Lemuel Johnson's conclusions on the consciousness of Islamic orthodoxy in West African fiction would have been more informed had he expanded his corpus to include Ahmadou Kourouma's *Les Soleils des indépendances* and Ibrahim Tahir's *The Last Imam*. Before undertaking a detailed study of Ibrahim Tahir's novel, we will briefly analyze *Les Soleils des indépendances* to highlight the theme of orthodoxy as it relates to the structure of conflict in that novel, and as it anticipates the crises dramatized in Tahir's text.

Johnson's study focuses on the works of Cheikh Hamidou Kane, Camara Laye, Sembène Ousmane, Ayi Kwei Armah, and Yambo Ouologuem. His readings of these texts lead him to the conclusion that

> thematic and narrative structures are more often resolved in syncretism and tension than in a return to orthodoxy. The reasons for such a tension parallel, and so may be deduced from, the general tendency in modern African literature to present religious phenomena primarily in terms of their contribution to crises of allegiance and identity.... We are, as a result, in a world coded to be unorthodox, whether for epic, tragic, or satirical reasons. Orthodox and formal propositions of dogma, imagery, and structure are set, modified or else ridiculed in the contexts provided by our "form resisting" island.[3]

Lemuel Johnson insists that the Afro-Islamic context is primarily accommodationist (*al-Mukhlit*). The only novel, among those he chooses to study, to come close to a purist concern with apostasy, heresy, and syncretism is Cheikh Hamidou Kane's *L'Aventure ambiguë*. On the other hand, Camara Laye's *L'Enfant noir* (1970) manifests a dual consciousness, seen in the apparent equanimity with which Camara Laye celebrates *Kondén Diara* and Mandingo totemism, and Allah and Ramadan. Although Camara Laye describes a cultural world in which Islamic and Mandingo practices blend very comfortably, with him one senses a consciousness of orthodoxy. This is notable in the passage depicting the strict adherence to Islam that the protagonist of *L'Enfant noir* observes in Mamadou, his uncle in Conakry:

> He was a Mohammedan—as we all are, I may add—but more orthodox than most of us. His observance of the Koran was scrupulously honest. He neither smoked nor drank and was absolutely honest. He wore European clothes only for work. As soon as he came home he undressed and put on a *boubou* which had to be immaculate, and said his prayers. On leaving the Ecole Normale he had taken up the study of Arabic.... It was simply his desire for a deeper knowledge of religion that had persuaded him to learn the language of the Prophet. The Koran guided him in everything. (Johnson: 241–242)

Still, observes Johnson, whatever tension may exist between Islam and ancestral Mandingo practices is muted.

Admittedly there is no place in *L'Aventure ambiguë for* a pre-Islamic worldview. This fact is not however indicative of a purist concern with syncretism. A concern with orthodoxy requires an awareness of heterodoxy. Such awareness is virtually absent in Kane's novel. There is no reference to syncretic practices in this novel, and no allusion to a pre-Islamic Diallobé cultural reality. Kane's text is therefore ironically similar to Sow Fall's works. For very different reasons, there is—to use Johnson's concept—no double consciousness. One discerns no tension between Islam and pre-Islamic Senegalese culture in Sow Fall's fiction because the Islamic culture she depicts is comfortably accommodationist, and in Kane's because Islam has simply obliterated all traces of the millennial Diallobé culture before it.

Camara Laye's cultural landscape is as syncretistic as Sow Fall's, with one significant difference between the two. As Lemuel Johnson himself observes, one does sense a consciousness of orthodoxy in Laye. Finally, Johnson's conclusion that the world of West African fiction is coded to be unorthodox and that propositions of dogma in this literature are "set modified or else ridiculed" can hardly apply to *Les Soleils des indépendances* and *The Last Imam*. Ahmadou Kourouma's novel undoubtedly depicts a heightened consciousness of Islamic orthodoxy that is not limited to the narrative perspective. And Ibrahim Tahir makes the confrontation between Islam and local custom a major theme of his novel.

Fama, the protagonist of *Les Soleils des indépendances,* belongs to the precolonial Mandingo aristocracy. He is first deprived of his traditional status as a prince by the colonial administration, and then independence deepens his frustration. He had struggled for independence in the hope of a better future only to discover that the postcolonial era has no place for idealists like him. He resides in the city with his "sterile" wife, Salimata. The first part of the novel deals with Salimata's desperate efforts at seeking a remedy for her "infertility." The narrator never really makes it clear whether in fact the problem is with her husband. Nevertheless, in a bid to get a child she regularly prays to Allah, performs charity, and consults marabouts and traditional seers.

Fama's cousin, Lacina, dies in Togobala, the seat of the Doumbouya dynasty, which Fama is now expected to inherit. In spite of the warm welcome that he receives upon his arrival in Togobala to participate in his cousin's funeral rites, Fama resolves to return to the city with a second wife. As soon as he arrives in the city he is falsely accused of complicity in a plot to overthrow the ruling government, incarcerated together with the other accused, and subjected to humiliation and torture. In a bizarre turn of events, the head of state not only offers clemency to the "coup plotters," he also offers them great wealth and prestige. The disillusioned Fama will have no such blood money. He soon learns that his wives were unfaithful to him while he was in jail. He finally decides to abandon the city and all it represents and return to his ancestral home. He arrives a dying man after violent confrontations with security forces on the way, and dies shortly afterward.

Islam is the dominant religion of the society depicted by Kourouma. The protagonist and the major players in this social drama identify themselves as Muslims. Even the narrative perspective is heavily Islamic. But this is also a society that is still firmly attached to a pre-Islamic view of life beyond the real. The syncretistic ethos is most apparent in the ways in which these Muslims deal with the problems of life: infertility, fear, insecurity, and general adversity.

It is tempting to say that there is no tension between Islam and Mandingo cultural beliefs in this novel. The syncretistic ethos comes out in the practices of Salimata, Fama's wife. The narrator presents her as a "Musulmane achevée" to emphasize her identity as a devout Muslim. She performs her prayers regularly and does charity work, sometimes at great personal risk. But this is not all. As a devout Muslim, she fasts for thirty days, prays four times a day, and gives to charity. She also consulted marabouts and witch doctors:

> Elle en tout et partout en pleine musulmane jeunait trente jours, faisait l'aumône et les quatre prières journalières. Et que n'a-t-elle pas éprouvé! Le sorcier, le marabout et les sacrifices et les médicaments, tout et tout. (*Soleils,* 25)

> She, like a true Muslim, fasted for thirty days, gave charity, and did the four daily prayers. And what has she not tried? The sorcerer, the marabout, ritual sacrifices, and medicines; she has tried everything.

That Salimata should indiscriminately seek the help of the marabout and the traditional seer with equanimity suggests that she is unaware of a contradiction in her actions. She is not the only character to betray this impression. Her mother, who had a similar problem of infertility, also had to make supplications to the "mont Tougbé" [Tougbé Mountain], dont le génie l'avait fécondée de Salimata. (*Soleils*, 34)

whose Spirit granted her the conception of Salimata.

In the morning of Salimata's circumcision, her prayers and gratitude are characteristically not exclusively addressed to Allah:

"Je remercie Allah que ce matin soit arrivé. Mais j'ai peur, et mon coeur saute, de ma peur, j'implore tous les génies que ce champ soit favorable à ma unique fille!" (*Soleils*, 31)

"I thank Allah that this morning has come, but I am afraid and my heart throbs due to my fear. I pray to all the spirits that this field be benevolent to my only daughter."

Similarly, the driver of the vehicle that takes Fama to his ancestral home to attend Lacina's funeral does not forget to make a thousand incantations

où se mêlaient les noms d'Allah et des mânes. (*Soleils*, 72)

where the names of Allah were intermingled with the names of spirits.

All these examples seem to underscore a total lack of awareness of the demands of Islamic orthodoxy. They do not, however, represent the full picture. There is already evidence of a consciousness of orthodoxy in the narrative relating Salimata's therapeutic rituals. Fama himself is very uneasy about these practices:

Qui pouvait le rassurer sur *la pureté musulmane* des gestes de Salimata? Trépidations et convulsions, fumées et gris-gris, toutes les pratiques exécutées chaque soir afin que le ventre se féconde? . . . Elle priait des sourates pieux et longs du marabout. . . . Finissait-elle? Avec la fièvre, elle déballait gris-gris, canaris, gourdes, feuilles, ingurgitait des décoctions sûrement amères . . . battait des mains et chantait *des versets mi-Malinké, mi-arabe.* (*Soleils*, 26, emphasis added)

Who could guarantee to her that Salimata's movements were *Islamically orthodox?* Gyrations and convulsions, smoke and amulets, all rituals carried out each evening to bring about the pregnancy? . . . She recited long and holy suras (Koranic chapters) selected by the marabout. . . . Was that all? When she had the fever, she displayed

> amulets, cowries, gourds, and leaves. She gulped concoctions that must be bitter, . . . clapped her hands, and sang *verses that were a mixture of Mandingo and Arabic.*

The narrator and Fama are demonstrating here a concern for orthodoxy and "purity." This concern takes the dimensions of a theme in Togobala, the seat of the Doumbouya dynasty. The syncretistic character of the Islam practiced in Togobala leads the narrator to ask an important question about the cultural self-definition of the Mandingo people. It is difficult to tell whether the people of Togobala are Muslims or animists:

> Sont-ce des féticheurs? Sont-ce des musulmans? Le musulman écoute le *Coran,* le féticheur suit *Koma;* mais à Togobala aux yeux de tout le monde, tout le monde se dit et respire musulman, seul chacun craint le fétiche. (*Soleils,* 93, my emphasis)

> Are these fetish worshippers? Are they Muslims? The Muslim listens to the *Koran,* the fetish worshipper follows *Koma.* At Togobala, everybody publicly professes Islam, but when they are alone, they only fear the fetish.

A clear distinction is made here between two seemingly irreconcilable religious-cultural identities, that of the *féticheur* and that of the Muslim. These two belief systems have equally irreconcilable sources of authority, the Koran and *Koma* respectively. The problem raised by the narrator touches on the issue of allegiance. One cannot both be Muslim and remain attached to non-Islamic beliefs. In the narrative perspective to do so amounts to hypocrisy (93), which in Islam is more damnable than pure disbelief.

It would appear from the foregoing analysis that Fama is an exponent of orthodoxy. Indeed, when he arrives in Togobala he stops the mourners because crying for a deceased person is not allowed in the Koran:

> "Non et non! Allah dans son livre interdit de pleurer des décédés." (*Soleils,* 91)

> "No, no! Allah has prohibited mourning for the dead in this book."

But the real test of his loyalty to Islam comes in the form of a very concrete question to which the two belief systems have diametrically opposite answers. The Koran states that the dead return to Allah, and have no further influence on the world of the living. For the animist Bambaras, however, the ghosts of the dead continue to dwell in their former houses:

> Le Coran dit qu'un décédé est un appelé par Allah, un fini et les coûtumes Malinké disent qu'un chef de famille couche dans la case patriarcale. . . . Mais chez les Bambara, les incroyants, les Cafres, on ne couche jamais dans la case d'un enterré sans le petit sacrifice qui éloigne esprits et mânes. (*Soleils*, 93)

> The Koran states that the dead have been summoned by Allah; they are departed (from this world). Mandingo customs say that the head of a family should sleep in the patriarch's house. . . . But among the pagan Bambara, one never sleeps in the house of one who has been buried without first performing a (ritual) sacrifice to ward off spirits and ghosts.

If Fama subscribed to the Koran then he would sleep in the patriarchal house where the deceased had lived without any fear of spirits and ghosts. If, on the other hand, he still believed, as do the pagans, in ghosts, then he would have to perform the sacrifices to sleep peacefully in the ancestral house. The *cafre* beliefs simply triumph here:

> En dépit de sa profonde foi au Coran, en Allah et en Mohamet, Fama toute la nuit, dans une petite case se recroquevilla entre de vieux canaris et un cabot galeux. (*Soleils*, 94)

> In spite of his deep faith in the Koran, in Allah and in Muhammad, Fama was huddled up all night long between old cowries and a dog with scabies in a small hut.

If Fama does not make the protective sacrifice it is because, instead of spending the night in the patriarchal house, he spends it in a small house making sure to get up early in the morning. He then appears in front of the ancestral house "comme s'il y avait dormi." He even subsequently makes a sacrifice to the *fétiches* of Balla, the self-declared non-Muslim and chief *sorcier* (sorcerer) of Togobala.

This episode is obviously significant. There is no doubt that Fama's primary cultural self-definition is that of a Muslim, and there is equally no doubt that he is aware of the puritanical demands of his faith. He compromises regardless. Islam has simply not been able to uproot the millennial cultural beliefs in the Mandingo society depicted in this novel. It is this accommodation to pre-Islamic beliefs that the narrator qualifies as Mandingo hypocrisy.

In fact not everybody in Togobala is Muslim. The most outspoken representative of traditional Mandingo culture is Balla:

> [Balla] avait toujours rejeté la pâte de la conversion et il avait bien fait. Fétichiste parmi les Malinkés, il devint le plus riche, le plus craint, le mieux nourri. (*Soleils,* 99)

> [Balla] had always rejected conversion, and he had done well. As a fetishist among the Mandingos, he became the wealthiest, the most feared, the one who had the best food.

Balla prospers because Muslims like Fama continue to solicit his services each time they feel that Allah is not answering their supplications on a specific matter (99). There is one notable exception to this generally accommodationist ethos: Diamourou, the old griot of the Doumbouya dynasty, is the voice of Islamic orthodoxy. While everybody else fears and needs Balla, Diamourou is opposed to the very presence of a pagan in Allah's village. (See the epigraph at the beginning of this chapter.)

Diamourou is no doubt the antithesis of Balla and stands out in his puritanical adherence to Islam. The narrative shows both him and Balla fighting to win Fama's absolute loyalties. Diamourou's efforts in this direction are more desperate, if futile. While the elders of the village observe silence on their way to the cemetery, Diamourou seizes the opportunity to proselytize and warn Fama against pagan practices:

> Il parlait parce qu'il avait à profiter de l'absence de Balla, pour placer près de son maître les appels à l'Islam, les conseils contre les pratiques Cafres du féticheur. . . . Fama n'entendait rien. (*Soleils,* 103)

> He spoke, because he had to benefit from Balla's absence by bringing to the attention of his master, the calls of Islam, advice against the pagan practices of the fetishist. . . . Fama did not pay attention.

Fama and the other Muslims in Togobala are simply not ready to give up the possibility of seeking the help and protection of dead ancestors and other forces of the spirit world when confronted with life's numerous problems.

Diamourou's voice is a lonely one. Nevertheless his presence together with the narrative perspective are significant. There is an awareness of the irreconcilability between the Koran and Koma, between Islam and the Mandingo traditional belief system. The tension that this awareness engenders in Kourouma's text does not, however, lead to open conflict. The voice of orthodoxy is simply too weak for such a conflict to develop.

Is Diamourou an Islamic reformer? The stature that Kourouma gives him does not enable him to be one. He wields very little influence in his society. There is not even any mention of the possibility of tajdid or jihad in the narrative. Kourouma's novel is nonetheless admittedly different from the other novels reviewed by Lemuel Johnson. Kourouma depicts a sharpened consciousness of orthodoxy in his fictional world and hints at the potential for conflict. It is in Ibrahim Tahir's *The Last Imam* that such a conflict is actualized and transformed into a central theme.

Tahir's narrative dramatizes, with great realism, the struggles of Alhaji Usman, the imam of the Bauchi empire, to implement a puritanical Islam in his personal life and in his family, and perhaps more significantly in the rest of the Bauchi empire. Many factors, some of which are personal, but more significantly having to do with his people's unreadiness to do away completely with their pre-Islamic beliefs, stifle his efforts. His uncompromising stance on many issues affecting the lives of his followers alienates him from them. At the end of the novel he is unturbaned by the pragmatic emir who, at the same time, recognizes that his empire will never again have an imam of Alhaji Usman's calibre. Alhaji Usman is replaced with a spiritual leader who will be more ready to accommodate the weaknesses of the people; all subsequent "imams" will be chosen with this imperative in mind. A detailed summary of the novel will underscore the central role of Islam in the plot.

The biography of the protagonist is strategically linked by the author to the legend of Shehu Dan Fodio's jihad. Alhaji Usman belongs to a lineage of Fulani scholars of great learning and devotion to Islam recruited by the emir of Bauchi during the jihad of Shehu Dan Fodio to be the spiritual leaders of the emirate. Alhaji Usman's succession of his father as imam is consecrated by a dream when the boy is still very young. He subsequently supersedes his father's other students in learning and piety. So great is his devotion to his calling that he has to be virtually coerced at twenty-five by his father to marry a Hausa girl, A'isha, offered to him in an alms marriage. This marriage stifles the spiritual flame of the young Usman. He nonetheless marries three other women (this time, Fulani) in rapid succession. But his passion for Islam will only come back while he is on pilgrimage with his father. The abstract catalyst to the spiritual rebirth is the view of the desert, but the passion itself finds concrete expression in Alhaji Usman's overpowering desire to marry Hasana, a slave girl in his household. As a Muslim, he could get a fifth consort only by kind permission of the Koranic verse "and take also what you may from what your right hands possess, your slave maidens" (*The Last Imam,* 34). For the following thirteen years, Alhaji Usman devotes himself exclusively to Hasana and the son she bears him, Kasim, ignoring the other wives and their children. This unhealthy domestic situation is made worse by the death of Hasana. For a long time the Imam is inconsolable; he feels abandoned by God and goes to the graveyard regularly to lament his loss. He just cannot reconcile God with the cruel death of his beloved. In this state of grief and near apostation, he demands to get a sign from God. When the answer finally comes, it is in the form of a "cold realisation that his sadness had led him into the blasphemous hands of Sheidan and unless he repented there and then he was a sinner and an apostate" (*The Last Ima*m, 3–4).

A'isha helps to reinforce this realization. She then enjoys some measure of closeness with the imam at the price of alienating Kasim. Kasim is accused by A'isha of being disrespectful to his "mothers." The imam, conscious of the Koranic verse commanding believers to show deference to their parents, loses his temper and beats Kasim inordinately. He thus breaks a promise he made to the boy's mother, that he would be kind to him. Guilt ridden, he starts going again to the graveyard to ask Hasana for forgiveness. He seeks to compensate for what he did by renewing his closeness to Kasim. The schemes of A'isha finally lead to the boy's running into the hands of a much less knowledgeable teacher whose reported maltreatment of the boy leads the people to doubt the imam's wisdom. Meanwhile the imam forces the hand of the emir to ban what he calls the heathen Hausa custom of the *gwauro*. This tradition involves the utter humiliation and torture of any married man whose wife is not home with him in the month of Ramadan.

The imam soon discovers that Malam Shu'aibu, whom he has despised for his lack of learning, is in fact his elder half-brother, the son of his father and a slave girl his father had raped. This discovery sends the imam into a frenzy. His disillusionment with his forebears is total: he cannot accept that one of his ancestors whom he considered pious and beyond reproach could have committed such an abomination. What is more significant about this revelation is that Malam Shu'aibu leads the imam to realize that he is no better than his father. By not respecting the Islamic principles regulating the days that each wife in a polygamous setting should share the night with the husband, the imam himself is guilty of what he accuses his father: "A child conceived in a stolen embrace was as much a bastard as if he had been conceived out of wedlock" (*The Last Imam*, 177).

With this realization, the imam's feeling of superiority vis-à-vis his ancestors is deflated. He seeks his wives' forgiveness and resolves to bring the empire to a strict observance of Islam's nuptial rules by giving a sermon on the nuptial and bastardy. This sermon angers many people in the empire, including members of the ruling class.

In spite of their adherence to Islam, the people of Bauchi are unwilling to give up all their ancient cultural beliefs and practices. When they hear the howl of the Bauchi hyena, they are certain that a foul crime has been committed in the land, and that there will be great disasters as a consequence. Coincidentally, thunder and lightning strike for seven consecutive days, killing many people each time. No amount of Koranic exegesis convinces the people that the hyena's noises have nothing to do with the tragedies. In fact, they believe that the imam's treatment of his son brought the calamity upon the people.

The people are seized with panic and some already undertake to risk abandoning their ancestral homes to flee from the curse that supposedly brought the deaths and the imminent drought. The emir summons the imam for a final confrontation. The imam categorically refuses to bring his child home, and dismisses as pagan superstition the belief that the hyena's call has anything to do with the tragedies that have occurred in Bauchi or that the deaths are a result of the sin committed by any one man. He bases all his arguments on scriptural exegesis. Making any concessions to the people's beliefs amounts in his opinion to catering to the fears and wishes of men and disregarding the will of God. Faced with the prospect of witnessing the disintegration of his empire, the emir judges on the side of the people, unturbans the intransigent imam, and replaces him with his "bastard" half-brother, who like the other spiritual leaders to come after him will be an agreeable imam "much better suited to the ways of some of us" (*The Last Imam*, 241).

This outline illustrates the thematic complexity of Ibrahim Tahir's narrative. The themes developed in the novel include the condition and role of women in a Northern Nigerian traditional Fulani-Hausa Muslim household; polygamy in Islam; the dynamic dialogue between Islam and pre-Islamic African beliefs; the role of Islamic education in a traditional African Muslim society; and the historical relationship between Islamic scholars (*ulama*) and political leadership. As in any well-written novel, Tahir's narrative does not present these themes as separate and discrete topics, but rather as an organic whole. One cannot therefore discuss any one of these themes to the exclusion of others without doing injustice to the novel as a work of art. The personality of Alhaji Usman underscores this thematic complexity. He is not only presented as an imam, he is also in the beginning a son and then a husband and a father. His desire to reform the Islamic practices of his people cannot be analyzed without taking into account his upbringing, the special relationship he had with his father, which is itself later developed in the novel; his great love for Hasana and his rather ambivalent relationship with their son, Kasim; the role of A'isha, his first wife; and the general dynamic of his polygamous household. All of these elements interact with each other to produce the complex personality of this warrior of Islam, Alhaji Usman, the imam, the last imam. The issue of the consciousness of orthodoxy has to be analyzed within this dynamic framework.

The subject of orthodoxy is best broached by analyzing the structure of conflict in the novel. Much of the social conflict in the novel arises from the discrepancies between the Muslim ideal and the actions and beliefs of the Bauchi Muslims. Significantly, in the novel of Alhaji Sir Abubakar Tafawa Balewa, *Shaiu Umar,*[4] the Muslim ideal is embodied by the protagonist Shaiu Umar, but in Ibrahim Tahir's novel the Muslim ideal remains by and large an idea that no one truly embodies. Although Alhaji Usman and his father come closest to this ideal, they themselves are shown to fall short of it. Alhaji Usman is quick to define his model: "For my part, I take my example as every true Muslim and every servant of God should do, from *Prophet Mohammad,* the Peace and Blessings of Allah be upon him" (*The Last Imam,* 199, emphasis added).

This absence of a model in the novel enables the narrative to deal with the issue of orthodoxy within a broad and general context without reducing the structure of conflict to a simple confrontation between the proponents of orthodoxy and the others.

The first conflict in the novel revolves around the old imam's desire to have his son accept the alms marriage with A'isha. Twenty-five at the time and totally devoted to his Islamic work, the son insists on staying celibate in order to dedicate his life to Allah's work. What is significant in this crisis is that no one seeks to resolve it except by reference to the *sharia*. The usual deference to age in general and automatic obedience to a father that one finds in African literature does not obtain here. The frame of reference remains unequivocally Islamic. The young Usman's fear that marriage will disturb his work is debunked by the evidence of his father's successful management of the duties of a husband and that of imam. On the other hand Usman's refusal is couched in religious terms: "I have told you I'm married to Allah's work and will marry nobody. That is real enough for me and I want to remain celibate" (*The Last Imam*, 19).

The old man finally prevails by using two arguments. The first one appeals to his son's love of the lifestyle of the Prophet. Just as Usman is being offered A'isha in an alms marriage so was the Prophet offered the legendary A'isha in an alms marriage. To refuse this offer will have one implication: "Will you tell the people that alms marriages are illegal, or that they are legal but that you, their Imam, disapprove?" (*The Last Imam*, 20).

The final blow comes when the father quotes a *hadith* condemning celibates as not being among the followers of the Prophet Mohammed (*The Last Imam*, 20). Usman has to capitulate. He "dared not protest because he knew that his father's arguments were unassailable, as indeed was everything the old man said" (*The Last Imam*, 20).

This tense exchange between father and son underscores at once the predominant role that Islam plays in the world depicted by Ibrahim Tahir and hence the power that comes with the possession of Islamic knowledge. The potential for the manipulation and abuse of such knowledge becomes more obvious in the next fight between father and son over a custom surrounding the taking away of the wife's virginity. According to this custom, the girl is expected to scream loud enough for her family members to hear when her virginity is being taken—that is, if she is found to be a virgin. This means much honor to the girl's family. One of the implications of this practice is that the first night is a public event. The narrator explains the cultural origins of this practice: "The taking away of the wife's chastity on the first nuptial night had been ritualised and had become part of the customs in the lower orders of society. . . . It was a distasteful practice which Usman's family and all houses of breeding had condemned and eschewed as a carry-over from darker days" (*The Last Imam*, 23).

"Darker days" is a translation of the Islamic concept of *jahiliya*, which is a denigrating term designating pre-Islamic cultural practices. The attitudes displayed here betray not only a consciousness of orthodoxy, but more significantly a resolve to erase the pre-Islamic past. Usman will have nothing to do with this custom. His father, however, does not see much harm in the practice and asks his son to do it to please the parents of the bride. To Usman the plea sounds like an invitation to honor *jahiliya* as opposed to obeying the laws of Islam: "So you want me to disobey the laws of my faith just to satisfy a common Hausa heathen custom?" (*The Last Imam*, 22). All attempts on the part of the old man to justify his stance only increases his son's feeling of shame that the father whose piety he clearly respects should so readily make concessions to pre-Islamic beliefs. Usman categorically denounces his father when the latter relates to his son the rumors that Usman's delay in taking his wife's virginity is due to impotence: "How can you father? It is not enough that you ask me to behave like a heathen? Must you go on to talk like vulgar market women?" (*The Last Imam*, 24). Not even the progressive Oumar Faye in Sembène Ousmane's *O pays, mon beau peuple!* could display such irreverence towards his father.

Usman's brutal taking of A'isha's virginity is an act of vengeance directed at all those who suppose him impotent. It is this act of violence that brings about Usman's loss of his passion for his faith that will ironically only return and be intertwined with his consummate love for Hasana when he comes back from his pilgrimage to Mecca.

This domestic saga between father and son anticipates the greater social crises that result from the conflict between puritanical concerns with orthodoxy and accommodationism. The narrator provides an interesting synopsis of the history of Islam in Bauchi. Islam arrived 300 years back:

> Yet only three hundred years ago, and maybe less, the Word of God and God Himself had not existed for the people who inhabited the land.... For Bauchi then was no more than a rocky trough in the mountainous country of the wild savannah, a no-prophet land of pagan tribes, each with its shrine sheltering behind a rocky grove. (*The Last Imam*, 121)

After giving a description of some of the aspects of the ancient religious practices of Bauchi, the narrator portrays the triumphant arrival of Islam and its washing clean of the souls of the men "with the waters of Islam" (*The Last Imam*, 122). Although much as in the case of Cheikh Hamidou Kane's Diallobé, Islam becomes the real nature of the people (*The Last Imam*, 122), some ancestral beliefs and practices resist erasure: "Even so they [the people of Bauchi] needed diversion like the *gwauro* ceremony and other rituals whose roots lay deeply buried in long-forgotten history" (*The Last Imam*, 123).

It is this major diversion of the *gwauro* ceremony that Alhaji Usman abolishes, much to the silent resentment of the people, as a carryover from pagan times (*The Last Imam*, 124). The real conflict between the orthodox quest and syncretism comes in the form of the interpretation of the world beyond the real. Legend has it that each time the hyena calls in Bauchi there is calamity in the air: "Long ago, they say, when the Hyena moaned, the emir and his entire household died" (*The Last Imam*, 206).

When the hyena emits its awesome howl for the people it portends an ill omen, but for the imam the hyena is nothing but a beast. While the people's interpretation of this apparently unusual occurrence is based on ancestral beliefs, the imam's frame of reference remains uncompromisingly scriptural. "To show Moses his power, Allah had turned the Mount Sinai into dust, to protect him he had parted the sea and to save Joseph he had sent down a ram from the sky . . . the miracles of the past had nothing to do with superstitions. Certainly not with the moan of a hyena" (*The Last Imam*, 207).

The conflict brought about by the interpretation of the hyena's noises is reminiscent of the legendary Askia Mohammed's report to the Egyptian scholar Al-Maghili on the beliefs of the Dogon, whom he had conquered:

> Then I released everyone who claimed that he was a free Muslim and a large number of them went off. Then after that I asked about the circumstances of some of them and about their country and behold they pronounced the *shahada:* "There is no god save God. Muhammed is the messenger of God." But in spite of that they believe that there are beings who can bring them benefit or do them harm other than God, Mighty and Exalted is He. They have idols and they say: "The fox has said so and so and thus it will be so and so." . . .
> So I admonished them to give up all that and they refused to do without the use of force.[5]

Alhaji Usman, in contrast to Askia Muhammed, and in spite of the militant tropes used to characterize him in the novel, is not a *mujahid*. He has to depend on persuasion and the cooperation of the emir to enforce orthodox Islamic beliefs and practices.

The differences between the imam's perspective and that of the people are not like those opposing Diamourou and Balla in Kourouma's novel. There is apparently no non-Muslim in Bauchi. Yet, the crisis in *The Last Imam*, resulting from differences between Muslims at different levels of commitment to Islamic orthodoxy, proves to be more intractable. Such a conflict between believers is possible precisely because the imam strategically constructs a definition of the Muslim that is so rigorous that many Muslims lose their credentials as Muslims and become *kufar* (infidels), at least in the sight of the imam.

This notion of *takfir,* the act of declaring someone to be an unbeliever, has been clearly explained by Nehemia Levtzion and John O. Voll in the context of eighteenth-century renewal and reform in Islam:

> The spread of Islam was greatly aided by a broad and inclusive definition of Muslims: whoever identified himself as such by proclaiming the *Shahada*. However, the reformists sought to separate Muslims from non-Islamic beliefs and practices and to delineate more clearly the boundaries of the Muslim community. For them, those who claimed to be Muslims but were associated with what the reformers believed to be non-Islamic beliefs and practices, were non-believers.[6]

This process of redefining the Muslim is one that is necessary in periods of reform. In such periods the definition of the Muslim as one who believes in Allah and Mohammed is simply not useful. The reformer needs to know who the adversary is, the one who refuses to adhere to the fundamentals of the faith. It is therefore significant that the imam sees himself first as a warrior against disbelief (*The Last Imam*, 208). To be a warrior against disbelief is, however, too abstract a formulation for a reformer. He needs to identify disbelief with those who practice it. In Tahir's novel, the imam considers as evidence of *kufr* (disbelief) the belief that the fate of Bauchi and its people lies in the moan of a hyena. He thus creates an unbridgeable opposition between this belief that he considers idolatrous and the embracing of the word of God (*The Last Imam*, 209). His sermon during the special prayers of rededication makes his new definition of the Muslim unambiguous if violent: "And the men who come here and join us in our acts of dedication to God and still believe in such things [as the traditional meaning of the hyena's moan] are nothing but heathens" (*The Last Imam*, 209).

He leaves the fate of such people in the hands of the Islamic judge, the *qadi,* and orders them to leave the congregation of the Muslims who are "unseduced by the temptations of blasphemy" (*The Last Imam*, 209).

The structure of the novel intensifies the conflict. The moan of the hyena is made to precede a period of heat and the signs of a devastating drought, thus the people interpret the moan of the hyena's call as the signal for a drought. Tragedy soon strikes in the form of lightning and thunder, which kill several people for seven consecutive nights. While everybody, including the imam, believes that the calamity is a divine punishment for some iniquity committed in Bauchi, the people are quick to believe that the culprit is the imam himself. He has provoked Allah's wrath by maltreating his son, Kasim. As A'isha tells him, "the Vizir and the rest are encouraging the people in their gossip, saying that you should have known better than to mention excessive sinning when you have a major sin hanging over your head unredeemed" (*The Last Imam,* 229).

The alleged sin, as we have already mentioned, is the imam's maltreatment of Kasim that rumor says is the reason for Kasim's running away from home to join Malam Shu'aibu. Rumor also has it that the malam is physically abusing Kasim. The imam refuses to bring his son home in spite of the personal pleas by the emir. When the emir, out of political expediency, unturbans the imam, the latter's reaction translates adequately the extent to which he has come to see the conflict opposing him and the people of Bauchi as a conflict between Islam and paganism. "Can you not see that it is not me that you have unturbanned, but the very Word of God that you have denied! Mohammmed himself might as well never have come into the world for the deed you have committed this day" (*The Last Imam,* 240).

This remark also points to the thematic merger between the imam as a public religious figure and the individual. None of the positions defended or promoted by Alhaji Usman can be divorced from his own personal life narrative. He is not just a reformer imbued with an ideal to purify the Islamic practices of his people, he is himself a character in process with personal frustrations and aspirations that inform in a significant way some of his major initiatives. His passion for his religious work earlier on in his career cannot be distinguished from his passion for Hasana. His love for acquiring Islamic knowledge cannot be separated from his desire for the power that comes with scholarly repute (150). His resolve to ban the *gwauro* diversion is significantly motivated by his awareness that he might himself become its victim.

To make these observations is not to suggest that the imam is a hypocrite who uses his position simply to protect himself and serve his own personal ambitions. He is indeed a reformer, but a reformer who is also a person with weaknesses and a potential for pettiness. His complex characterization is first of all a testimony to Ibrahim Tahir's mature realism. It is also perhaps an indication that great historical figures do not fit single neat descriptions such as "jihadist" or "reformer."

That *The Last Imam* is imbued with a consciousness of orthodoxy even goes beyond the puritanical program represented by the protagonist. The all-pervasiveness of the Islamic discourse is first of all evidenced by Tahir's use of Islamic scriptural models and motifs. The physical appearance of the protagonist himself is, as the narrative suggests, based on the scriptural model of Moses: "He was very tall: with his long beard and his white robe hanging on so majestically around him, he looked like a Hausa or Fulani idea of Moses in all his dignity" (*The Last Imam*, 1).

This messianic appearance is stressed throughout the narrative, but Moses is not the only model used to construct the personality of the Imam. In fact the many tribulations that the imam faces in his life create an affinity between him and the prophet Job, although one can arguably say that the Biblical Job rather than the Koranic one comes out clearly in the imam's feeling of being abandoned by his God when Hasana dies (*The Last Imam*, 3). The Prophet is also not only a personal spiritual model for Alhaji Usman, just as he ought to be for every Muslim, significant aspects of his *seera* (biography) are also used by Ibrahim Tahir to develop the character of the imam. The narrative continuously stresses the parallels between the Imam's marriage with A'isha and the Prophet's marriage with A'isha, Abu Bakar's daughter. Both are alms marriages, and both women's fathers' names are Abu Bakar (rendered Bukar in Hausa). Moreover, neither woman has had children of her own. Tahir's A'isha, like many of the characters in the novel, is very aware of these parallels. This awareness only increases her frustrations, for "she had come into the Alhaji's hands as the bride of the Prophet Mohammed, and when she felt she needed Allah and Mohammed most, they had rebuffed her" (*The Last Imam*, 173).

The all-pervasiveness of the Islamic ethos could also be seen in the presence of the Koran in the text. Ibrahim Tahir uses the Koran more extensively than any other sub-Saharan African writer. To use Lemuel Johnson's terms, we find none of the "exuberant Koranic inversions of Yambo Ouologuem" (Johnson: 242) in *The Last Imam*. Tahir's use of Koranic references and allusions is altogether reverential. Moreover, unlike Cheikh Hamidou Kane, whose Koranic culture has been shown by Morita Knicker to manifest itself in his style rather than in any direct references to the Koran, Ibrahim Tahir has used the Koran to the extent that his narrative would lose much of its length if all the Koranic quotations were removed. In fact, in no other sub-Saharan African novel does the Koran actually assume the status of *furgan,* the ultimate yardstick by which all human actions are judged to be good or evil, wise or unwise. The Koran, and not the wisdom of men, is presented in this novel as the final arbiter. One can thus understand the power that those who have mastered its interpretation wield in Ibrahim Tahir's text. Part of the conflict in the novel is due to the fact that many believers of Bauchi still subscribe to other cultural frames of reference apart from the Koran, without necessarily disputing the authority of the Koran in their lives as Muslims.

Tahir's novel is, as a result, perhaps the least charitable among sub-Saharan African novels to pre-Islamic indigenous African culture. The narrator's presentation of the history of the triumphant spread of Islam in Bauchi is not only simplistic, it also translates a celebration of the wiping out of indigenous cultures by Islam. In fact Islam is presented as a liberator and cleanser of wicked traditions. In pre-Islamic times, for example, certain days were set aside during which no man could show his face. "The man who dared to show his face, for whatever reason, was caught, at once, set upon, torn apart and ritualistically laid out in the Juju shrine for all to see and to learn, to feel the enslaving grip of their terror" (*The Last Imam,* 122). It is such wanton barbarism that Islam came to eradicate, "and the new God arrived, emerged from hiding, banished the idols with their fetish priests and their shrines, and washed clean the souls of the men with the waters of Islam" (*The Last Imam,* 122).

The narrator will accord little space to a more detailed presentation of the so-called juju religion in the novel. Aspects of this culture occasionally appear between the cracks of the Islamic canvas, but then such apparitions of the past come in very grotesque forms. It is, for example, difficult for a reader to identify with the *gwauro* tradition. The ugliness of the *gwauro* is metaphorically linked to the ugliness of the ancestral deities: "When the man [the *gwauro* victim] was stood up he looked to Kasim like the pagan mask gods he had seen coming in Bauchi on sallah and Empire day to dance their ritual dances" (*The Last Imam,* 97).

This passage is significant in many respects. First of all it supports our observation regarding the negative associations with the ancestral religion. These metaphorical associations are found in many other places in the novel. For example, the somber aspect of the wives of the imam who await their husband to tell him about their disgust at Kasim's behavior evokes the image of ancestral carvings. The imam is reported to see on his return home "the grim circle of women sitting there like ritual carvings in a juju shrine" (*The Last Imam,* 59).

Elsewhere ancestral religion is disnarrated.[7] The imam is not tempted to revert to traditional religious practice when he loses Hasana, his beloved. "No ritual drums roared, no horns blew, no 'bori' spirit dancers who had held the people captive long ago came, and the *magajiva,* the spirit dance queen and arch seductress of the delinquent young and the unrepentant old, did not lay out her idolatrous mat for him" (*The Last Imam,* 37).

That traditional practices are inscribed in the narrative by negation illustrates the tendency to relegate them to the irretrievable past in Ibrahim Tahir's novel. Moreover, the constructed identification between the traditional religion and images of enslavement, debauchery, and idolatry is also obvious.

One of the most peculiar characteristics of this novel is its refusal to define itself relative to anything having to do with the geopolitical realities of postjihad Nigerian history. Not once is Africa or Nigeria mentioned in this narrative. In fact the *gwauro* passage is one of only two occasions in which the historical reality of the Nigerian colonial experience is vaguely and dismissively hinted at. The other instance relates to the abolition of slavery. "Her people [Hasana's] had been made free by the British, but that had been a mere technicality. To himself and to everyone, slaves not free-born could not legally wed without bringing scorn upon his own head" (*The Last Imam,* 34).

The absence of any reference to Nigeria or Africa and the scanty reference to the Nigerian colonial experience cannot be fortuitous. It has to be read within the context of an overall denial of anything not directly related to the Islamic ideal. For all sub-Saharan writers the question of the cultural and political rehabilitation of the continent is a major preoccupation, but Ibrahim Tahir's text is primarily concerned with that part of Northern Nigeria that was part of the Islamic state founded by Usman Dan Fodio in the late eighteenth and early nineteenth centuries.

Ibrahim Tahir also establishes, to use Sulayman Nyang's terms, the classical Islamic division of the world into bipolar camps of Darul Islam and Darul Harb.[8] The former is the land of the Muslims, and is supposed to enjoy peace and stability and is governed by the rules of Islam. The latter, meaning literally the land of war, is the land of the non-Muslims governed by the customs of *jahiliya,* in tension with the Muslims and therefore unsafe. Hence in *The Last Imam* we have the dwellers of Dar-ul-Islam, primarily the Fulani and the Hausa, on one hand and the dwellers of Dar-ul-Harb on the other. The latter are lumped together under the anonymous designation of the *Asabe* or men of the south. When Kasim runs away from home and spends a night in the jungle, these are the men he fears most because "child thieves, too, were lurking in the jungles, ready to pounce on any stray child and sell him to the men of the south, the Asabe, as they called them" (*The Last Imam*, 65).

The image of the non-Muslim as savage and barbarian is clearly constructed in Tahir's text. One is left to imagine what happens to the unfortunate children who are sold to the men of the south. Will they be used as slaves or, worse still, will they be eaten?

Even Muslims who live in the periphery of the Muslim state are very readily categorized as bushmen. Yako, one of the men from Kangere, who comes to Bauchi to report the sighting of the new moon for the month of Ramadan, is immediately referred to as a bushman and his report is dismissed when he fails to tell the difference between the *farli* (obligatory prayers) and the *nafila* (supererogatory prayers) (*The Last Imam*, 87). The real news, the credible news, will have to come from Dar-ul-Islam, not from Kangere: "It was just as well to stay awake, in case Sokoto, Kano or Katsina sent wires that they had seen the moon" (*The Last Imam*, 88).

The land beyond the Muslim city-state is the origin of all pagan practices, such as the mask gods who come into Bauchi on Sallah and Empire day, or at best the home of Muslims whose commitment to and knowledge of Islam is doubtful.

Beyond the use of the Koran, the biography and traditions of the Prophet, and the structure of dichotomy between Dar-ul-Islam and Dar-ul-Harb, one Islamic motif dominates the entire novel of Ibrahim Tahir, the personality of Usman Dan Fodio. The reform movement that the latter started and the Islamic society that he succeeded in establishing are always invoked in the text with a sense of nostalgia. The jihad itself is remembered as a time of valor and Islamic heroism: "It was a long time, a long time indeed since the Jihad when the men rode out to hunt down the pagans for the God of man and came back crippled, scarred and bloodied but proud in their victorious robes" (*The Last Imam*, 144).

The family history of the imam is traced back to the jihad. His struggle to purify Islam and revive a strict adherence to its fundamentals is modeled on the cause of Usman Dan Fodio, who in the imam's estimation fought for the preservation of the word of God against the wills of men (*The Last Imam*, 199). The struggle between him and the Bauchi leadership is in many ways reminiscent of the protracted struggle between Usman Dan Fodio and the Habe kings. Although the imam never considers taking up arms to uphold the supremacy of Islam as his historical model did, the tropes used to describe his personal vocation are unmistakably militant. During one of his meetings with Bauchi's political leadership at the emir's palace, the imam is described as "a warrior of Islam thrusting the sword into the infidel flesh and hearing the pagan's groans" (*The Last Imam*, 77).

The same image of the *mujahid* is used to describe the imam's final struggle with the political establishment bent on unturbaning him due to his radical Islamic intransigence. "I see before me fighting men in battle dress and I am a warrior King. But Allah is with me and I fight not for the glory of the world but for the Kingdom of God" (*The Last Imam*, 242).

Admittedly the war evoked here is metaphorical, but the struggle it connotes is no less real. Unlike his historical model and homonym, Alhaji Usman does not take up the sword against those he considers enemies of Allah, and he also loses in the struggle. However, his stance against open accommodation to local practices is much better articulated than that of Diamourou in Ahmadou Kourouma's *Les Soleils des indépendances*. Moreover, Tahir's protagonist is not totally crushed at the end of the novel. He vows to get back his son, Kasim, who henceforth represents his "hope for the future" (*The Last Imam*, 244). The struggle for the establishment of an Islamic fundamentalist state will be passed on to a new generation of Muslims. Will these new Muslims limit themselves to preaching peacefully, or will they model the struggle more concretely on legendary figures like Usman Dan Fodio, whose memory is still fresh in the mind of Muslim Northern Nigerians? The *Yan Tatsine* insurrections of the 1980s and the violent interreligious conflicts of 1987 in Kaduna portend a future of militant Islamic activism in Ibrahim Tahir's real Northern Nigeria.

The foregoing analysis demonstrates that sub-Saharan African writers of the Muslim tradition textualize varying degrees of consciousness of Islamic orthodoxy in their works. Ibrahim Tahir most fully articulates this consciousness and makes it the central theme of his work. *The Last Imam* is bound to be categorized as fundamentalist and totalitarian by many. It comes as no surprise that critics have been reluctant to approach it, and to date, virtually no study has been devoted to it. Given, however, the current trend toward radical Islam in sub-Saharan Africa, notably but by no means exclusively in Sudan and Nigeria, *The Last Imam* needs to be studied.

Indeed, Diamourou's definition of Togobala as a village of Allah, where pagans should not be welcome, and Alhaji Usman's insistence that Bauchi is a Muslim kingdom in which Allah's laws must be observed are a fictional translation of the growing radicalization of Islamic consciousness and of calls for the implementation of *sharia* in a number of sub-Saharan countries. In our concluding chapter we shall examine the implications of this trend towards radical (fundamentalist?) Islam in black Africa as it relates to the important question: What does it mean to be black or African in an Africa where religious loyalties turn out to be more important than ethnic, racial, and national loyalties?

## Notes

1. Ahmadou Kourouma, *Les Soleils des indépendances* (Montréal: Les Presses de l'Université de Montréal, 1968), 98. All subsequent references to this novel will be indicated parenthetically in the text.

2. Ibrahim Tahir, *The Last Imam* (Boston: Routledge & Kegan Paul, 1984), 110. All subsequent references to this novel will be indicated parenthetically in the text.

3. Lemuel Johnson, "Crescent and Consciousness: Islamic Orthodoxies and the West African Novel," in Kenneth Harrow, ed., *Faces of Islam in Sub-Saharan African Literature* (London, Portsmouth: Heinemann, 1991), 240. Subsequent references to this study will be indicated parenthetically in the text.

4. In his introduction to Tafawa Balewa's novel, Hiskett makes the correct observation that the character of Umar, the protagonist, "is both an Islamic and Hausa ideal." *Shaiu Umar* (New York: Markus Wiener Publishing, 1989), 4.

5. John O. Hunwick, *Sharia in Songhay: The Replies of al-Maghili to the Questions of Askia al-Hajj Mohammed* (New York: Oxford University Press), 77.

6. Nehemia Levtzion, in Nehemia Levtzion and John O. Vol, eds., *Eighteenth-Century Renewal and Reform in Islam* (Syracuse: Syracuse University Press, 1987), 12.

7. Gerald Prince defines the *disnarrated* as a category that includes "all the events that do not happen but, nonetheless, are referred to in a negative or hypothetical mode by the narrative text." "The Disnarrated," *Style* 22, no. 1 (Spring 1988): 2.

8. Sulayman Nyang and Samir Abed Rabbo, "Bernard Lewis and Islamic Studies: An Assesment," in Asaf Hussain, ed., *Orientalism, Islam, and Islamists* (Brattleboro, Vt.: Amana Books, 1984), 264.

# 7

•

## Conclusion

In this book, I have examined many key arguments on the characteristics of contemporary African(ist) writings on Islam and Muslims in black Africa. The historical connection between Orientalist discourse and colonial scholarship on Muslim societies in sub-Saharan Africa has been established, thus expanding the scholarship on Western Orientalism to include Western writings on African Muslim societies. The affinities between the two "intellectual" traditions are unmistakable. The scholarship they produced was politically motivated, serving the political interest of an imperial Europe. Thus Islam was studied from a logic that is external to it, as a focus of resistance to colonial designs. As a result of its political nature, this scholarship lacked internal consistency, its perceptions being largely the result of the political preoccupations of the colonizing powers. Moreover the scholarship exhibited considerable ideological hostility toward Islam. All these factors account for the distortions of Islam we have exposed in this study.

The interesting question to be asked is why these ideas about Islam survived the colonial era and are still in vogue in contemporary African(ist) writing, for the continuity between colonialist distortions of Islam and contemporary "facts" about Muslim societies is unmistakable. Islam is still viewed as a fatalistic religion that shows no interest in the material and economic improvement of human society; Islam is the religion of the sword, a violent superstition that was forced down the throats of the Africans; Islam is such an austere religion that it had to be considerably diluted by proselytizers for it to be accepted by the otherwise spiritually immature Africans; Islam is more successful than Christianity in Africa because of its lax ethical standards.

It is easy to understand why such contradictory ideas have survived when one realizes that most commentators on Islam have no access to the vast intellectual tradition of Islam nor to the available informed sources on the history of Islam in sub-Saharan Africa. For many, European-language writings are still the dominant academic resources on Islam. Scholars wanting to gain access to Islamic material often have to rely on layers and layers of translations. And even translations of the intellectual masterworks of the Islamic tradition are still few. The French colonial attitudes toward Arabic, as spelled out by Mariani, can be interpreted not simply as a superstitious belief in the inherent subversiveness of Arabic, but as indicating an awareness of the dangers of sustaining the African Muslims' direct access to Islamic sources. The latter interpretation is in fact more viable, given the efforts made to ban Arabic publications from French West Africa for fear that they might promote the idea of pan-Islamism in the colony and incite Muslim subjects to rebellion.

Moreover, some scholars select sources that reinforce their own ideological convictions, not bothering to complicate their neatly packaged analyses by paying attention to alternative views. It is of little surprise then that when contemporary critics of African literature discuss Islamic views on charity, political tyranny and social injustice, or gender roles and polygamy, they hardly ever use the founding texts of Islam (the Koran and the Sunna) or writings on the subject by the reputed scholars of Islam and interpreters of Islamic law. A quote from Orientalist sources or from the fictional works such critics are studying seems sufficient.

Our analysis of Debra Boyd-Buggs's study clearly illustrates the survival of colonial distortions of Islam. Even though we could not discern any hostility to Islam in her writing, her views on the subject of polygamy in Islam, for example, were shown to be problematic. First of all, she chose not to consult the rich and elucidating Islamic literature on the subject. Instead a single and, as we have illustrated, nondefinitive verse of the Koran was chosen. And even then she relied on a clearly distorting French translation of a Koranic verse. Such casual discussion of Islam as a subject not requiring any special intellectual preparation translates at the very least a condescension vis-à-vis Islamic culture. What was more significant, however, was the way that her failure to acquaint herself with the basics of Islamic beliefs negatively affected her readings of novels with an Islamic subtext, and more specifically of Cheikh Hamidou Kane's *L'Aventure ambiguë*.

There is much evidence of ideological hostility to Islam in the writings of Wole Soyinka, Pierrette Herzberger-Fofana, and Martin Bestman. But the verbal brawl between Wole Soyinka and Ali Mazrui not only shows how Soyinka's secularist ideology makes him vehemently unsympathetic to religious traditions such as Islam with its sharia ambitions, it also underscores the ambiguous situation of an African Muslim intellectual, Ali Mazrui, who is forced to reconcile the imperative of paying tribute to Africa's indigenous cultural past and his Islamic identity. In the process, Mazrui virtually pleads to have his evidence of fidelity to African culture accepted in Wole Soyinka's high court designed to try Africa's cultural apostates.

But to be accepted as an African, does Mazrui have to commit the gravest sin according to Islam by calling for the celebration of deities other than Allah? And why does he make such reductive statements on Islam and the gender issue? These questions lead to the mother of all questions: Can one be a faithful Muslim and a proud African at the same time? This issue is a fundamental though subliminal concern in our analysis of the works of four African writers of the Muslim tradition: Cheikh Hamidou Kane, Sembène Ousmane, Aminata Sow Fall, and Ibrahim Tahir.

There is no denying that Sembène Ousmane is not a promoter of Islam. His ideological option is Marxism. His attitudes toward Islam, Christianity, and Senegalese traditions are therefore thoroughly informed by his socialist orientation. In other words, he is impatient with any cultural belief or practice he suspects of hindering the Senegalese from assuming total responsibility for the political and economic emancipation of their society. Admittedly, there is in his work a latent criticism of the misinterpretation of the Islamic concepts of *tawakul,* the belief that Muslims must steadfastly rely on Allah for help. Interpreted negatively, it may very well be taken to mean that one must not struggle to improve one's lot in life. This is the interpretation of which Sembène Ousmane is critical. We have also highlighted many episodes in Ousmane's fiction that vindicate the vitality of the Islamic faith in Senegal. There is, therefore, a whole range of attitudes toward Islam in Ousmane's fiction, depending on the specific texts' thematic orientations. For example, as Mohamadou Kane has correctly observed, polygamy is positively portrayed in *O pays, mon beau peuple!* The father of Omar Faye, the imam in the novel, heads a peaceful polygamous household. As well, *Le Mandat* depicts a very cohesive traditional family structure. It is as if Ousmane were actively promoting (Islamic?) polygamy in these two works. On the other hand, *Xala* and many of

Ousmane's fictional works give an utterly negative picture of polygamy.[1]

One should expect this kind of complexity in the work of a man who sees himself not only as the cultural chronicler of his overwhelmingly Muslim people, but who also feels a great attachment to that culture. But as a socialist ideologue, Sembène Ousmane is also aware that culture itself can be repressive, hence his selective satirical targeting of certain aspects of Senegalese culture and history (e.g., the caste system, male chauvinism, passivity). By and large there is much ambiguity in Ousmane's attitudes toward Islam. What I have tried to highlight in this study is the failure of critics to acknowledge the heterogeneity of Sembène Ousmane's textual relationships to Islam.

Moreover, my analysis leaves no doubt that Ousmane's fictional world is animated by Muslim characters of varying attitudes toward Islam as it affects their lives. Almost all the protagonists in his fictional world carry Muslim names and constantly use an Islamic frame of reference to give meaning to their world. The villains are also for the most part Muslims and use Islam in pursuing their less-than-honorable goals. For all the challenges that these observations present for commentators desirous of identifying "good guys" and "bad guys" in terms of Muslims and non-Muslims, one has to admit that Ousmane's characterization is realistic. If, as he claims, he wants to show contemporary Senegalese society as it is, Muslims have to be shown to be both good and bad, honest and dishonest, progressive and reactionary, given the fact that Senegalese society is overwhelmingly Muslim. The invention of non-Muslims, atheists, or Marxists to be consistently the spokespersons of Sembène Ousmane in his fiction would have been grossly unrealistic.

The societies that Ousmane presents in his work are recognizably Islamic. In fact it could be said that he cannot escape from the reality of Islam's historical grip on Senegalese society. The historical prologue of *Blanche-Genèse* foregrounds this problem. In it, Ousmane speaks of an almost pre-historic Senegalese utopian past. One would have thought that indeed we have here a window on pre-Islamic Senegalese society. On the contrary, Islam was even then the religion of the people of Santhiu Niaye:

> L'histoire que je vous conte aujourd'hui est aussi vieille que le monde. . . . Aussi longtemps qu'on "descend" ou que l'on "remonte" pour s'approcher de nos ancêtres, du temps de nos grands-parents . . . il n'y eut jamais de maison en dur dans le Niaye. . . . Pourtant ils croyaient ferme, leurs genoux à la prière: cinq fois par jour. (*Ciosane*, 22)

> The story I am telling you today is as old as the world. . . . As far "back" or "forward" one can go to get close to the era of our ancestors, the epoch of our grandparents, . . . there never had been houses built with rocks or concrete in Niaye. . . . Nevertheless, they (our ancestors) believed firmly; their knees were bent in prayer five times a day.

Significantly, his attempt to portray Alimami Samori as a legendary pre-Islamic African figure in *Les Bouts de bois de Dieu* fails, a point that Wole Soyinka fails to reckon with.

Regardless of her extraliterary self-definition as a Muslim, and contrary to the assertions of many of her commentators, Aminata Sow Fall does not come out as a promoter of Islam in her narratives. I must state, however, that our conclusion that she deemphasizes the Islamic cultural context of Senegalese society in her works can at best be taken as a hypothesis that has to be tested in light of all her literary production, including *L'Ex-père de la nation* (1987) and her most recent works, *Le Jujubier du patriarche* (1993) and a video recording, *Touki-Bouki: Magaye niang, mareme niang* (1993). These works need to be incorporated into a future study focusing exclusively on Aminata Sow Fall. Needless to say, a change in her textual relationship to Islam will not refute the thesis advanced here; contrast will only further support my case. Then it will be interesting to probe into the significance of the change in creative strategies, and the ideological implications of such a shift, should such a shift be found.

In these my concluding remarks on Sow Fall, it is important to draw attention to a study of William Hemminger on the difficulties of translating *L'Ex-père de la nation* into English.[2] This otherwise interesting work by one who actually translated this novel, under the title *The Former Father of the Nation,* further illustrates the failure of scholars to reckon with the Islamic factor in studies on contemporary African cultures such as that of Senegal.

First of all, Hemminger's study is not interested in the problem that I addressed, the artistic challenges faced by African writers to articulate their cultures in foreign imperialist languages. Instead, he struggles with the issue of translating a written text from one language to another: "Translation of such a work as *L'Ex-père de la nation* poses unique problems for the translator: how to bridge the distance between two very different cultures without destroying the ethos of the original text or betraying its language" (Hemminger: 302).

According to this approach, the original language of the novel is French (Hemminger: 301). Although Hemminger recognizes that

French itself is a foreign language, which in the text is infused with parables and interjections from the author's native Wolof, he fails to acknowledge the reality that the French text itself is a "translation," and not strictly speaking an original. Hence when Hemminger speaks of the distance between *two* very different cultures, one is led to the erroneous conclusion that the cultures in question are those of French and English. The language of the original text whose ethos is betrayed in an English translation is French. We wish to argue that in Sow Fall's case, the "culture-bound significance of the original text" (Hemminger: 303) that an English translation has to transmit is not primarily related to French, but to Wolofo-Senegalese culture. In other words, any translations of Sow Fall's French texts into other European languages are translations not of a French text alone, but of Senegalese culture. Such translations are translations of a translation. They are therefore doomed to distort significantly the culture of the text they are translating if they do not pay attention to the cultural horizons of the original "text."

An example of this failure is Dorothy Blair's translation of a passage in *La Grève des Bàttu* that reads: "Dieu l'a dit: il ne faut pas éconduire les pauvres."[3] Dorothy Blair translates this text as "God has said: 'Let the poor come unto me.'"[4] The French text does not have the idea of God's telling human beings to allow the poor to come to him. Instead, God exhorts the believers not to turn away the poor. There are many verses in the Koran that the original French statement paraphrases. Perhaps the better known is an address by Allah to the Prophet reminding him to be kind to the poor, just as he, Allah, has been kind to him in his time of need as a poor orphan. The text reads thus:

> Did He [Allah] not find thee
> An orphan and give thee
> Shelter [and care]?
> And he found thee
> Wandering, and He gave
> Thee guidance
> And he found thee
> In need, and made
> Thee independent.
> Therefore, treat not
> The orphan with harshness,
> *Nor repulse him who asks;*
> But the Bounty
> Of thy Lord
> Rehearse and proclaim. (Koran, 93: 6–11, emphasis added)

How appropriate this divine reminder and commandment is to Mour Ndiaye in light of his humble beginnings! The idea of God's inviting the poor to come unto him is so foreign to Islamic belief, and yet so perfectly normal in Christian culture, according to which God, in the person of Jesus, did physically dwell on earth, especially among the weak, the poor, the downtrodden, and the children. In fact anyone with any knowledge of Christian scriptures will automatically link Dorothy Blair's statement to an episode in the scriptures in which Jesus chastises his disciples for not "suffering the little children to come to him." Thus Dorothy Blair's translation ends up suggesting a Christian cultural framework for Sow Fall's narrative, ironically on one of those rare occasions in which Islamic culture is tentatively asserted by Sow Fall.

To use Hemminger's terminology, Dorothy Blair's heinous transcriptive crime (Hemminger: 303) naturally leads me to Hemminger's own blindness to the Islamic factor in Senegalese culture. I find the same simplistic binary oppositions between African culture and the foreign reader in his analysis. Hemminger alludes, if only summarily, to the fact that such greeting formulas as those involving the use of *al hamdoulillah*, used by Sow Fall in the novel he translated, are "invested with religious overtones that seldom resound in the translated tongue" (Hemminger: 304). But he overlooks the fact that such formulas are not readily understood by all Africans and that their use is not restricted to Africa, by saying that "similar extended greetings occur elsewhere in the text and to the *Western audience* must appear quaint. . . . Yet to an *African reader,* the greetings are not only typical, they betoken the 'necessary' and popular form of address" (Hemminger: 306, emphasis added).

The informed reader clearly knows that such expressions as *assalamu alaikum* or *al hamdoulillah,* if they have become naturalized in such Islamized cultures as those of the Sahel, still belong to the wider cultural world of Islam, to which belong an ever-increasing number of Westerners who profess Islam as a faith. It is clear from these observations that scholars interested in the language question for African writers are still yet to fully reckon with the Islamic factor, especially when this involves writers of the Muslim tradition.

I have documented the distortions of Islam in the criticism that pertains to works of the imagination by sub-Saharan African writers. I have not, however, documented similar distortions or inaccuracies in the literature itself. This decision must not leave the impression that writers of the Islamic tradition have been uninfluenced by colonialist writings on Islam, or that they have a solid understanding of Islam. In fact many of these writers display considerable ignorance of some of the very basic facts of their faith. That francophone writers especially exhibit such shortcomings is of little surprise: these writers' intellectual exposure to Islam is very limited.

In fact, the story of Samba Diallo is to a large extent that of many francophone Muslim writers. For the most part, they spend relatively few years in the rote memorization of the Koran, without ever getting to the stage of understanding the meaning of the Koranic verses. Hence they never gain access to those books of *hadith,* Islamic law (*sharia*), and Islamic jurisprudence (*figh*), let alone to the vast intellectual literature of Islam. Their progress in the French schools often meant their early abandonment of Islamic education. The French schools in colonial Muslim French West Africa, especially the French-built Muslim schools (*medrasa*), were deliberately designed to produce a Muslim elite class that would have a very watered-down interpretation of Islam that enabled them to look favorably on French rule.[5] A study of the impact of such assimilationist French educational policies on the way Islam is presented in the works of francophone Muslim writers is yet to be done. Such a study will involve extensive archival research into French educational policy pertaining to French West Africa and a study of the curricula used in the schools attended by such writers, as well as interviews with the latter. The time and material resources required for such a project explain, at least partly, the choice of focus in this study. Nonetheless, it would be parochial, during this era of Islamic political activism in Africa, not to discuss the political content of Islam as articulated by the various writers I have studied. This observation should now lead me in these concluding notes from my focus on the politics of representation to the representation of politics and the Islamic factor in the works I have studied.

To those who still continue to believe that Islam is a fatalistic religion showing no real interest in worldly matters, the ever-increasing attempts by Muslims in sub-Saharan Africa to present Islam as a political ideology must be a rude awakening. The ongoing war in the Sudan that is threatening to tear the country apart cannot be understood without taking into account the religious factor. The recent politics of Cameroon and Guinea have also shown Islam as a powerful political platform. The situation is even more dramatic in other sub-Saharan countries with an Islamic presence.

The Tanzanian parliament, for example, has recently passed a motion in favor of setting up a separate Tanganyikan parliament despite the efforts of Julius Nyerere to save "his" union: "One of the motivating factors behind the nationalists has been the rising tide of fundamentalism and the religious tension that has ensued. . . . Another factor was when the Zanzibar government secretly joined the Organization of Islamic Conference."[6] Although Zanzibar has since withdrawn its membership under pressure, the relationship between Tanzanian Christians and Muslims remains strained over the issue.

Perhaps more surprising are the recent political developments in neighboring Kenya. Who could have imagined that an Islamic political party, the Islamic Party of Kenya (IPK), would ever come into existence in a country like Kenya where Muslims, concentrated mainly in the coastal province, are clearly a minority community? The *New African* reports that over the past two years a number of scuffles ending in pitched battles have created significant divisions among the coastal peoples.[7] The most recent violence is largely attributed to the anti-Arab and anti-Swahili campaign led by Emmanuel Karisa Maitha, the Kenyan African National Union (KANU) candidate, who claimed to champion the cause of his Miji Kenda ethnic group. His main opponent, Professor Rashid Mzee of the Ford-Kenya ticket, had gained considerable popularity among both the Muslims and the Luo communities. To make the situation even more explosive, the Muslims themselves are divided between those who support Daniel arap Moi's government and those who oppose it. The most outspoken critic of the government is Sheikh Balala, the strongman of IPK. It is speculated that the government backed the creation of the United Muslims of Africa (UMA) as a foil to the IPK. The leader of UMA, Umari Masumbuko, claims to fight for the rights of African Muslims as opposed to Arabs and Swahilis.

Many of the conflicts that Nigeria has experienced in the past two decades are linked to religious unrest. The systematic riots organized by the Maitatsine sect in Kano that resulted in many deaths, including those of Muslims outside the sect, readily come to mind. There were subsequent resurgences of the movement in Maiduguri (1981), Yola (1984), and Gombe (1985). The movement's declared agenda was reformist; it saw it as its duty to cleanse Nigerian Islam of the corrupt condition into which it had descended.[8] It is, therefore, an ill-affordable luxury to discuss the subject of Islam in African literature without reflecting on what novels of the Muslim tradition tell us about the origin and nature of religious conflicts on the continent.

This broadly political question manifests itself at the primary social level in two forms: interfaith antagonisms and, in the case of Islam, conflicts within the ranks of Muslims that are closely related to the issue of *tajdid* and *takfir*. On the wider state level, the dominant question is the issue of the imposition of the Islamic sharia laws. To start with, which of our authors discuss Islam from a political point of view?

Of all the authors reviewed in this study, Aminata Sow Fall demonstrates the least awareness of the political content of Islam. The only cultural framework that has principles pertaining to the conduct of the individual in society as she depicts it is cosaan. But the wisdom of tradition is just what it is—wisdom, not law. Likewise, the enunciations of God's commandments of "charity" made notably by the marabout Birama are not meant to be enforced. It is up to the believer to comply or not.

The issue of zakat is particularly significant in the history of Islam, because it is the issue that led to the first war waged by Abu Bakr, the first caliph of Islam. The war was initiated against a rich man who decided to discontinue his payment of zakat after the death of the Prophet. By fighting to enforce the observance of zakat, Abu Bakr set a historic precedent. The Islamic state can indeed force believers to obey such laws of Allah as the payment of zakat. But there is absolutely no question of the legislative ambitions of Islam in Sow Fall's narratives. It is simply a nice thing to help the less fortunate members of society: failure to do so is a moral shortcoming, but it does not call for any social or political sanctions.

Just as there is no sharia consciousness in these works, so also is there a total absence of an Islamic identity as separate and distinct from other religious identities or identities based on ethnicity. This observation is best substantiated by the curious fact that in *La Grève des Bàttu,* even Europeans partake in the apparently religious practice of alms giving. The society described by Sow Fall is so perfectly syncretic that the sources of conflict (actual or potential) are cast in terms of class. The only cultural tension articulated is between adherence to cosaan and the blind assimilation of Western materialism and culture.

Perhaps surprisingly, Sembène Ousmane shows greater sharia consciousness in his narratives than does Sow Fall. We have demonstrated how various characters in *Les Bouts de bois de Dieu* are always eager to use Islam as a framework to justify their opinions on the strike. The legislative power of Islam is also acknowledged in this novel. That is why the European authorities enlist the help of an imam in Dakar to issue a *fatwa* (Islamic ruling) on the strike. (Such an action would make no sense in a society like the one depicted by Aminata Sow Fall, where there is no sharia consciousness.) The trial of Diarra can even be considered somewhat a sharia trial; the decision not to kill him is based on Fa Keita's *fatwa*. But there is also an interesting example of sharia implementation in Ramatoulaye's decision to force the water vendor to engage in charity upon his declaring himself to be a believer—a kind of fictional reenactment of Abu Bakr's zakat war. On a wider level, the strikers themselves are *ansarullah* (God's helpers) who are used by God as agents for the establishment of justice on earth. This is the significance of the title of the novel, a significance that Ousmane commentators have so far failed to grasp.

Of all the works by Ousmane, *Véhi-Ciosane* is probably the novel that demonstrates the greatest sharia consciousness. That the narrator establishes unambiguously the difference between the Koran and adda, the pre-Islamic Senegalese cultural framework, is a case in point. The debate surrounding the judgment of Guibril is, as we have illustrated, centered on the legal system to be applied, the Koran or the adda. Massar's argument in favor of the use of the adda sounds very much like the indictment of a society that claims to be Muslim and yet fails to apply the laws of the sharia in the practical matters of life. Never in his village, remonstrates Massar, nor as a matter of fact in the whole of Senegal where mosques proliferate, are the *hudud* (Islamic corporal punishments) applied. While we cannot say that Ousmane is advocating here the implementation of sharia in Senegal, it is at least obvious that he is aware of a contradiction in a Senegalese society that claims to be Muslim and believes in the eternal validity of the Koran as a legislative scripture, while refusing to apply its laws (*Véhi-Ciosane*, 71). This observation underscores the complexity of the sharia debate, which is sometimes seen only in light of opposition to it by non-Muslim minorities in Muslim societies. Not all Muslims are ready to accept the systematic application of sharia in their societies. This is in itself a source of conflict in many contemporary Muslim societies where significant segments of the population are calling for the application of sharia.

From Lemuel Johnson's analysis, one would expect Cheikh Hamidou Kane's *L'Aventure ambiguë* to be imbued with the sharia ethos. Indeed, in the fictional world of the Diallobé, there is no distinction between the spiritual and the temporal. In other words, secularism as a political ideology is not presented as a viable option in *L'Aventure ambiguë*. The Diallobé utopia is precisely that time in history when the Diallobé were at once the spiritual and temporal guides for a third of the continent. The maître understands the unfortunate historical circumstances that led to Europe's adoption of secularism, the division between the "church and the state." The political ideal thus presented by Hamidou Kane is theocratic. The interesting thing in this theocratic conception is the way it purports to deal with dissidence. Which legal system will be adopted in this hypothetical theocratic state? If, as one would expect, it is sharia, how then does it handle noncompliance with sharia?

Kane does not directly deal with this issue. First, the society he presents is confessionally homogeneous, unlike many real sub-Saharan nation states. Apart from the French colonialists, everybody is Muslim. As well, Islam does not have to compete with indigenous African belief systems. Samba is the only character who comes anywhere close to questioning some of the values of his faith, as when he refuses to pray at the end of the novel. The fact is that in Kane's fictional Islamic state, people are free to love, hate, and therefore obey or disobey God. In the words of the maître, man's right to love or hate God is God's ultimate gift to man, which no man (not even a caliph?) can take away from him. That it is a fool who compels Samba to pray, and literally applies the Islamic punishment for apostasy—death—signifies, at least to us, a discomfort if not a total rejection of the application of sharia laws in Kane's fictional world. This observation leaves us with a truly ambiguous picture of the political ideology that is asserted by the novel. How does one reconcile theocracy with total freedom of religious thought and conduct? What does it in effect mean to love and hate God? How does hatred for God manifest itself?

Even though we might not be able to answer these questions, the fact that the maître defines man's relationship to God in terms of love and hate, instead of obedience and disobedience, gives us a clue to understanding the apparent political paradox discerned above. What is being elaborated in Kane's text is a certain quietist mystical (Sufi) understanding of man's relationship to God, what Nehemia Levtzion and John O. Voll describe as "the predominance of love over law and of the spirit over the letter."[9]

Hence, if there are any laws governing Kane's theocratic state, they are the laws of love, which paradoxically depend for their efficacy on the right not to love. This is not the world of sharia. By murdering Samba, the *fou,* in a twist of irony, has chosen to express his love for God by destroying one who, in his estimation, has chosen to hate God by not praying to him. Are there any laws in Hamidou Kane's political system to safeguard the right of man to love or hate God, or is this deemed unnecessary in his political utopia? This question is not really addressed by Kane, thus leaving us with a feeling that in light of the current religious conflicts bedeviling the Muslim world, the political theory expounded in Kane's text remains thoroughly utopian.

Of the novels we have examined, Ahmadou Kourouma's *Les Soleils des indépendances* and Ibrahim Tahir's *The Last Imam* are the ones that best articulate a sharia consciousness and hint at the political implications of this consciousness. The narrator of Kourouma's novel clearly constructs a Muslim identity that defines itself as being separate and distinct from the ethnic identities in the novel. This Muslim identity calls for nothing less than a total rejection of the notion of traditional tribal heritage. The Koran and *koma* are irreconcilable. This position is far more radical than the one presented by Sembène Ousmane in the dichotomy between the Koran and the adda. In *Les Soleils des indépendances,* subscribing to the two cultural codes at the same time simply amounts to hypocrisy. The most uncompromising stance taken by Diamourrou calls for no less than sectarian cleansing. In his village of Allah there can be no place for non-Muslims. Islam is not presented in this novel as a political ideology in the sense that it is not shown to have any role in the broader political drama of Kourouma's fictional African state. This is of little surprise, since at the time Kourouma wrote this novel the Islamic presence in his country, the Ivory Coast, was not politically very significant. That Islam is presented here in ethnic terms, as the religion of the Mandingos, as against the pagan Bambaras, dates this portrayal of Islam in the Ivory Coast. Peter Clarke's study has indicated the fast growth of Islam in that country, a trend that is continuing.

Certainly, Diamourrou and the narrative persona in Kourouma's text seem to represent a minority voice regarding the exclusivist definition of the Muslim and the Muslim territory that they advance. The questions that remain to be asked are: How long will their voice continue to be a minority voice in the Ivory Coast? When will Allah's village become Allah's nation, Allah's empire?

In Ibrahim Tahir's novel, the Muslims have an empire of their own. Islam is no longer only discussed at the level of the village or the chiefdom or the tribe, as in *Les Soleils des indépendances.* It is the de facto religion of the state. But so it was in the country of the Diallobé. The significant difference here is that, unlike the Diallobé, not all the inhabitants of Bauchi share the same commitment to the Islamic ideal. In fact the Islamic ideal itself is significantly different. Although a Sufi ethos informs the imam's desire for intimacy with Allah, and initial resolve to shun the world (including marriage) and dedicate himself entirely to Allah's work, here man's relationship to Allah is cast in terms not of love or its opposite, but of obedience and total submission to the laws of Allah. Moreover, obedience to Allah is not a question of personal choice, it has to be legislated. The laws of God, the sharia, and not the wishes and wisdom of men, must be upheld. Moreover, the imam is unambiguously aware of the political imperatives of Islam.

The political questions raised in *The Last Imam* are to some extent similar to those raised by Ousmane in *Véhi-Ciosane.* What must be the role of sharia in a society that claims to be Muslim? But there is a difference. While in *Véhi-Ciosane,* the scriptures are treated as *lettre morte* (a dead letter), having no impact on the legislative institutions of Senegal, the politics of Bauchi present the case of the imperfect application of sharia. The concept of sharia is mentioned frequently in the narrative. Sharia courts actually function. Thus, the imam is able, by a simple *fatwa,* to ban the tradition of *gwauro.* The emir has to implement the ban reluctantly. The society depicted by Tahir has still not defined clearly the boundaries of the powers of the imam, who is more than just the spiritual leader of the empire, since he also passes legislation affecting the worldly life of his congregation, and the emir, who is not just a temporal leader, but also the *amir al muminin,* the leader of the believers. The undeclared war between the emir's courtiers and the imam is thus a struggle for power. In the words of the emir to the imam, "they [the courtiers] are men of power, men who want to rule and are born to rule. Such men never forget when they are made to live the shadow and not the substance of what they believe to be their rights. They are men of power and so are you" (*The Last Imam,* 242).

One dimension of the conflict in Tahir's novel is, therefore, the classical struggle between the *ulama* (Islamic scholars) and those who wield power in the Islamic state. Sub-Saharan Islamic history provides many examples of this struggle. The most notorious examples are probably the tensions between Sonni Ali Ber and the ulama of Timbuktu, and later the protracted conflict between Usman Dan Fodio and the Habe kings that resulted in the jihad and the creation of the Sokoto caliphate. The other dimension of the conflict is between the imam's puritanical and exclusivist Islamic ideal and the resistance to that ideal by the people of Bauchi. The two dimensions are related. The courtiers only made their assault against the imam when they were sufficiently certain that he had been estranged from the people due to his radical and unaccommodating *tajdid* stance. The astute emir clearly understood this dialectic when he warned the imam:

> And there are others, the Vizir and the other vassals at my Court. They too are men. In the past they accepted the rigid discipline your insistence on doctrine imposed on their conduct of the affairs of the Emirate. But their acceptance was based only on the spirit of give and take between men who understand the affairs of state and who knew they needed you and you needed them. Now they know that the people are not with you. (*The Last Imam,* 199)

Diamourrou and Imam Usman are solitary figures, and the causes they espouse, the clear delineation of the boundaries of Dar-ul-Islam, the exclusivist definition of the Muslim, and, especially in the case of Alhaji Usman, the total implementation of sharia (if necessary by force) in Muslim societies, remain the mere articulation of a forlorn ideal. The two writers have denied them the possibility of immediate victory, and yet have left us with the feeling that somehow a battle is lost, not the struggle. For the struggle is a product of the inherent contradictions of the modern African nation-states. What are these contradictions?

Sudan and Nigeria illustrate the problems of sub-Saharan countries faced with the problem of creating modern nation-states out of societies composed of diverse religions, cultures, and histories precisely at a time when, as John Hunwick puts it, "at both the individual and societal levels, a primary identification as Muslim or Christian often seems to override other loyalties."[10]

The option of secularism that is championed by scholars like Wole Soyinka is contested not only because, for many Muslims, the Western-style constitutions adopted in many African countries are imbued with a Euro-Christian ethos but also because the separation between "church and state," as it is generally understood, is untenable for many Muslims. In the words of Francis Deng, "to appreciate the pivotal role of religion in the [Sudanese] conflict, it should be remembered that Islam welds together all aspects of life, public and private, into a composite whole that is ideally regulated by Sharia."[11]

How Nigeria and Sudan resolve this problem will show whether in fact the modern sub-Saharan African state bedeviled with interreligious conflicts can manage to resolve this contradiction.

It is an interesting fact that when Sembène Ousmane and Ahmadou Kourouma wrote *Véhi-Ciosane* and *Les Soleils des indépendances,* respectively, Islamic "fundamentalism" had not yet become an issue in modern sub-Saharan African politics. This fact underscores the prophetic quality of literature. It must, however, be noted that these works only dealt with the relationship between Islam and local African traditional belief systems. There is no Christian resident in Diamarrou's village, nor is there apparently any Christian in Santhiu Niaye. Generally speaking, Christian-Muslim antagonism is yet to become a thematic preoccupation for sub-Saharan African writers. The closest we can come to it are the self-styled political novels of Francis Deng, *Seed of Redemption* (1986) and *Cry of the Owl* (1989), in which the author seeks to neutralize divisive myths and shed light on unifying realities (Deng: 46).

Nonetheless, the contradictions highlighted by Sembène Ousmane in Senegalese society regarding the marginal role accorded to Islamic sharia in Senegalese politics—Diamourrou's sharp consciousness of a contradiction in Mandingo ethnic and religious loyalties, and Ibrahim Tahir's neo-jihadist suggestions—represent a literary paradigm for the role that Islam is poised to play in contemporary African politics.

Literary critics have a contribution to make in analyzing this role and its implications by paying attention to the representation of politics and the Islamic factor by sub-Saharan Africa's literary visionaries. For critics to perform this task well, in addition to the general business of interpreting meaningfully the imaginative responses to Islam by sub-Saharan African writers, they must not repeat the critical shortcomings that I have analyzed in this study.

The first suggestion to critics interested in the study of sub-Saharan African literature of Islamic inspiration is to acquire some familiarity with the Islamic framework. Any discussion of the teachings of the Prophet must be informed by a familiarity with the two most widely accepted collections of the prophetic tradition, *Al-Bukhari* and *Muslim*. Knowledge gained by a study of what Muslims believe to be the authentic teachings of their Prophet will significantly help honest scholars from presenting some of the more obvious distortions of Islam analyzed in this study.

Such knowledge must however not lead to the danger of essentialism. First, if Muslims do argue that there is only one Islam, there is no denying the fact that there are different expressions of Islamic practice in the Muslim world, a fact that must put us on guard against making reified generalizations about Islamic practice. Moreover, one must not assume that Muslims live outside of history. The actions of Muslim individuals and groups may sometimes be determined more by real concrete social and political pressures than by the fact of their being Muslim. Edward Said put this observation more eloquently when he wrote:

> The fundamental question raised by such contemporary Orientalist texts as *The Cambridge History* is whether ethnic origin and religion are the best, or at least the most useful basic and clear, definitions of human experience. . . . Does it matter more in understanding that X and Y are disadvantaged in certain very concrete ways, or that they are Muslims or Jews?[12]

One must clearly take into account both the religious-ethnic and socioeconomic descriptions, and not just capitalize on the religious category, as some of the commentators we have studied clearly do. The work of determining which category to emphasize can only be performed well by one who, in our specific area of focus, has a very good understanding not only of Islam, but also of its history and sociology in sub-Saharan Africa.

Admittedly, the paradigms I have established call for interdisciplinary competence. The competent scholar should be equipped with linguistic skills, not only to be able to read the primary texts as well as historical and scriptural texts in the original, but also to have access to the many African Islamic cultures to which the texts refer more or less explicitly. I cannot claim to have demonstrated these competences in this study, but I hope that my exposing the shortcomings in traditional criticism has been a useful exercise.

Indeed, more remains to be done in this field. An expanded study of the subject covering sub-Saharan fiction and its criticism will pay attention, for example, to the fictional writings of Francis Deng, one of the leading intellectuals of southern Sudan. Of particular interest will be the writer's interpretation of the role of Islam in Sudan's civil war. Also, the chapter on Sembène Ousmane can be expanded to include a study of his films in both Wolof and French. Is there internal consistency in the image of Islam that emerges from his works? All possibilities will be explored from the point of view of his extraliterary pronouncements, the medium/language used, the targeted readership/viewers, the sociopolitical context in which the works are produced, and the specific thematic orientation of each work. In other words, how have the images of Islam in the different works been influenced by some or all of these variables?

My work, which is a tentative beginning, opens up many areas for further investigation. One can, for example, study the criticism of novels of the Maghreb to look for parallels and differences in the way Islam is represented in this criticism. Is there any concept of *l'Islam berbère* (Berber Islam) in these writings? Are there any significant differences in the way francophone Muslim writers of the Maghreb relate textually to Islam? How do they deal with their composite identities, that of the Berber, the Arab, and the religious one? Is their relationship to French different from that of their sub-Saharan colleagues? How do they deal with the ambivalence of articulating the integrity of their cultures using the ex-colonizer's language? All these questions and more provide exciting fields for further study of Islam and African fiction, to which my study, in its present form, has been but a modest contribution.

## Notes

1. Mohamadou Kane, *Roman africain et tradition* (Dakar: Nouvelles Editions Africaines, 1982), 399–400.
2. William Hemminger, "The Translator's Task: Crossing Cultural Bounds," *Southern Humanities Review* 26, no. 4 (Fall 1992). Subsequent references to this article will be indicated parenthetically in the text.
3. Aminata Sow Fall, *La Grève des Bàttu* (Dakar, Abidjan, Lomé: Les Nouvelles Editions Africaines, 1979), 26.
4. Aminata Sow Fall, *The Beggars' Strike,* trans. Dorothy Blair (Essex: Longman, 1990), 17.
5. Christopher Harrison, *France and Islam in West Africa, 1860–1960* (Cambridge: Cambridge University Press, 1988), 61.
6. "Nyerere Fights for Union," *New African* 316, 18 February 1994, 17–18.
7. "Mombasa in Ferment," *New African* 316, 18 February 1994, 16.
8. Ibrahim Gambari, "The Role of Religion in National Life: Reflections on Recent Experiences in Nigeria," in John O. Hunwick, ed., *Religion and National Integration in Africa: Islam, Christianity and Politics in the Sudan and Nigeria* (Evanston: Northwestern University Press, 1992), 90.
9. Nehemia Levtzion and John O. Voll, eds., *Eighteenth-Century Renewal and Reform in Islam* (Syracuse: Syracuse University Press, 1987), 9.
10. John O. Hunwick, ed., *Religion and National Integration in Africa: Islam, Christianity and Politics in the Sudan and Nigeria* (Evanston: Northwestern University Press, 1992), xi.
11. Francis M. Deng, "A Three-Dimensional Approach to the Conflict in the Sudan," in John O. Hunwick, ed., *Religion and National Integration in Africa: Islam, Christianity and Politics in the Sudan and Nigeria* (Evanston: Northwestern University Press, 1992), 41. Subsequent references to this article will be indicated parenthetically in the text.
12. Edward Said, *Orientalism* (New York: Vintage Books, 1979), 305.

# Glossary

*Cosaan:* Pre-Islamic Senegalese culture.

*Fatwa:* A formal legal opinion given by a *mufti,* a legal scholar of Islam. In common usage the term designates any scripturally derived opinion or advice.

*Figh:* The science of jurisprudence in Islam.

*Hadith* (plural: *ahadith*): An account related to the actions and teachings of the Prophet. After the Koran, and in conjunction with it, the *ahahdith* collectively constitute the fundamental sources for Islam.

*Jihad:* "Holy war," but essentially meaning personal effort and sacrifice in the path of Allah.

*Kafir* (plural: *kufar*): a disbeliever.

*Mufti:* A professional giver of *fatawa* (plural of *fatwa*).

*Mujadid:* See *tajdid.*

*Mujahid:* One undertaking *jihad,* usually involving military engagement. See *jihad.*

*Seera:* The biography of the Prophet.

*Sunna:* The way of life of the Prophet as it is expressed in the *ahadith.*

*Tafsir:* The science of interpreting the Koran.

*Tajdid:* The action of renewal, generally referring to Islamic reform or renewal undertaken by a *mujadid.*

*Takfir:* The action of considering someone a disbeliever (*kafir*).

# Bibliography

Abdalati, Hammudah. *Islam in Focus.* Indianapolis: Islamic Trust Publications, 1977.
Abdalla, Raqiya Haji Dualeh. *Sisters in Affliction: Circumcision and Infibulation of Women in Africa.* London: Zed Press, 1982.
Abel, Armand. *Les musulmans noirs de Maniema.* Bruxelles: Centre pour l'étude des problèmes du monde musulman contemporain, 1960.
Abrahman, Ervand. *Khomeinism: Essays on the Islamic Republic.* Berkeley: University of California Press, 1993.
Abu-Lughod, Ibrahim. *Arab Rediscovery of Europe: A Study in Cultural Encounters.* Princeton, N.J.: Princeton University Press, 1963.
Achebe, Chinua. *Hopes and Impediments.* London: Heinemann, 1988.
Adotevi, Stanislas. *Négritude et négrologues.* Paris: UGE, 1972.
Afrahmi, Mahnaz, ed. *Faith and Freedom: Women's Human Rights in the Muslim World.* Syracuse: Syracuse University Press, 1995.
Afshar, Haleh. *Women, State and Ideology: Studies from Africa and Asia.* Basingstoke, U.K.: Macmillan, 1987.
Ahmad, Mumtaz, ed. *State Politics and Islam.* Indianapolis: American Trust Publications, 1988.
Akakuru, Iheanacho A. "Islam as Infrastructure: A Reading of Cheikh Hamidou Kane's *Ambiguous Adventure.*" *Neohelicon: Acta Comparisionist Litterarum Universarum* 18, no. 2 (1990). 105–120.
Al Hilli, Al-Hassan Ibn Yusuf. *Al-Babu l-Hadi 'Ashar: A Treatise on the Principle of Shi'ite Theology.* Translated by William McElwee Miller London: Royal Asiatic Society, 1928.
Al-Nawawi. *Gardens of the Righteous: Riyadh as-Salihin of Imam Nawawi.* Translated by Muhammad Zafrullah Khan. London: Curzon Press, 1975.
Al-Nouty, Hassan. *Le Proche-Orient dans la littérature française de Nerval à Barrès.* Paris: Nizet, 1985.
Al Shafi'i, Muhammad Ibn Idris. *Islamic Jurisprudence: Shafi'i's Risala.* Translated by Majid Khadduri. Baltimore: Johns Hopkins University Press, 1961.

Ali, A. Yusuf, trans. *The Koran: Text, Translation and Commentary.* 1934, various reprintings.
Amadiume, Ifi. *Male Daughters, Female Husbands: Gender and Sex in an African Society.* London: Zed Books, 1987.
Anozie, Sunday O. *Sociologie du roman africain: réalisme, structure et détermination dans le roman ouest-africain.* Paris: Aubier-Montaigne, 1970.
Anyidoho, Kofi. "African Creative Fiction and a Poetics of Social Change." *Komparitistische Hefte* 13 (1986): 67–81.
Appiah, Kwame Anthony. *In My Father's House: Africa in the Philosophy of Culture.* New York: Oxford University Press, 1992.
Arberry, A. J. *British Orientalists.* London: William Collins, 1943.
———. *The Koran Interpreted.* London: Allen & Unwin, 1955; New York: Macmillan, 1964.
Arkoun, Mohammed. *Rethinking Islam: Common Questions.* Translated by Robert D. Lee. Boulder: Westview Press, 1994.
Arkoun, Mohammed, Jacques Le Goff, Tawfiq Fahd, and Maxime Rodinson. *L'étrange et le merveillux dans l'islam médiéval.* Paris: Jeune Afrique, 1978.
Armstrong, Karen. *Muhammad: A Biography of the Prophet.* San Francisco: Harper, 1992.
Arnold, Stephen H., ed. *African Literature Studies: The Present State/L'Etat présent.* Washington D.C.: Three Continents Press, 1985.
Ascroft, Bill, Gareth Griffiths, and Helen Tiffin. *The Empire Writes Back: Theory and Practice in Post-Colonial Literatures.* London: Routledge, 1989.
Astier-Loufti, Martine. *Littérature et colonialisme: l'expansion coloniale vue dans la littérature romanesque française, 1871–1914.* Paris: Mouton, 1974.
Athar, Shahid. *Reflections of an American Muslim.* Chicago: Kazi Publications, 1994.
Auddouin, Jean, and Raymond Daniel. *L'Islam en Haute-Volta à l'époque coloniale.* Paris: L'Harmattan; Abidjan: Inades, 1978.
Augue, Marc. *Théories des pourvoirs et idéolgie: étude de cas en Côte d'Ivoire.* Paris: Hermann, 1975.
———, ed. *La construction du monde: religion, répresentation, idélogie.* Paris: Maspero, 1974.
Bâ, Amadou Hampaté. *Aspects de la civilisation africaine.* Paris: Présence Africaine, 1972.
———. *L'etrange destin de wangrin.* Paris: Union Generale d'Editions, 1973.
———. *Jésus vu par un musulman.* Abidjan/Dakar: Nouvelles Editions Africaines, 1976.
———. *Vie et enseignement de Tierno Bokar, le sage de Bandiagara.* Paris: Le Seuil, 1980.
Bâ, Amadou Hampaté, and Jacques Daget. *L'Empire peul du Mecina.* Bamako: I.F.A.N., 1955.
Bakhtine, M. *Esthétique et théorie du roman.* Paris: Gallimard, 1978.
Balewa, Tafawa. *Shaiu Umar.* New York: Markus Wiener Publishing, 1989.
Bannerman, Patrick. *Islam in Pesrpective: An Introduction to Islamic Society, Politics and Law.* London: Routledge, 1988.

Barry, Boubacar. *Le royaume du waalo*. Paris: Maspero, 1975.
Barth, Heinrich. *Voyages et découvertes dans l'Afrique septentrionale et centrale pendant les années 1849 a 1855*. Traduction française. Paris: Bruxelles, 1861.
Beck, Lois Grant, and Nikkie Keddie, eds. *Women in the Muslim World*. Cambridge: Harvard University Press, 1978.
Beier, Ulli, ed. *Introduction to African Literature: An Anthology of Critical Writing from Black Orpheus*. London: Longmans, 1967.
Bestman, Martin. *Sembène Ousmane et l'esthétique du roman négro-africain*. Sherbrooke, Canada: Naaman, 1981.
Bhabha, Homi. *The Location of Culture*. London: Routledge, 1994.
Binger, Captaine. *Du Niger et Golfe de Guinée*. Paris: Hachette, 1982. Reédition par la société des Africanistes, 1980.
Blair, Dorothy S. *African Literature in French: A History of Creative Writing in French from West and Equatorial Africa*. New York: Cambridge University Press, 1976.
———. *Senegalese Literature: A Critical History*. Boston: Twayne Publishers, 1984.
Blyden, Edward. *Christianity, Islam and the Negro Race*. Original edition 1887. Edinburgh: Edinburgh University Press.
Boilat, Abbé. *Esquisses Sénégalaises*. Paris: Kathala, 1984.
Bonaparte, Napoléon. *Compagnes d'Egypte et de Syrie, 1798–1799: Mémoires pour servir à l'histoire de Napoléon*. Paris: Bossagne, 1821.
Boni-Sierra, Jacqueline. "Littérature et société: Etude critique de *La Grève des Bàttu* d'Aminata Sow Fall." *Revue de littérature et d'esthétique négro-africaines* 5 (1984): 59–89.
Bosworth-Smith, R. *Mohammed and Mohammedanism*. Lahore, Pakistan: Sind Sagar Academy, 1974.
Boyd-Buggs, Debra. "Baraka: Marboutism and Maraboutage in the Francophone Senegalese Novel." Ph.D. diss., Ohio State University, 1986.
Brasseur, Paule. "A la recherche d'un absolu missionnaire: Mgr Truffet, Vicaire apostolique des Deux-Guinées (1812–1847)." *Cahiers d'Etudes Africaines* 58, no. 15-2 (1976): 259–285.
Breckenridge, Carol A., and Peter van der, eds. *Orientalism and the Postcolonial Predicament*. Philadelphia: University of Pennsylvania Press, 1993.
Brevié, I. *Islamisme contre "Naturisme" au Soudan français*. Paris: E. Leront, 1923.
Brown, Ella. "Reactions to Western Values as Reflected in African Novels." *Phylon: The Atlanta University Review of Race and Culture* 48, no. 3 (Fall 1987): 216–228.
Cailler, Bernadette. "L'Aventure ambiguë: Autobiographie ou histoire d'un peuple?" *The French Review: Journal of the American Association of Teachers of French* 55, no. 6 (May 1982): 742–751.
Caillie, René. *Travels through Central Africa to Timbuktu*. London: Cass, 1968.
Calverly, E. E. *Worship in Islam*. Rev. ed. London: Luzac, 1957.
Cardaire, Marcel. *L'Islam et le terroir africain*. Bamako: I.F.A.N., 1954.

Carrabino, Victor. "Kane and Badiane: The Search for the Self." *Rocky Mountain Review of Language and Literature* 41, no. 1–2 (1987): 65–72.

Case, Frederic. "Worker's Movements: Revolution and Women's Consciousness in God's Bits of Wood." *Canadian Journal of African Studies* 15, no. 2 (1981): 277–292.

———. "Le Discours islamique dans les romans d'Aminata Sow Fall." In *Commentaries on a Creative Encounter: Proceedings of a Conference on the Culture and Literature of Francophone Africa*. Albany: African American Institute, 1988, pp. 17–32.

Cazenave, Odile. "Gender, Age, and Reeducation: A Changing Emphasis in Recent African Novels in French as Exemplified in *L'Appel des arènes* by Aminata Sow Fall." *Africa Today* 38, no. 3 (1991): 54–62.

Cham, Mbye. "Islam in Senegalese Literature and Film." In Kenneth Harrow, ed., *Faces of Islam in African Literature*. London, Portsmouth: Heinemann, 1991, pp. 163–186.

———. "Art and Ideology in the Work of Sembène Ousmane and Haile Gerima." *Présence Africaine: Revue Culturelle du Monde Noir* [*Cultural Review of the Negro World*] 129, no. 1 (1984): 79–91.

Chambers, Ross. *Story and Situation: Narrative Seduction and the Power of Fiction*. Minneapolis: University of Minnesota Press, 1984.

Chateaubriand, Françoise-René de. *Oeuvres romanesques et voyages*. Edited by Maurice Regard. Paris: Gallimard, 1969.

Chew, Samuel. *The Crescent and the Rose: Islam and England During the Renaissance*. New York: Oxford University Press, 1937.

Chinweizu et al. *Toward the Decolonisation of African Literature*. Washington, D.C.: Howard University Press, 1983.

Cissoko, Sekene Mody. *Tombouctou et l'empire songhai*. Abidjan/Dakar: Nouvelles Editions Africaines, 1975.

Claire-Jaccard, Anny. "Les visages de l'Islam chez Mariama Bâ et chez Aminata Sow Fall." *Nouvelles du sud: Islam et littératures africaines*. Paris: Silex, 1987, pp. 171–182.

Clarke, Peter B. "Islam, Development and African Identity: The Case of West Africa." In Kirsten Holst Peterson, ed., *Religion, Development and African Identity*. Uppsala: Nordiska Afrikaninstitutet, 1987, pp. 125–143.

Cohn-Sherbor, Dan, ed. *Islam in a World of Diverse Faiths*. New York: St. Martin's, 1991.

Coquery, Catherine. *La découverte de l'Afrique*. Paris: Julliard, 1965.

Corcoran, Patrick. "Critical Introduction." In Sembène Ousmane, *O Pays, mon beau Peuple!* London: Methuen, 1986.

Cragg, Kenneth. *The Event of the Qur'an: Islam in Its Scripture*. London: Allen & Unwin, 1971.

Cromer, [Lord]. *Modern Egypt*. New York: MacMillan, 1908.

Crosta, Suzanne. "Les structures spatiales dans *L'Appel des arènes* d'Aminata Sow Fall." *Revue Francophone de Louisiane* 3, no. 1 (Spring 1988): 58–65.

Cuoq, Joseph M. *Les Musulmans en Afrique*. Paris: Maisonneuve et Larose 1975.

Dailly, Christophe. "The Novelist as a Cultural Policy Maker." *Présence*

*Africaine: Revue Culturelle du Monde Noir* [*Cultural Review of the Negro World*] 125 (1983): 202–213.

Daniel, Gibon. *The Arabs and Medieval Europe*. London: Longman's Green & Co., 1975.

Daniel, Norman. *Islam and the West: The Making of an Image*. Edinburgh: Edinburgh University Press, 1960.

Darthorne, O. R. *The Black Mind: A History of African Literature*. Minneapolis: University of Minnesota Press, 1974.

Delafosse, Maurice. "De l'animisme nègre et sa résistance à l'islamisation en Afrique occidentale." *Revue du monde musulman* (1922): 121–163.

Deng, Francis M. "A Three-Dimensional Approach to the Conflict in the Sudan." In John O. Hunwick, ed., *Religion and National Integration in Africa: Islam, Christianity and Politics in the Sudan and Nigeria*. Evanston: Northwestern University Press, 1992, pp. 39–62.

Dia, Mamadou. *Islam et civilisations négro-africaines*. Dakar: Nouvelles Editions Africaines, 1980.

———. *Islam, sociétés africaines et culture industrielle*. Dakar: Nouvelles Editions Africaines, 1975.

Diop, Chiekh Anta. *L'unité culturelle de l'Afrique Noire*. Paris: Présence Africaine, 1959.

Duchet, Claude, ed. *Sociocritique*. Paris: Nathan, 1979.

Dumont, Fernand. *L'anti-Sultan ou al-Hajj Omar Tal du Fouta, combattant de la foi*. Dakar/Abidjan: Nouvelles Editions Africaines, 1974.

———. *La pensée religieuse d'Amadou Bamba fondateur du muridisme Sénégalais*. Dakar/Abidjan: Nouvelles Editions Africaines, 1975.

Eagleton, Terry. *Criticism and Ideology: A Study in Marxist Literary Theory*. London: N. L. B., 1976.

———. *Walter Benjamin: Or Towards a Revolutionary Criticism*. London: Verso Press, 1981.

Egonu, I. T. K. "Aminata Sow Fall: A New-Generation Female Writer from Senegal." *Neophilologus* 75, no. 1 (January 1991): 66–75.

Escarpit, R. *Le Littéraire et le Social*. Paris: Flammarion, 1970.

Esposito, John, *Islam: The Straight Path*. New York, Oxford: Oxford University Press, 1988.

Fakhry, Majid. *A History of Islamic Philosophy*. New York: Columbia University Press, 1970.

Fick, Johann W. *Die Arabischen Studien in Europa bis in den Anfag des 20 Jarhunderts*. Leipzig: Otto Harrassowitz, 1955.

Fischer, Michael M. J., and Medi Abdi. *Debating Muslims: Cultural Dialogues in Postmodernity and Tradition*. Madison: University of Wisconsin Press, 1990.

Fisher, H. J. *Ahmadiyya: A Study in Contemporary Islam on the West African Coast*. New York: Oxford, 1963.

Foucault, Michel. *L'Ordre du discours*. Paris: Gallimard, 1971.

Froelich, Jean-Claude. *Les Musulmans d'Afrique Noire*. Paris: L'Orante, 1962.

Fyzee, Asaf Ali Asghar. *Outline of Muhammadan Law*. 3rd ed. London: Oxford University Press, 1964.

Gadjigo, Samba. "Literature and History: The Case of Cheikh Hamidou Kane's

*Ambiguous Adventure.*" *Research in African Literature* 22, no. 4 (Winter 1991): 29–38.

———. "Social Vision in Aminata Sow Fall's Literary Work." *World Literature Today: A Literary Quarterly of the University of Oklahoma* 63, no. 3 (Summer 1989): 411–415.

Gambari, Ibrahim. "The Role of Religion in National Life: Reflections on Recent Experiences in Nigeria." In John O. Hunwick, ed., *Religion and National Integration in Africa: Islam, Christianity and Politics in the Sudan and Nigeria.* Evanston: Northwestern University Press, 1992, pp. 85–100.

Gardet, Louis. *Les hommes de l'islam.* Paris: Hachette, 1977.

Garnette, David, ed. *The Letters of T. E. Lawrence of Arabia.* London: Spring Books, 1964.

Garrot, Daniel. *Léopold Sedar Senghor, critique littéraire.* Dakar: Les Nouvelles Editions Africaines, 1978.

Gassama, Makhily. *Kuma: Intérrogation sur la littérature nègre de langue française.* Dakar/Abidjan: Les Nouvelle Editions Africaines, 1978.

Gates, Henry Louis, Jr. *Black Literature and Literary Theory.* New York and London: Methuen, 1984.

Gatje, Helmut. *The Qur'an and Its Exegesis.* Translated by Alford T. Welch. London: Routledge & Kegan Paul, 1976.

Geertz, Clifford. *Work and Lives.* Stanford: Stanford University Press, 1979.

Genette, Gérard. *Figures III.* Paris: Seuil, 1972.

Gérard, Albert. "Sembène's Progeny: A New Trend in the Senegalese Novel." *Studies in Twentieth Century Literature* 4, no. 2 (Spring 1980): 133–145.

Gibb, H. A. R. *Area Studies Reconsidered.* London: School of Oriental and African Studies, 1964.

———. *Modern Trends in Islam.* Chicago: University of Chicago Press, 1947.

———. *Mohammedanism: A Historical Survey.* London: Oxford University Press, 1949.

Gilsenan, Michael. *Recognizing Islam: An Anthropologist's Introduction.* London and Canberra: Croom and Helm, 1983.

Glele, Maurice Ahanhanzo. *Religion, culture et politique en Afrique Noire.* Paris: Présence Africaine, 1981.

Gouilly, Alphonse. *L'islam en Afrique occidentale française.* Paris: Larose, 1952.

Grousset, René. *L'Empire du Levant: Histoire de la question d'Orient.* Paris: Payot, 1946.

Guisse, Youssouph Mbargane. *Philosophie, culture et devenir social en Afrique noire.* Dakar/Abidjan/Lome: Les Nouvelles Editions Africaines, 1979.

Gunn, Giles. *The Interpretation of Otherness: Literature, Religion and the American Imagination.* New York: Oxford University Press, 1979.

Haddad, Adnan. *L'Arabe et le Swahili dans la République du Zaïre: Etudes islamiques, histoire et linguistique.* Paris: Sedes, 1983.

———. *Pourquoi L'Islam?* Paris: Sedes, 1987.

Haddad, Yvonne. "Islam, Women and Revolution in Twentieth-Century Arab Thought." *Muslim World* LXXIV (1984): 137–160.

Hale, Thomas. *Scribe, Griot, and Novelist: Narrative Interpreters of the Songhay Empire*. Gainesville: University of Florida Press, 1990.
Hamidullah, Muhammad. *Muslim Conduct of State*. 7th rev. ed. Lahore, Pakistan: Sh. Muhammad Ashraf, 1977.
Hammond, Thomas. "Entretien avec Aminata Sow Fall." *Présence Francophone: Revue Internationale de Langue et de Littérature* 22 (Spring 1981): 191–195.
Harrison, Christopher. *France and Islam in West Africa, 1860–1960*. Cambridge: Cambridge University Press, 1988.
Harrow, Kenneth W. "Art and Ideology in *Les Bouts de bois de Dieu:* Realism's Artifices." *The French Review: Journal of the American Association of Teachers of French* 62, no. 3 (February 1989): 483–493.
———. "Camara Laye, Cheikh Hamidou Kane, and Tayeb Salih: Three Sufi Authors." In Kenneth Harrow, ed., *Faces of Islam in African Literature*. London and Portsmouth: Heinemann, 1991, pp. 261–298.
———, ed. *Faces of Islam in African Literature*. London: Heinemann, 1991.
———. *The Marabout and the Muse: New Approaches to Islam in African Literature*. London: Heinemann, 1996.
Haschmi, Mohamed Yahia. "Spirituality, Science, and Psychology in the Sufi Way." In Rushbrook Williams, ed., *Sufi Studies: East and West*. New York: Dutton, 1973, pp. 114–132.
Hawkins, Peter. "An Interview with Senegalese Novelist Aminata Sow Fall." *French Studies Bulletin: A Quarterly Supplement* 22 (Spring 1987): 19–21.
Hemminger, William. "The Translator's Task: Crossing Cultural Bounds." *Southern Humanities Review* 26, no. 4 (Fall 1992): 301–312.
———. "Les Influences religieuses dans la littérature féminine d'Afrique noire." *Nouvelles du sud: Islam et littératures africaines*. Paris: Silex, 1987, pp. 191–199.
Herzberger-Fofana, Pierrette. "Sembène Ousmane, forgéron de caractères: Une interviue avec le romancier et cinéaste sénégalais." *Komparatistische Hefte* 8 (1983): 55–63.
Heykal, Muhammad Husayn. *The Life of Muhammad [Hayat Muhammad]*. Translated by Ismail R. al-Faruqi. Indianapolis: American Trust Publications, 1976.
Hirsch, E. D., Jr. *The Aims of Interpretation*. Chicago: University of Chicago Press, 1976.
Hiskett, Mervyn. *The Sword of Truth: The Life and Times of the Shehu Usman Dan Fodio*. New York: Oxford University Press, 1973.
———. *A History of Hausa Islamic Verse*. London: School of Oriental and African Studies, 1975.
———. *The Development of Islam in West Africa*. New York: Longman, 1984.
Hodgkin, Thomas. *Nigerian Perspectives*. 2d ed. New York: Oxford, 1975.
Hogben, S. J., and A. H. M. Kirk-Greene. *The Emirates of Northern Nigeria*. London: Oxford University Press, 1966.
Hourani, Albert. *Islam in European Thought*. Cambridge: Cambridge University Press, 1991.
Huannou, Adrien. "L'Islam et le Christianisme face à la domination coloniale dans Les Bouts de bois de Dieu." *Nouvelles du Sud* 6 (1986–1987): 41–48.

Hunwick, John O. *Sharia in Songhay: The Replies of al-Maghili to the Questions of Askia al-Hajj Mohammed*. New York: Oxford University Press, 1985.

———, ed. *Religion and National Integration in Africa: Islam, Christianity and Politics in the Sudan and Nigeria*. Evanston: Northwestern University Press, 1992.

Ibn Babawayh, Muhammad Ibn 'Ali. *A Shiite Creed. A Translation of Yzee*, Asa A.A. Risalat l-l'tiqadat. London: Oxford University Press, 1942.

Ibn, Battuta. *Voyages*. Translated by C. Defremery and B. R. Sanguinetti. Paris: Anthropos, 1979.

Ibn, Ishaq. *The Life of Muhammad. A Translation of Ishaq's Sirat Rasul Allah*. Translated by Alfred Guillaume. London: Oxford University Press, 1967.

Ibn, Khaldun. *Discours sur l'histoire universelle* [*Al-Muqaddima*]. Translated by Vincent Monteil. Paris: Sindbad, 1978.

Ibn, Taimiya. *Ibn Taimiya on Public and Private Law in Islam* [*Al-Siyasa al-Shar'iya*]. Translated by Omar A. Farrukh. Beirut: Khayyat, 1966.

Ijere, Muriel. "La Condition féminine dans Xala de Sembène Ousmane." *Revue de Littérature et d'Esthétique Négro-Africaine* 8 (1988): 36–45.

Innes, Gordon. *Sunjata: Three Mandinka Versions*. London: School of Oriental and African Studies, 1974.

Iyam, David Uru. "The Silent Revolutionaries: Sembène Ousmane's Emitai, Xala, and Ceddo." *The African Studies Review* 29, no. 4 (December 1986): 79–87.

Izutsu, Toshihihko. *Ethico-Religious Concepts in the Qur'an*. Montreal: McGill University Press, 1966.

Jansen, J. J. G. *The Interpretation of the Koran in Modern Egypt*. Leiden: E.J. Brill, 1974.

Jauss, H. R. *Pour une Esthétique de la réception*. Paris: Gallimard, 1978.

Jeffery, Arthur. *The Qur'an as Scripture*. New York: Russell F. Moore, 1957.

Johnson, Lemuel. "Crescent and Consciousness: Islamic Orthodoxies and the West African Novel." In Kenneth Harrow, ed., *Faces of Islam in Sub-Saharan African Literature*. London, Portsmouth: Heinemann, 1991, pp. 239–260.

Kaba, Lansine. *The Wahhabiya Islamic Reform and Politics in French West Africa*. Evanston: Northwestern University Press, 1974.

Kane, Cheikh Hamidou. *L'Aventure ambiguë*. Paris: Julliard, 1961.

———. *The Ambiguous Adventure*. Oxford: Heinemann, 1972.

Kane, Mohamadou. *Roman africain et tradition*. Dakar: Nouvelles Editions Africaines, 1982.

———. "L'écrivain africain et son public." *Présence Africaine* 58 (1966): 8–31.

Kati, Mahmoua. *Tarikh el-Fettash*. Translated by O. Houdas and M. Delafosse. Paris: Adrien-Maisonneuve, 1964.

Kattan, Naïm. "Peut-on traduire les civilisations?" *Meta* 27, no. 4 (1982): 401–403.

Kesteloot, Lylian. *Les Ecrivains noirs de langue française: Naissance d'une littérature*. Bruxelles: Editions illustreés de Bruxelles, 1983.

Khadduri, Majid. *War and Peace in the Law of Islam*. Baltimore: Johns Hopkins University Press, 1955.

Khatibi, Abdelkedir. *Figures de l'étranger dans la littérature française.* Paris: Denoel, 1987.

Killam, G. D. *African Writers on African Writing.* Evanston: Northwestern University Press, 1973.

Kimoni, Iyay. *Destiné de la littérature négre-africaine ou problématique d'une culture.* Sherbrooke, Canada, and Kinshasa: Editions Naaman & Presses Universitaires du Zaïre, 1975.

Klein, Martin. *Islam and Imperialism in Senegal.* Stanford: Stanford University Press, 1968.

Knicker, Morita. "Le Coran comme modèle littéraire dans *L'Aventure ambiguë* de Cheikh Hamidou Kane." *Nouvelles du sud: Islam et littératures africaines.* Paris: Silex, 1987, pp. 183–90.

Kourouma, Ahmadou. *Les Soleils des indépendances.* Montréal: Les Presses de l'Université de Montréal, 1968.

Lang, George. "Through a Prism Darkly: 'Orientalism' in European-Language African Writing." In Kenneth Harrow, ed., *Faces of Islam in African Literature.* London, Portsmouth: Heinemann, 1991, pp. 299–311.

Last, Murray. *The Sokoto Caliphate.* London: Longman, 1967.

Latour Da Veiga Pinto, Françoise. *Le Portugal et le Congo au XIXe siècle.* Paris: Presse Universitaire de France, 1972.

Laye, Camara. *L'Enfant Noir.* Paris: Plon, 1953.

———. *Le Regard du Roi.* Paris: Plon, 1954.

———. *Dramouss.* Paris: Plon, 1966.

———. *Le Maître de la parole*: *Kouma lafolo Kouma.* Paris: Plon, 1978.

Lemotieu, Martin. "Interférence de la religion musulmane sur les structures actuelles de la société négro-africaine: L'Exemple de *La Grève des Bàttu* d'Aminata Sow Fall." *Nouvelles du sud: Islam et littératures africaines.* Paris: Silex, 1987, pp. 49–60.

Lesseps, Ferdinand de. *Lettres, journal et documents pour servir à l'histoire du Canal de Suez.* Paris: Didier, 1881.

Levtzion, Nehemia. *Muslims and Chiefs in West Africa.* New York: Oxford, 1968.

———. *Islam in West Africa: Religion, Society and Politics to 1800.* Great Yarmouth: Galliard Printers, 1994.

Levtzion, Nehemia, and John O. Voll, eds. *Eighteenth-Century Renewal and Reform in Islam.* Syracuse: Syracuse University Press, 1987.

Levy, Reuben. *The Social Structure of Islam.* Cambridge: Cambridge University Press, 1957.

Lindfors, Bernth, ed. *Research Priorities in African Literatures.* Oxford: Zell, 1984.

Lings, Martin. *Muhammad: His Life Based on the Earliest Sources.* London: George Allen & Unwin, 1983.

Linkhorn, René. "L'Afrique de demain: Femmes en marche dans l'oeuvre de Sembène Ousmane." *Modern Language Studies* 16, no. 3 (Summer 1986): 69–76.

Macherey, P. *Pour une théorie de la production littéraire.* Paris: Maspero, 1970.

Mage, Eugene. *Voyage au Soudan occidental [1863–1866].* Paris: Karthala, 1980.

Makouta-M'boukou, J. Pierre. *Le Français en Afrique noire*. Paris: Bordas, 1973.

———. *Introduction à l'étude du roman négro-africain de langue française: problèmes culturels et littéraires*. Abidjan: Les Nouvelles Editions Africaines, 1980.

Makward, Edris. "Women, Tradition and Religion in Sembène Ousmane's Work." In Kenneth Harrow, ed., *Faces of Islam in African Literature*. London, Portsmouth: Heinemann, 1991, pp. 187–200.

Martin, B. G. "Notes sur l'origine de la tariqa des Tijaniyya et sur le débuts d'Al-Hajj Umar." *Revue des Etudes Islamiques* (1969): 267–290.

Marty, Paul. *L'Emirat des Trarzes*. Paris: Leroux, 1919.

———. *L'Islam en Guinée, le Fouta Djallon* Paris: Leroux, 1921.

———. *Etudes sur l'Islam et les tribus Maures, les Brakna*. Paris: Leroux, 1921.

Massignon, Louis. "Causes et modes de la propagation de l'islam parmi les populations païennes de l'Afrique." *Opera Minora* 1 (1938): 317–324.

Maududi (Mawdoodi), Abu Ala. *The Meaning of the Qur'an*. Lahore, Pakistan: Sh. Muhammad Ashraf, 1967.

Mazrui, Ali. "Wole Soyinka as a Television Critic: A Parable of Deception." *Transition* 54 (1991): 165–177.

———. "The Dual Memory: Genetic and Factual." *Transition* 57 (1992): 134–146.

Mbabuike, Michael. "Cheikh Hamidou Kane's *Ambiguous Adventure*: Dichotomy of Existence and the Sense of God." *The Journal of Ethnic Studies* 8, no. 4 (1981): 114–120.

McCaffrey, Kathleen M. "Images of Women in West African Literature and Film: A Struggle Against Dual Colonisation." *International Journal of Womens Studies* 3 (1980): 76–88.

Metlitzki, Dorothee. *The Matter of Araby in Medieval England*. New Haven, Conn.: Yale University Press, 1977.

Meyers, Jeffrey. "Culture and History in Things Fall Apart." *Critique* 11, no. 1 (1968): 25–32.

Midouhan, Guy O. "Exotique? Coloniale? Ou quand la littérature africaine était la littérature des français d'Afrique." *Peuples noirs, Peuples Africains* 29 (1982): 119–126.

Miller, Christopher L. *Blank Darkness: Africanist Discourse in French*. Chicago and London: The University of Chicago Press, 1985.

Miller, Elinor S. "Contemporary Satire in Senegal: Aminata Sow Fall's *La Greve des Bàttu*." *French Literature Series* 14 (1987): 143–151.

Miller, Hugh. "*L'Aventure ambiguë* vue de dedans: Perspectives islamiques." *French Studies in Southern Africa* 19 (1990): 52–70.

Minh-ha, Trinh. "Aminata Sow Fall et l'espace du don." *The French Review* 55, no. 6 (May 1982): 780–789.

———. *Woman, Native, Other*. Bloomington: Indiana University Press, 1989.

Mohanty, Tapalde Chyandra. "Under Western Eyes: Feminist Scholarship and Colonial Discourse." *Boundary* 2, nos. 12.3 and 13.1 (Spring/Fall 1984): 333–358.

Monteil, Vincent, *L'Islam noir.* Paris: Le Seuil, 1964.
Moore, Gerald. *Seven African Writers.* London: Oxford University Press, 1962.
———. "Towards Realism in French African Writing." *Journal of Modern African Studies* 1, no. 1 (1963): 61–73.
———. *The Chosen Tongue: English Writing in the Tropical World.* New York: Harper and Row, 1969.
Moreau, René-Luc. "Les marabouts de Dori." *Archives de Sociologie des Religions* 17 (1964): 113–134.
———. "Note sur le pélerinage de La Mekke vécu au Sénégal aujourd'hui." *M.I.D.E.O.* 9 (1967): 215–220.
———. "Les chances d'un dialogue en Afrique noire entre le Christianisme et l'Islam." *Concilium* 126 (1977): 141–137.
———. *Africains musulmans: Des communautés en mouvement.* Paris: Présence Africaine, 1982.
Moukoko, Gobina. "Entretien avec Aminata Sow Fall." *Cameroun littéraire* 1 (1983): 53–56.
Mudimbe, Boyi M. E. "Harlem Renaissance et l'Afrique: Une Aventure ambiguë." *Présence Africaine: Revue Culturelle du Monde Noir* [*Cultural Review of the Negro World*] 147, no. 3 (1988): 18–28.
Mudimbe, V. Y. *L'autre face du royaume: Une introduction à la critique des langages en folie.* Lausanne: L'Age d'Homme, 1973.
———. "African Literature: Myth or Reality?" In Stephen H. Arnold, ed., *African Literature Studies: The Present State/L'Etat présent.* Washington D.C.: Three Continent Press, 1985, pp. 7–15.
———. *The Invention of Africa: Gnosis, Philosophy, and the Order of Knowledge.* Bloomington: Indiana University Press, 1988.
Muslim ibn al-Hajjaj al-Qushayri. *Sahih Muslim: Being Sayings and Doings of the Prophet Muhammad as Narrated by His Companions and Compiled Under the Title al-Jami-us-Sahih by Imam Muslim.* Translated by Abdul Hamid Siddiqi. Lahore, Pakistan: Sh. Muhammad Ashraf, 1971–1973.
Nazareth, Peter. *The Third World Writer: His Social Responsibilities.* Nairobi: Kenya Literature Bureau, 1978.
Nevakiui, Jukka. *Britain, France, and the Arab Middle East, 1914–1920.* London: Athlone Press, 1969.
Ngate, Jonathan. "And After the 'Bolekaja' Critics?" In Stephen H. Arnold, ed., *African Literature Studies: The Present State/L'Etat présent.* Washington D.C.: Three Continent Press, 1985, pp. 101–114.
Nicolas, Guy. *Dynamique sociale et appréhension du monde au sein d'une société hausa.* Paris: Institut d'Ethnologie, 1975.
Nnuruka, Matiu. "La Fonction idéologico-religeuse dans *L'Aventure ambiguë* de Cheikh Hamidou Kane." *Présence francophone: Revue internationale de langue et de littérature* 24 (Spring 1982): 77–87.
Nyang, Sulayman, and Samir Abed Rabbo. "Bernard Lewis and Islamic Studies: An Assesment." In *Orientalism, Islam, and Islamists.* Brattleboro, Vt.: Amana Books, 1984, pp. 259–284.
Obielo-Okpala, Louis. "L'Islam dans l'oeuvre de Sembène Ousmane." *L'Afrique Littéraire* 85 (1989): 14–24.

Ojo, S. Ade. "Revolt, Violence and Duty in Sembène Ousmane's God's Bits of Wood." *Nigeria Magazine* 53, no. 3 (July–September 1985): 58–68.
Ousmane, Sembène. *O pays, mon beau peuple!* Paris: Presses Pocket, 1957.
———. *Les Bouts de bois de Dieu.* Paris: Presses Pocket, 1960.
———. *Voltaïque.* Paris: Présence Africaine, 1962.
———. *Xala.* Paris: Présence Africaine, 1962.
———. *L'Harmattan.* Paris: Présence Africaine, 1964.
———. *Véhi-Ciosane ou Blanche-Genèse.* Paris: Présence Africaine, 1966.
———. *Le Dernier de L'Empire.* Paris: L'Harmattan, 1981.
———. *Niiwam Suivi de Taaw.* Paris: Présence Africaine, 1987.
Parekh, Pushpa N., and Siga N. Jagne. *Postcolonial African Writers: A Bio-Bibliographical Critical Sourcebook.* Westport, Conn.: Greenwood Press, 1998.
Park, Mungo. *Voyage dans l'intérieur de l'Afrique.* Paris: Maspero, 1980.
Peters, F. E. *A Reader on Classical Islam.* Princeton, N.J.: Princeton University Press, 1994.
Peters, Jonathan A. "Aesthetics and Ideology in African Film: Ousmane Sembène's Emitai." In Eileen Julien, ed., *African Literature in its Social and Political Dimensions.* Washington, D.C.: Three Continents, 1986, pp. 69–75.
Pfaff, Françoise. "Aminata Sow Fall: L'Ecriture au féminin." *Notre Librairie* 81 (1985): 135–138.
———. "Enchantment and Magic in Two Novels by Aminata Sow Fall." *College Language Association Journal* 31, no. 3 (March 1988): 339–359.
Pirenne, Henri. *Mohammed and Charlemagne.* Translated by Bernard Miall. New York: W.W. Norton & Co., 1939.
Prince, Gerald. "The Disnarrated." *Style* 22, no. 1 (Spring 1988): 1–8.
Rahbar, Daud. *God of Justice: A Study of the Ethical Doctrines of the Qur'an.* Leiden: E.J. Brill, 1960.
Rahimieh, Nasrin. *Oriental Responses to the West: Comparative Essays in Select Writers from the Muslim World.* Leiden: Brill, 1990.
Rahman, Fazlur. *Islamic Methodology in History.* Karachi, Pakistan: Central Institute of Islamic Research, 1965.
Rahnema, Zeinolabedin. *Payambar the Messenger.* Translated from Persian by L.P. Elwell-Sutton. Lahore, Pakistan: Sh. Muhammad Ashraf, 1964.
Rauf, Muhammad Abdul. *The Islamic View of Woman and the Family.* New York: Robert Speller, 1977.
Ricoeur, Paul. *Interpretation Theory: Discourse and the Surplus of Meaning.* Fort Worth: Texas Christian University Press, 1975.
Robinson, C. H. *Mohammedanism: Has It Any Future?* London: Gardener, Darton, 1897.
Roded, Ruth. *Women in Islamic Biographical Collections: From Ibn Sa'd to Who's Who.* Boulder: Lynne Rienner Publishers, 1994.
Rosenthal, E. I. J. *Political Thought in Medieval Islam: An Introductory Outline.* Cambridge: Cambridge University Press, 1958.
Royster, James E. "The Study of Muhammad: A Survey of the Approaches from the Perspective of the History of Phenomenology of Religion."

*Muslim World* 62 (1972): 49–70.
Ryan, Patrick J. *Imale: Yoruba Participation in the Muslim Tradition.* Cambridge: Harvard University Press, 1978.
Said, Edward. *The World, the Text and the Critic.* Cambridge: Harvard University Press, 1983.
———. *Orientalism.* New York: Vintage Books, 1979.
———. *Beginnings: Intention and Method.* New York: Basic Books, 1975.
Scholes, Robert. *Semiotics and Interpretation.* New Haven: Yale University Press, 1982.
Sharfman, Ronnie. "Fonction romanesque féminine: Rencontre de la culture et la structure dans *Les Bouts de bois de Dieu*." *Ethiopiques* 1, nos. 3–4 (1983): 134–144.
Siddiqui, Abdul Hamid. *Major Themes of the Qur'an.* Minneapolis and Chicago: Bibliotheca Islamica, 1980.
———. *The Life of Muhammad.* Lahore, Pakistan: Islamic Publications, 1969.
Southern, R. W. *Western Views of Islam in the Middle Ages.* Cambridge: Harvard University Press, 1962.
Sow Fall, Aminata. "Pratiques langagières dans la littérature négro-africaine de langue française." *Ethiopiques* 3, nos. 1–2 (1985): 61–66.
———. *Le Revenant.* Abidjan: Nouvelles Editions Africaines, 1982.
———. *La Grève des Bàttu.* Dakar, Abidjan, Lomé: Nouvelles Editions Africaines, 1979.
———. *L'Appel des arènes.* Abidjan: Nouvelles Editions Africaines, 1982 edition.
———. *L'Ex-père de la nation.* Paris: Harmattan, 1987.
Soyinka, Wole. *Myth, Literature and the African World.* Cambridge: Cambridge University Press, 1976.
———. "Religion and Human Rights." *Index on Censorship* 17, no. 5 (1988): 82–85.
———. "Triple Tropes of Trickery." *Transition* 54 (1991): 178–183.
———. "Footnote to a Satanic Trilogy." *Transition* 57 (1992): 148–149.
———. *The Burden of Memory, the Muse of Forgiveness.* Oxford: Oxford University Press, 1999.
Spivak, Gayatri Chakravorty. "The Politics of Interpretations." In Gayatri Chakravorty Spivak, ed., *Other Worlds: Essays in Cultural Politics.* New York: Routledge and Kegan Paul, 1987.
Starratt, Priscilla E. "Oral History in Muslim Africa: Almaghili Legends in Kano." Ph.D. diss., University of Michigan, 1993.
Steiner, George. *Language and Silence: Essays on Language, Literature and the Inhuman.* New York: Atheneum, 1967.
Stringer, Susan. "Aminata Sow Fall." *SAGE: A Scholarly Journal on Black Women* (1988): 36–41.
Tahir, Ibrahim. *The Last Imam.* Boston: Routledge & Kegan Paul, 1984.
Thiong'o, Ngugi wa. *Detained: A Writer's Prison Diary.* London: Heinemann, 1981.
Tine, Alioune. "Wolof ou français, le choix de Sembène Ousmane." *Notre Librairie* 81 (1985): 43–50.

Todorov, Tzvetan. *Nous et les autres: la réflexion française sur la diversité humaine*. Paris: Seuil, 1989.
Tompkins, Jane P., ed. *Reader-Response Criticism: From Formalism to Post-Structuralism*. Baltimore: The Johns Hopkins University Press, 1981.
Vignala, Daniel. "Sembène Ousmane, nouvelliste." *Peuples Noirs–Peuples Africains* 19 (1981): 141–147.
Waardenburg, Jacques. *L'Islam dans le miroir de l'Occident*. The Hague: Mouton & Co., 1963.
———. "Official and Popular Religion as a Problem in Islamic Studies." In Pieter Hendrik Vrijhof and Jacques Waardenburg, eds., *Official and Popular Religion as a Theme in the Study of Religion*. The Hague: Mouton, 1979.
Wallace, Karen Smyley. "A Search for Identity: The Alienated Female Persona in some Francophone African Novels." *Rendezvous: Journal of Arts and Letters* 22, no. 2 (Spring 1986): 32–38.
Watt, W. Montgomery. *Muhammad at Mecca*. Oxford: Clarendon Press, 1953.
———. *The Faith and Practic of al-Ghazali*. London: Allen & Unwin, 1953.
Williams, Raymond. *Politics and Letters: Interviews with New Left Review*. London: New Left Books, 1979.
Wolfson, Harry Austryn. *The Philosophy of the Kallam*. Cambridge: Harvard University Press, 1976.
Yetiv, Isaac. "Acculturation, aliénation et émancipation dans les oeuvres d'Albert Memmi et de Cheikh Hamidou Kane." *Présence Francophone: Revue Internationale de langue et de littérature* 34 (1989): 73–90.
Zabus, Chantal. "Othering the Foreign Language in the West African Europhone Novel." *Canadian Review of Comparative Literature* 17 (September/December 1990): 348–366.
———. *The African Palimpsest: Indigenization of Language in the West African Europhone Novel*. Amsterdam: Rodopi, 1991.
Zimma, Pierre V. *Pour une Sociologie du texte littéraire*. Paris: U.E.G., 1978.
Zwemer, S. M., ed. *The Mohammedan World of Today*. New York: F. H. Revell, 1906.

# Index

Achebe, Chinua, 81, 84
*Adda* (pre-Islamic legal system), 70–72, 141
African culture, indigenous: environmental concerns in, 25–26; gender roles and, 26–27; and Islamic cultures, 107–109, 115, 119–121, 125–126; introduction of Islam and, 23–28. *See also* Senegalese culture
African Islam: colonial scholarship on, 5, 10–15, 19–20, 31, 33–34, 131–132; contemporary African politics and, 145–146; European biased studies of, 9–10; indigenous cultural heritage and, 23–28; as Islam noir, 7, 12, 30–31, 43, 46–47, 107; missionary scholarship on, 15–19; modes of conversion, 43–45; as syncretism and simplification of Islam, 7, 31, 42–43, 45–48; violent propagation of, 24–25, 28, 43, 45
Africanist literary criticism, 23–52; balanced treatment of Islam in, 50–52; colonial perceptions and, 10–15, 19–20, 33–34, 49; cross-cultural analysis in, 4; essentialism in, 38–40, 41; and European-language resources on Islam, 132; Islamic religious determinism in, 39–42; Orientalism and, 2, 38, 40–41; treatment of Islamic subtext in, 2–3, 5, 6, 30–36, 49–52, 131–132
African literature: consciousness of Islamic orthodoxy in, 108, 109–115; distortions of Islam in, 137–138; Islamic inspiration and voice in, 29, 36–38, 51; linguistic differentiation in, 4, 82, 85, 87, 92, 101–103; model Muslim in, 33; politics of language in, 82–85; sharia consciousness in, 139–146; syncretic ethos in, 92–93, 95, 108, 109–115; Western Orientalist scholarship and, 1–2
*Africans: A Triple Heritage, The* (television series), 23
Ahadith (teachings of the Prophet), 32, 40, 77
*Al-Bukhari,* 146
Algerian colonialism, Muslims and, 11, 14
Arabic publications, banning of, 132

Bestman, Martin, 3, 30, 57, 73–74
Blair, Dorothy, 103, 136–137
*Blanc-Genèse* (Ousmane), Islamic subtext in, 134
Blyden, Edward, 18–19
Bonaparte, Napoleon, 14
Boni-Sierra, Jacqueline, 38
*Borrom Sarret* (Ousmane), 57
Boyd-Buggs, Debra, 5, 31–33, 34–38, 40, 132
Burkina Faso, Islam in, 45

Caillé, René, 14–15
Carrère, Frédéric, 11

Catholic Church, 15–16, 17
*Ceddo* (Ousmane), Islamic conversion in, 28
Cham, Mbye, 56–57, 66, 81, 102
Christianity: in colonial Africa, 15–19, 24; compared to Islam, 45–46; and missionary scholarship on Islam, 15–19; morality and, 3, 25; women's status in, 26, 41
Christian-Muslim antagonism, as literary theme, 145
Claire-Jaccard, Anny, 51, 94
Clarke, Peter, 45, 46, 77
Colonial scholarship, 19–20, 33–34; in Africanist literary criticism, 20, 31, 49; and contemporary African writing, 131; Orientalism and, 5, 131; overview of, 10–15
Coppolani, Xavier, 11
Corcoran, Patrick, 30, 57–58, 62, 63
*Cry of the Owl* (Deng), 145

Davidson, John, 39
Deng, Francis, 145, 147
Depont, O., 11
Duveyrier, Henri, 15

Environment, and African indigenous values, 25–26

Faideherbe, Louis, 12, 13
Francophone Muslim literature, distortions of Islam in, 137–138
French colonialism: Christian missionaries and, 17; scholarship of, 11–12, 13–15

Ghattas-Soliman, Sonia, 39
Glottopolitics. *See* Language politics

Haddad, Yvonne, 76
*Hadith*. *See* Ahadith
Herzberger-Fofana, Pierrette, 40–42
Holle, Paul, 11, 15

Islam: activism and revolutionary character of, 76–78; charity in, 92, 94–95; classical divisions of Darul Islam and Darul Harb in, 126–127; communal spirit in, 66–67; compared to Christianity, 45–46; diversity and mixing of approach in, 38–39; divine providence in, 61–63, 75–76; essentialist approach to, 38–40; European-language resources on, problems with, 132–133; fatalism and passivity in, 6, 41, 55–61, 66, 68–71, 78; ideological debates on, 78–79; maraboutism and maraboutage in, 30–31; Marxism and, 6, 55, 59, 76; nuptial rules in, 116–117, 119–120; orthodox, *see The Last Imam*; as political ideology, 138–146; powers of imam and emir in, 144; predestination in, 55, 62, 68–71; racial determinism and, 47; radical, 128–129; as reactionary religion, 33–34, 60, 63–64, 74–75; sharia and, 140–145; syncretism of animism and Islamic practices in, 30–31; women's status in, 26–27, 39, 41, 133; work ethic in, 77; worship and prayer in, 63–66, 100. *See also* African Islam
Islamic Conference, Organization of, 138
Islamic identity, and African identity, 133
Islamic Party of Kenya (IPK), 139
Ivory Coast, Islam in, 45, 143

*Jahilya,* concept of, 119
*Jihad*: concept of, 149; of Usman Dan Fodio, 7, 49, 115, 127–128
Johnson, Lemuel, 108–109, 141

Kane, Cheikh Hamidou: Koranic culture in, 124, 141–142; syncretism and, 108, 109. *See also L'Aventure ambiguë*
Kattan, Naïm, 100–101
Kenya, political Islam in, 139
Knicker, Morita, 51
Koran, 61, 79, 88, 132, 136, 138; *adda* (pre-Islamic Senegalese law) and, 70–72, 141; *ahadith* and, 32, 40; charity and, 92, 94–100, 102; fatalistic interpretation of, 78; as frame of reference, 51, 124–125; Islamic work ethic and, 77; polygamy/monogamy and, 31–32, 53n.6

Kourouma, Ahmadou. *See Soleils des indépendances*

*La Grève des Bàttu* (Sow Fall), 86; concept of charity in, 7, 92–93, 94–100, 102; critical misreading and translations of, 41–42, 91–92, 136–137; Islamic subtext and voice in, 37–38
Lang, George, 49, 51–52, 94
Language politics: *décentrement* and *annexion* concepts in, 82, 103–104n.4; linguistic differentiation in, 82, 85, 87, 92, 101–103; othering of European languages in, 83–86; relexification, cushioning, and contextualization in, 84, 85; and translation of African/Islamic culture into ex-colonizers' languages, 82–83, 84, 100–101
*L'Appel des arènes* (Sow Fall), 85, 86, 90–91; cultural conflict in, 87; Islamic practices in, 88–89
*Last Imam, The* (Tahir): confrontation between orthodoxy and syncretism in, 107, 115, 119–121; consciousness of Islamic orthodoxy in, 7, 107, 118–128; imam's characterization in, 123–124; Koranic references and allusions in, 124–125; Muslim ideal in, 118; non-Muslim image in, 126–127; personality of Usman Dan Fodio in, 115, 127; pre-Islamic indigenous religion and culture in, 125–126; setting, 126; sharia consciousness in, 7, 143–144; structure of conflict in, 118–121; thematic complexity of, 117–118; women's condition and roles in, 115–117, 119–120
*L'Aventure ambiguë* (Kane), 78; apostasy, heresy, and syncretism in, 108, 109; critique of, 29, 33–36, 50, 132; intertextual study of, 51; model Muslim in, 33; political paradox in, 141–142
Laye, Camara, 93, 108–109
*Le Jujubier du patriarche* (Sow Fall), 135
*Le Mandat* (Ousmane), 133
Lemotieu, Martin, 37, 95
*L'Enfant noir* (Laye), syncretism in, 108–109
*Le Revenant* (Sow Fall), 41, 85, 86–90; Islamic practices in, 88–90; linguistic variance used in, 87–88; principle of charity in, 92, 94–102; untranslated word experimentation in, 92–93
*Les Bouts de bois de Dieu* (Ousmane), 35, 135; dialogic structure in, 56; Islamic versus materialistic viewpoint in, 59–62, 74–76; sharia consciousness in, 140–141
*L'Ex-père de la nation* (Sow Fall), translation of, 135
Linguistic differentiation, 82–83, 87
Literary criticism. *See* Africanist literary criticism
Lubeck, Paul M., 77

Mage, Eugene, 12–13
Makward, Edris, 50–51
*Marabout and the Muse: New Approaches to Islam in African Literature, The*, 50, 52
Maraboutism/maraboutage, 30–31
Marty, Paul, 47
Marxist ideology, Islam and, 6, 55, 58, 59, 76
Massignon, Louis, 77–78
Mazrui, Ali, 23–28, 133
Miller, Walter, 16–17
Mocher, Gaspard Théodore, 14
Mohammedanism, 40
Mohanty, Tapalde, 4, 26
Monteil, Vincent, 77–78
Moreau, René-Luc, 47, 49
Morocco, French colonial rule in, 13
Muslim identity: Islamic reform and, 122; Muslim ideal and, 33, 118; traditional tribal heritage and, 142–143 *See also* Islam
*Myth, Literature and the African World* (Soyinka), 28–29

Nigeria, political Islam in, 139, 145. *See also The Last Imam*
Noruka, Matiuu, 78
Nyerere, Julius, 138

*O pays, mon beau peuple!* (Ousmane), 55, 57–58, 62–67; dialogic structure

in, 56; Islam's communal spirit in, 66–67; polygamy in, 133
Obielo-Okpala, Louis, 58–59, 68
Orientalism: and Africanist europhone literature and criticism, 1–2; and colonial scholarship, 5, 131; critique of, 9–10; political nature of, 131
"Othering the Foreign Language in the West African Europhone Novel" (Zabus), 83
Ousmane, Sembène, 29, 55–79; as apostate, 29, 30, 55–57; Christianity and, 3; films of, 147; and Islam, textual relationship to, 28, 50–51, 55, 56–59, 60–76, 85; Islamic voice in, 75–76; Marxist ideological orientation of, 6, 55, 58, 59; reasons for misreadings of, 6; religious symbolism in, 67; Senegalese culture depicted by, 133–135; sharia consciousness of, 140–141; writing stance of, 56. *See also Les Bouts de bois de Dieu; O pays, mon beau peuple!; Véhi-Ciosane*

Pan-Africanism, 18
Polygamy, 31–32, 45–46, 132, 133–134
Ponty, William, 9
Pope Nicholas V, 15

Rinn, Louis, 11
Rumi, Jalalud din, 67
Rushdie, Salman, 1
Ryan, Patrick, 45

Said, Edward, 2, 4, 9, 10, 38–39, 146
Salih, Tayeb, 39
*Satanic Verses, The* (Rushdie), 1
*Seasons of Migration to the North* (Salih), 39
*Seed of Redemption* (Deng), 145, 147
*Seera* (biography of the Prophet), 149
Senegalese culture: *adda* (pre-Islamic Senegalese cultural framework) and, 72, 141; glorification of, 7, 81–82, 86–87, 90, 91, 133–135; islamization of, 30–31, 133–135, 137; untranslated Islam-Arabic concepts in, 83
Senegalese fiction, Islam and, 33, 56.
*See also* Ousmane, Sembène; Sow Fall, Aminata
Sharia ethos, 7, 140–145
Sokoto caliphate, 77, 144
*Soleils des indépendances, Les,* (Kourouma): orthodoxy and syncretism in, 108, 109–115; as prophetic, 145; sharia consciousness and Muslim identity in, 142–143
Sow Fall, Aminata, 81–103; Catholic/Euro-Christian cultural framework in, 88–89; critical misreading of, 41–42, 91–92, 136–137; and Islam, textual muting of, 6–7, 85–86, 87–91, 100–102, 109, 135, 139–140; Islamic voice in, 37–38; linguistic differentiation of, 82, 85, 87, 92, 101–103; as promoter of Islam, 7, 81, 82; readership of, 92–93; syncretic ethos in, 7, 92–93, 95; themes of cultural alienation/authenticity in, 87, 91; traditional Senegalese culture (*cosaan*), 7, 81–82, 86–87, 90, 91, 135; translation of Islamic concepts in, 82, 85–86, 101–102, 135–137; translations of, 135–137; untranslated word experimentation in, 92–94.
*See also La Grève des Bàttu; L'Appel des arènes; Le Revenant*
Soyinka, Wole, 23–30, 50, 59, 74–75, 76, 133
Spivak, Gayatri, 4
Sudanese conflict, role of religion in, 145
Sufiism, colonial writing on, 11
Sulaiman, Ibraheem, 77
Syncretism, in African fiction, 92–93, 95, 108–109

Tahir, Ibrahim, as literary Islamic fundamentalist, 7. *See also The Last Imam*
*Tajdid,* Islamic concept of, 48–49, 139, 144, 149
*Takfir,* Islamic concept of, 122, 139, 149
Tanzania, political Islam in, 138–139
*Tatauwu,* Islamic concept of, 100, 133
"Through a Prism Darkly: 'Orientalism' in European-Language African Writing" (Lang), 51–52

*Touki-Bouki: Magaye niang, mareme niang* (Sow Fall), 135
Translation: of African culture into European languages, 7, 82, 83, 101–102; annexing versus decentering model of, 82, 103–104n.4; and cultural distortion, 32, 135–137
"Triple Tropes of Trickery" (Soyinka), 28

United Muslims of Africa (UMA), 139
Usman Dan Fodio, 49, 115, 127–128

*Véhi-Ciosane* (Ousmane), 57, 67–73, 141; dialogic structure of, 56; prophetic quality of, 145; sharia ethos in, 143–144
*Voltaique* (Ousmane), Islamic subtext in, 57

Western Orientalism. See Orientalism
"Wole Soyinka as a Television Critic: A Parable of Deception," 23–30
"Women, Tradition and Religion in Sembène Ousmane's Work" (Makward), 50–51
Women's status, Islam and, 4, 26–27, 39, 41, 133

*Xala* (Ousmane), 133–134

Zabus, Chantal, 83–85

# About the Book

Ahmed Bangura argues that a deeply ingrained pattern of prejudice toward Islam in European-language writing on Africa has led to serious misreadings of many West African novels.

Extending Edward Said's study of the Orientalist tradition in Western scholarship, Bangura traces the origins of contemporary misunderstandings of African Islam to the discourse of colonial literature. Western critics and writers, he observes, typically without access to Islam except through the colonialist tradition, have perpetuated unfounded, politically motivated themes.

Bangura discusses the historical and sociological contexts of Islam in sub-Saharan Africa, providing a framework for the study of West African novels with an Islamic subtext. Contrasting his own reading of the novels of Sembène Ousmane, Aminata Sow Fall, and Ibrahim Tahir with that of traditional Western critics, his analysis also features Wole Soyinka, Debra Boyd-Buggs, Mohamadou Kane, Ali Mazrui, Cheikh Hamidou Kane, Ahmadou Kourouma, Mbaye Cham, and Kenneth Harrow.

**Ahmed S. Bangura** is assistant professor of modern languages at the University of San Francisco.